Common Tree Fruit Pests

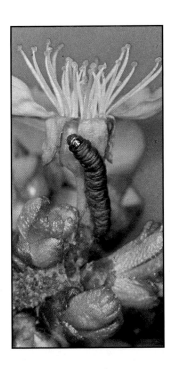

Angus J. Howitt
Department of Entomology (Retired)
Michigan State University Extension
NCR 63
October 1993

MICHIGAN STATE UNIVERSITY

Table of Contents

Index to Tables

Note on the emergence graphs: Where pheromones or trapping devices were suitable to use with an insect, emergence patterns were tracked and graphed. These emergence graphs are not indexed here — when available, they are included with the discussion of the individual insect.

Key to Fruit Identification

 APPLE

 APRICOT

 CHERRY

 NECTARINE

 PEACH

 PEAR

 PLUM

THIS BOOK IS THE COMPILATION OF NOTES GATHERED IN 28 YEARS WORKING AS A fruit entomologist and teaching a course on fruit entomology in Lifelong Education at Michigan State University. This course was taught off campus in various fruit-growing areas in Michigan and was intended for growers, chemical industry and commodity groups, Extension staff members and others who felt a need for information on the recognition, biology and control of pests attacking deciduous fruit trees. The information was not readily available to the audience for which this publication is intended.

This, then, is an attempt to bring together in one publication some of the priceless observations made by numerous entomologists and naturalists, living and deceased, whose observations and studies have been responsible for our present knowledge and control of fruit pests.

Currently, there is a great concern about chemicals in the environment, insect resistance to chemicals, chemical pollution that endangers health and the environment, and a rapidly diminishing supply of effective pesticides available to growers. No attempt has been made to make specific chemical recommendations because they would soon be out of date. Principles of control, based on attacking the pests at the most susceptible stage of their life history, have been stressed. New techniques such as pheromones will continue to be introduced and will greatly advance the science of fruit pest control. However, the biology of arthropod pests is generally immutable, and optimum use of any new technology or control agent must be based on a thorough knowledge of the pest involved. It is my wish that the material presented here will be helpful in this respect.

Angus J. Howitt

1993

Introduction

Acknowledgments

I AM GREATLY INDEBTED TO DR. RAY KRINER OF CLOSE-UP PHOTO, BLACK Mountain, N.C., for permission to use many of his outstanding slides in this publication.

I am also indebted to Dr. Henry W. Hogmire of the University of West Virginia for his critical review of the manuscript, as well as Larry Olsen, pesticide education coordinator, Michigan State University, for his contributions and suggestions on integrated pest management. Grateful acknowledgment is due to David Biddinger, Pennsylvania State University, for his work on the American plum borer and dogwood borer and his excellent review and many suggestions on the manuscript. Special thanks also goes to Alfred Pshea for his invaluable assistance in establishing Michigan State University's Trevor Nichols Research Complex, Fennville, Mich., where most of the research for this book was conducted, and for his efforts in the study and biology of the beneficial insects and mites reported on in this work.

I would like to express my thanks and appreciation to Allan Hays, Matthew Daly, Janis Howard, Wayne McFarland and Douglas Kronemeyer, who were or are employed at the Michigan State University Trevor Nichols Research Complex, and who provided valuable assistance in the study of many of the pests described in this publication.

A.J.H.

T HIS CHAPTER* DISCUSSES THE BASIC PRINCIPLES OF ARTHROPOD GROWTH. THE CONCEPTS HOLD FOR ALL INSECTS AND MITES, PESTS AS WELL AS BENEFICIALS. THIS INFORMATION REPRESENTS IMPORTANT BUILDING BLOCKS OF KNOWLEDGE THAT MUST BE GRASPED BEFORE MORE COMPLEX AND CRITICAL CONCEPTS OF PEST CONTROL CAN BE MASTERED.

Insects and mites belong to a group of organisms referred to as arthropods. Examples of other common arthropods are crabs, spiders, ticks, scorpions and harvestmen (daddy long-leg spiders). All arthropods reproduce and grow in a similar manner. In the following discussion of insect and mite growth, most examples are drawn from insects. Mite growth is similar. Where differences do occur, they are pointed out.

■ *Life Cycles*

Where did these insects come from? Though you may be able to identify an insect or mite, you may not know its specific life stages. Though insects seem to suddenly appear in hordes to ravage crops, they have natural origins similar to our own, as well as limits on their ability to increase population size.

Insect growth progresses through specific successive stages. A simplified life cycle of an insect is outlined in Fig. 1. The adult female lays eggs that hatch into an immature stage. After a growth

* by J. Brunner and A. Howitt

Excerpted and revised from NCR 63, "Tree Fruit Insects," 1981.

period when the insect passes through a series of successive immature stages, an adult emerges. Mating follows and the entire process begins again. The adult insect is the reproductively mature stage and is usually responsible for dispersal, host plant selection and colonization of new habitats.

All insects start as eggs, which vary in size, shape, color and placement on hosts. Eggs can be deposited singly, as in the case of the rosy apple aphid, or in compact masses, which is how red-banded leafroller eggs are laid. Insects also use various means of concealment. Eggs may be deposited in the soil or inserted

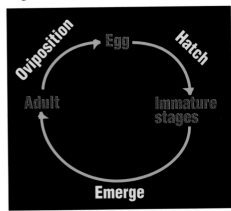

Fig. 1 Simplified insect or mite life cycle.

into plant tissue. Eggs left exposed are often covered with a coating that protects them against the elements and natural enemies. The eastern tent caterpillar, for example, lays its eggs in masses on cherry and other trees and covers them with a spittlelike substance, which hardens to a consistency of polyurethane foam. This protection helps eggs survive the winter.

Eggs may be flattened ovals, barrel-shaped or suspended on long stalks, but all have the same basic structure. The outside surface is a tough, elastic layer designed to prevent water loss and protect the developing embryo. Inside the egg, a rich and plentiful supply of yolk provides nutrients for the embryo. Egg hatch, or eclosion, occurs when the first immature stage ruptures the shell and struggles free. Significant dispersal to new trees or orchards may occur at this time by the new larvae, which "balloon" in the wind on extruded strands of silk. This is especially true of leafroller larvae.

As the young insect grows, it passes through specific life stages marked by molting (Fig. 2). The life stage between molts is called an instar. Each instar is successively numbered as the insect grows. When the insect hatches from the egg, it is referred to as a first instar or neonate. After molting to the next immature stage, it is a second instar, and so on until it reaches the pupal or adult stage.

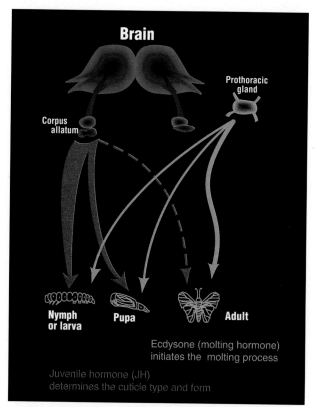

Fig. 3 Diagrammatic representation of how hormones control the growth and form of insects. Ecdysone stimulates the molting process while juvenile hormone determines which form the insect shall take.

Fig. 2 Sequence of events in the life cycles of insects and mites.

Not all insects have the same number of instars. The green apple aphid, for example, has five instars (stages) between egg hatching and adult emergence, while the apple maggot has only three.

Molting is distinctive of the insect and other arthropod anatomies. Unlike vertebrates, whose bodies are supported by internal skeletons, insects and other arthropods possess an outer skin called an exoskeleton. The exoskeleton is often hard, such as that of beetles and ants. Though the exoskeleton provides the insect protection from dessication (drying up) and physical crushing and support for internal muscles and organs, it does not expand. Thus, the insect is locked within its exoskeleton. To grow, it must shed the old exoskeleton and produce a new, larger one.

Molting is controlled by the insect's hormone system. To initiate molting, the insect's brain releases a substance called brain hormone. This hormone stimulates the prothoracic gland, which then releases the molting hormone, or ecdysone (Fig. 3).

Ecdysone permits the insect's epidermal, or outer, skin cells to partially dissolve the old exoskeleton and begin making a new one beneath it. The protective outer layer of the insect's old skin is retained to prevent water loss until the new skin is well formed. When

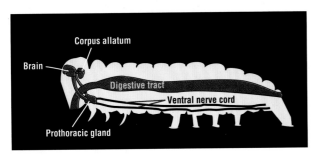

Fig. 4 Internal anatomy of an insect, showing the locations from which molting hormones are released.

ready, the insect pushes through the remaining old skin, which parts at predetermined weak lines.

Molting is also referred to as ecdysis. During ecdysis, the insect looks, and is, very soft and susceptible to injury. The new skin is larger than the old one but is soft and flexible and allows expansion of the insect's body.

Soon after the insect emerges from the old skin, a process called sclerotization, or hardening of the new skin, begins. The insect is relatively quiescent (inactive) during this period, lacking sound structural support for muscular movements. Within an hour or more, the sclerotization process is complete, and the insect starts consuming more food to fill the new, larger skin.

Molting is traumatic for insects. Many things can go wrong, resulting in death or deformity. Each time the insect molts, it increases in size. The process is repeated until the insect reaches the adult stage.

Though most insects damage fruit crops or trees in only one stage, it is important to recognize and associate the stages that precede and follow the damaging stage so proper pest management practices can take place.

■ *Metamorphosis*

When insects molt, they not only grow larger, but their bodies also undergo form changes. A change in form, such as a caterpillar changing into a moth, is called metamorphosis. Like molting, insect metamorphosis is controlled by hormones. The change at each

molt is dictated by a substance called juvenile hormone (JH), which is located in glands just behind the brain (Fig. 4).

JH is released from the glands during each molt. It is the relative ratio of JH to ecdysone, rather than the lack of JH, that prompts an insect into a particular metamorphosis stage. JH is present in large amounts in early immature stages. These concentrations gradually decrease as the insect matures. JH is nearly absent in the final stage, permitting full expression of adult characters (Fig. 3).

Normal growth can be disrupted if the JH is introduced at the wrong time or in the wrong concentration during the insect's life cycle. This can often lead to death. Some new "third generation" insecticides mimic juvenile hormones and use this principle to achieve pest control. These insecticides are part of a group known as insect growth regulators (IGRs). Another type of IGR is the chitin synthesis inhibitors, which interfere with eggs' development into unhatched larvae and molting of larvae into subsequent instars.

A new class of insect growth regulators mimics the molting hormone ecdysone and causes larvae to undergo molts prematurely. Because the insect's physiology is not yet ready for a molt, abnormalities occur at ecdysis and the larva soon dies.

There are two basic types of insect metamorphosis: gradual and complete. Gradual metamorphosis is considered a more primitive form, whereby the insect grows larger at each molt, but little external change is visible. In these insects, the immature stages, or nymphs (Fig. 5), resemble the adults, though nymphs have undeveloped external wing pads that will develop when the insect reaches the adult stage. Nymphs are found in the same habitat and usually feed on the same host as adults. Adults differ from nymphs in that adults possess wings and reproductive organs. Common tree fruit pests exhibiting gradual metamorphosis include rosy apple aphid, white apple leafhopper and tarnished plant bug. (See Exhibit A in this chapter for a more complete list, along with

Fig. 5 Gradual metamorphosis of insects.

Fig. 6 Events and stages in complete metamorphosis.

some characteristics of insect species exhibiting gradual metamorphosis.)

Complete metamorphosis involves greater changes in body shape and lifestyle (Fig. 6) than gradual metamorphosis. The differences between the immature and adult stages are obvious, because larvae, which are another segment of the immature stage, do not resemble the adult stage. Wings develop internally in the larvae and can't be seen until the pupal stage. The pupa is a special resting stage that is needed to complete the transformation.

The feeding habits and host plants of immature and adult forms usually differ as well. It is not as easy to associate immature and adult stages of insects that undergo complete metamorphosis as it is to make such associations with gradually metamorphosing insects. Many extremely destructive tree fruit insects, such as the apple maggot, codling moth, plum curculio and cherry fruit fly, experience complete metamorphosis. Consult Exhibit A for more information on characteristics and a list of these pests.

■ *Life Histories*

It is becoming increasingly important for fruit growers and consultants to know the life histories of arthropod pests that attack fruit crops. Knowing the number of generations completed per year, host plants utilized, the timing of various life stages, overwintering stages and movements between host plants is critical to make optimum use of resources to combat pest organisms.

The primary tactic currently used to maintain pests below economic injury levels is chemical control. To be effective, pesticide applications must coincide with the presence of the pest. Many pests invade orchards from outside sources. Others remain in the orchard continuously. In either case, they are present for only a short time in a life stage that is susceptible to chemical control. Therefore, it is to your advantage to be aware of these life stages so you can properly time chemical controls.

In addition, recent non-chemical pest control tactics implemented by fruit pest management projects (e.g., biological control, mating disruption, sterile male releases, genetic control, etc.) demand that growers and field advisors have more detailed knowledge of insect life histories than ever before. Many insecticides being developed for future use are extremely stage-specific and must be timed even for particular larval instars.

Most tree fruit arthropod pests complete one or two generations per year. A few, such as aphids and mites, complete several generations, continuing to reproduce until conditions become unfavorable. Because arthropods are poikilothermic (cold-blooded), they cannot continue activity during winter months. Each pest species usually has one life stage especially adapted for surviving the winter.

Insect life histories differ in complexity. The apple maggot, for example, completes one generation and utilizes only a few host plants. The European red mite, on the other hand, completes six to eight generations, usually on the same plant, though this species is

Insects exhibiting gradual metamorphosis

Plant Bugs	Leafhoppers	Aphids	Scale	Mites

Plant Bugs

Antennae visible, usually half as long as body, head smaller than abdomen, color variable, medium-sized insect (³⁄₁₆ to ⅜ in.), active flier.

• **Tarnished plant bug**

Leafhoppers

Antennae not readily visible, head wider than abdomen, color light cream to green, found on undersides of leaves, active jumpers and fliers, small to medium-sized (¹⁄₁₆ to ¼ in.).

• **Potato leafhopper**
• **White apple leafhopper**

Aphids

Antennae visible, head smaller than abdomen, soft-bodied, occur in colonies, not active fliers or jumpers, small to medium-sized (¹⁄₁₆ to ⅜ in.).

• **Apple grain aphid**
• **Rosy apple aphid**
• **Woolly apple aphid**
• **Black cherry aphid**
• **Green peach aphid**

Scale

Crawlers yellowish and small, other stages legless, flat, covered with scale, immobile, usually dark brown to blackish, small.

• **San Jose scale**
• **European fruit lecanium scale**
• **Oystershell scale**

Mites

No antennae, 8 legs, color variable, very small and active, head reduced in size, usually many found on a leaf.

• **European red mite**
• **Twospotted mite**
• **Apple rust mite**
• **Pear rust mite**
• *A. fallacis*
• *Z. mali*

Insects exhibiting complete metamorphosis

Larval stages

Grub-like	Caterpillars	Worms or maggots
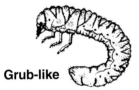		

Grub-like

Head capsule well formed, thoracic legs usually present, body often C-shaped and white or cream-colored, usually found in plant tissue or soil (not exposed foliage feeder).

Caterpillars

Head capsule well formed, thoracic legs and usually abdominal legs present, body not C-shaped and coloration variable; external foliage and internal fruit feeders.

Worms or maggots

Head capsule absent, body tapers toward head end where internal mouth hooks may be seen, body usually white or cream-colored; feed internally on fruit.

Adult stages

Beetles	Moths	Flies

Beetles

• **Plum curculio**
• **Apple curculio**
• **Japanese beetle**
• *Stethorus punctum*
• **Ladybird beetles**

Moths

• **Codling moth**
• **Redbanded leafroller**
• **Green fruitworm**
• **Tentiform leafminer**
• **Obliquebanded leafroller**
• **Peachtree borer**
• **Oriental fruit moth**
• **Tufted apple bud moth**
• **Lesser peachtree borer**
• **American plum borer**
• **Lesser appleworm**
• **Casebearers**

Flies

• **Apple maggot**
• **Cherry fruit fly**
• **Black cherry fruit fly**
• **Syrphid flies**

capable of developing on a number of host plants. Still another pest, the pear psylla, completes three to four generations, all restricted to a single host plant (pear).

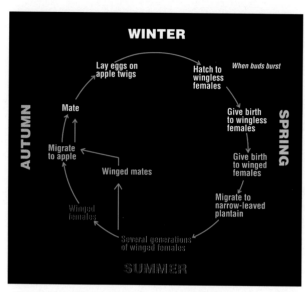

Fig. 7 Life history of the rosy apple aphid.

The most complex of all life histories are those of aphids. Rosy apple aphids initiate their seasonal life history as wingless aphids on apples, where three to four generations are completed. Winged forms are then produced, which migrate to summer hosts, where several generations of wingless aphids occur. As fall approaches, winged forms are again produced. These fly back to apples, where they mate and deposit overwintering eggs (see Fig. 7).

Since memorizing all the life histories of fruit pests is a formidable task, you may find it more practical to segregate the growing season into important growth stages (e.g., silver tip, bloom, shuck-split, etc.) and indicate the important pests that are active during these stages. This way, pest life histories could be compartmentalized by growing-season stages, and the orchard could be monitored only for those pests deemed important during each period. Regardless of how you choose to master information on insect and mite life histo-

ries, its importance to efficient, safe pest control cannot be underrated.

■ *Factors Affecting Growth*

To predict the growth of an insect population or the occurrence of a particular stage within an insect's life history, you must know what factors influence growth and how those factors affect growth. Like all cold-blooded organisms, insects' and mites' activity and growth are regulated by the physical environment. Conditions such as rain, humidity, photoperiod (day length) and evaporation all affect growth, but temperature appears to be the dominant factor in determining growth rate.

Insects do not respond to temperature as we do. Human body temperature remains constant, and the rate of growth is determined by factors other than air temperature. Insect response to daily temperatures is por-

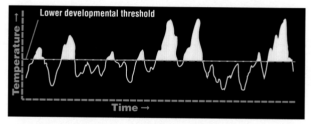

Fig. 8 Daily temperature trace showing how an insect's growth is influenced by daily temperature fluctuations.

trayed in Fig. 8. The horizontal line passing through the daily temperature trace represents the insect's growth or lower developmental threshold (LDT). Also known as base temperature, LDT varies from insect to insect. At temperatures below this threshold, the insect does not grow, or growth is so slow that its rate is essentially zero. Growth occurs at temperatures above the LDT; the higher the temperature, the more rapid the growth. The shaded area above the LDT and below the temperature trace approximates the growth occurring each day. The size of this shaded area varies from day to day in relation to the temperature and can be considered a measure of physiological time. On some days, no physiological time is accumulated, and no growth occurs; on other days, the amount varies, depending on how high the temperature is and the length of time it remains above the LDT. Some insects have an upper temperature threshold where growth completely stops and at which they may die if that temperature persists over extended periods.

The importance of considering insect growth in terms of physiological time as opposed to chronological time (days) can be made clear by a simple example. In Fig. 9, the period from April 15 through May 25 is presented in chronological and physiological time. The top line represents the chronological time scale and is the same for both years. The middle line represents the same time period for Year One, presented as physiological time. The bottom line is a physiological time scale for Year Two. Assume that the insect's LDT is 50 degrees F. When temperatures exceed 50 degrees F, insect growth proceeds as an accumulation of physiological time.

insect growth occurs (e.g., April 21–27, Year One, or April 17–25, Year Two). The periods of slow and rapid growth rate do not coincide during each year. As a result, a particular insect life stage may occur on different dates in different years.

To carry this example further, consider for a moment only the effect that chronological time has in timing insecticide sprays. Suppose that the critical event in the life history of a pest is egg hatch and the best chronological estimate of this event is May 3. The selection of this date would be the result of observing the pest for several years and using the average date of egg hatch as the predicted date for egg hatch in the coming season. Placing a vertical line through the chronological (top) timeline at May 3 shows how this predicted date compares with the actual development of the pest.

In Year One, the chronological prediction date for egg hatch would be fairly close to the actual event in the field (May 5 on the physiological time scale). In Year Two, however, egg hatch did not occur until May 16, or two weeks after the predicted date based on chronological time. In this case, applying a pesticide on May 3 would have been futile, because the insect was still in the non-susceptible egg stage. This example emphasizes the importance of using physiological time to determine the most effective timing for applications rather than using the more traditional calendar or chronological scheduling of these control procedures.

For years, fruit growers have indirectly used the accumulation of physiological time to correctly apply insecticide sprays. They associate the arrival or development of a particular insect pest with flower bud or leaf development of the fruit tree. Since temperature influences tree growth much as it affects insect growth, growers use the tree as a natural indicator (or accumulator) of physiological

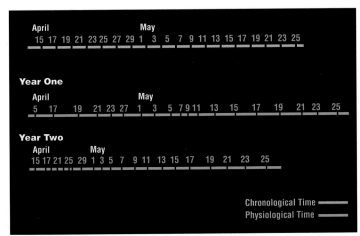

Fig. 9 Comparison of chronological and physiological time for a period of time during two years.

The accumulation of time on the chronological scale is the same for every day. On the physiological time scale, however, there are periods each year when little or no

time. In addition, this accumulator provides distinct cues (e.g., green tip, pink and petal-fall stages) when the time is right to apply controls. This natural timer is most useful early in the growing season when the tree growth stages are readily observable. However, a system for making accurate predictions

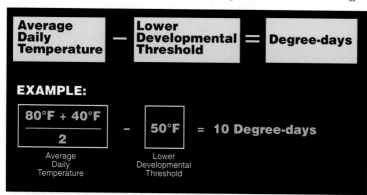

Fig. 10 Example of how to calculate degree-days to measure time in physiological units.

of insect life history events is needed throughout the growing season.

Entomologists have established methods of measuring physiological time and can estimate the rate of insect growth in response to daily temperatures. Each insect stage requires the accumulation of a certain number of physiological time units, called degree-days (DD), before molting to the next stage. The degree-day concept is an important one. Fig. 10 outlines a simple method of computing degree-days, given daily high and low temperatures. Calculating degree-day totals for each day provides an accurate estimate of physiological time accumulations. Several other accurate ways have been developed to determine degree-days, including the sine curve method, which involves hourly maximum-minimum temperature readings.

By studying insect development in the field and laboratory, entomologists have determined the LDTs (base temperatures) and degree-day totals for the life stages of some insects. The codling moth provides an example of how this information can be used to manage an insect pest. The LDT for the

codling moth is 50 degrees F. Exhibit B summarizes the degree-day totals associated with critical events in the life history of this pest. Degree-days are accumulated from first male catch in a pheromone trap. By starting the DD accumulation after this easily observed biological cue, growers can make a more accurate prediction of subsequent events in the insect's life history than if DD were accumulated from some arbitrary chronological starting date such as January 1. (NOTE: Traditionally, this starting date for insects and mites has been March 1 or April 1.) Assuming the optimum timings of insecticide controls were at first egg hatch, 50 percent egg hatch of the first generation and 50 percent egg hatch of the second generation, sprays would be applied after the accumulation of approximately 240, 460 and 1,302 degree-days, respectively. (NOTE: The degree-day model in Exhibit B is based on DD starting with the first male catch [biofix] instead of DD starting on March 1 or April 1. All DD models used in the biology text of this manual were taken from MSU PETE, a computer physiology model that figures DD starting March 1 or April 1.)

Exhibit B

Events in the life history of the codling moth, predicted by physiological time (degree-day accumulations)[1]

Life stage or event	DD accumulation from Biofix 1 [2]
First Generation	
First spring adults	0
First egg hatch	243 ± 21
Peak adult emergence	252 ± 38
50% egg hatch	465 ± 16
Second Generation	
50% egg hatch	1302 ± 44
Peak adult emergence	1329 ± 80

[1] Data from Riedl and Croft (1978). Management of the Codling Moth In Michigan.

[2] Biofix 1 refers to the first male codling moth catch in a pheromone trap.

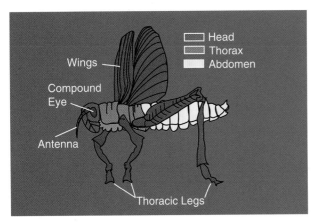

Fig. 11 Basic morphology of an adult insect.

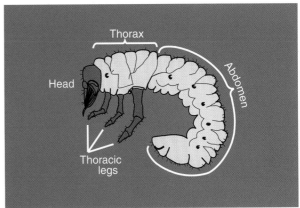

Fig. 12 Morphology of scarab beetle larva.

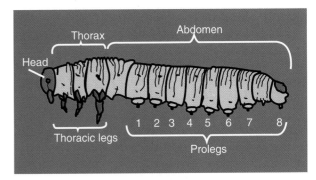

Fig. 13 Morphology of caterpillar-like insect larva that shows the abdominal prolegs.

■ *Identification*

Most decisions concerning insect and mite control are made in the field after infestations are detected. It is essential to correctly identify pests before taking control actions. When attempting to identify pests threatening your crops, you should consider three main categories of information — morphology, ecology and temporal considerations.

Morphology

Morphology refers to the insect's physical appearance, which includes but is not limited to color, size and shape. All insects have a similar shape. Adult insects are composed of three body regions — the head, containing the sense organs (eyes, mouth, antennae); the thorax, to which the legs and wings are attached; and the abdomen, which contains the sex organs (Fig. 11). Immature insect stages have the same body regions (Fig. 12), although some have leglike structures on the abdomen (Fig. 13), and some lack legs altogether and have reduced head capsules.

The head and thorax are fused and reduced in mites. This structure is referred to as the cephalothorax, and four pairs of legs arise from it. The abdomen of mites is not distinctly segmented, and it is large and bulbous relative to the rest of the organism.

Body shape and color are the two most useful morphological characteristics to consider when identifying pests. The shape of the body can be used to rapidly separate insects or mites, thus greatly reducing the candidates. Exhibit A in this chapter groups pest insects and mites by body form and may be useful in helping make such determinations. With a little practice, the beginner should be able to tell an adult fly from a moth, or a maggot from a caterpillar.

Once the insect's body is correctly categorized, color becomes an important determining character. This book contains color pictures of pests and some beneficial insects to help you compare and differentiate between insects with similar body forms.

Ecology

Ecology has different meanings for different people. We use the term inclusively to mean the location where an insect is found, which fruit trees it inhabits, where it occurs on trees, and what types of feeding injury or other injury it produces.

Many pests feed on a variety of plants, including different fruit trees, though a few have a restricted host plant range. Knowing the potential pests of each fruit tree crop helps eliminate many possibilities when attempting to identify an insect.

Insect location on the fruit tree can provide a clue to identity. Most insects feed on certain parts of the tree or fruit. For example, apple aphids are found on growing terminals, while rosy apple aphids prefer spur leaves. Understanding where an insect is most likely to be found also helps streamline monitoring by reducing the area to be examined.

This book contains many examples of typical feeding damage caused by primary and secondary pests. The type of damage to the fruit tree often helps determine the responsible pest. Many times the damage is not observed until after the insect is gone; however, it is important to associate damage with the insect to implement controls against subsequent generations.

Feeding behavior can also be used to differentiate between pests. Internal feeders of apple, for example, include the codling moth, lesser appleworm, apple maggot and plum curculio. All of these insects leave different clues, however, in their feeding habits. The codling moth usually enters the apple from the calyx end or side, and the larva feeds at the center of the apple on the flesh and developing seeds. The lesser appleworm larva resembles that of the codling moth, but it generally does not feed as deeply. The apple maggot larva tunnels erratically through the fruit flesh, leaving brown trails. The plum curculio larva also tunnels through the apple, but the trails are much larger and are indicated by a granule-like brown frass.

Temporal Considerations

It is helpful to know the time of year when you might encounter a particular life stage of a specific insect in the orchard. For example, suppose you find a small caterpillar in an apple orchard at the petal-fall stage. You could quickly eliminate the obliquebanded leafroller, green fruitworm or fruittree leafroller as the culprit because larvae of these pests would be nearly mature at this stage. Codling moth could also be eliminated because egg hatch would not yet have occurred by petal-fall. The only common pest caterpillar that would be present as a young larva at that time during the growing season would be the redbanded leafroller.

Agro-ecosystems are much less diverse than wild habitats or abandoned agricultural areas, and the fruit tree orchard is no exception. Insecticides and miticides used in orchards are intended to maximize production by minimizing fruit loss to insect and mite pests. In so doing, they eliminate many species — both pests and beneficials — that would normally occur on the crop under pesticide-free conditions. This alone makes pest identification easier.

The insects and mites that remain or most commonly reappear in the orchard are those that are either most chemical-tolerant or most abundant.

Occasionally, you may find insects in the orchard that are not discussed in this book. They may be harmless, accidental visitors that should cause you no concern, or they could be a new pest or secondary pest increasing in numbers in response to changed orchard practices. Most Cooperative Extension Service (CES) agricultural agents or state university entomologists can identify insects that puzzle growers or consultants. If you run across such a pest, consider contacting these specialists or sending specimens to the proper location for positive identification. Once the specimen is identified, you may wish to save it for future reference.

ARTHROPOD PESTS *OF* POME FRUITS

- *Apple Pests*
- *Pear Pests*

APPLE BUD DEVELOPMENT STAGES

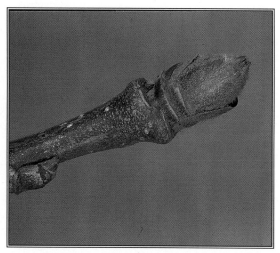

1. Dormant

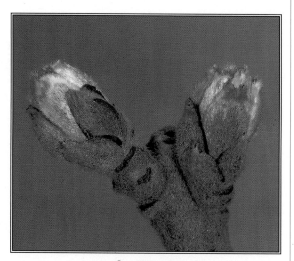

2. Silver tip

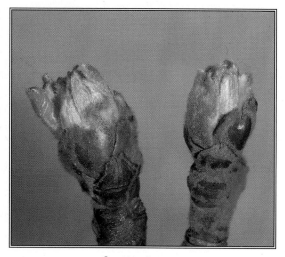

3. ¼ inch green

4. ½ inch green

5. Tight cluster

6. Pink

7. Full pink

8. King blossom

9. Full bloom

10. Petal fall

Apple Pests

Insects that burrow into or feed inside the fruit

THESE ARE SOME OF THE MOST DAMAGING AND COSTLY PESTS THAT attack fruit. Because most of the damage they cause is directed against the fruit, these insects are referred to as direct pests. A single feeding incident by these insects will make a fruit unsalable or render it to cull, where it may be used only for juice. It will also reduce the storability of processing apples and increase storage rot and disease.

Codling moth, apple maggot and plum curculio probably rank as the three most important pests of apples. Codling moth can be readily controlled by chemicals if the proper chemical in the proper dosage is applied at the right time. However, the codling moth may be the most expensive pest of apples to control because of the number of times in a season that pesticides are applied to control it.

Apple maggot is one of fruit growers' most feared pests. A few females have the potential to infest many apples. This insect is an insidious pest in that the damage it inflicts may not be apparent for some time after the fruit is infested.

Plum curculio is considered one of the most difficult apple pests to control. There are no good survey methods or pheromones available to time or estimate its populations. Pesticides for this insect are generally applied at petal fall and first cover. However, the lack of good monitoring methods, as well as the presence of rapidly changing meteorological conditions, make plum curculio a troublesome pest.

Chapter 1

Common Name—
Codling Moth

Scientific Name—
Cydia pomonella (Linnaeus)

Family—
Tortricidae

THE CODLING MOTH ORIGINATED IN ASIA Minor. It was carried into Europe by invading migrants and from this point was disseminated to all apple-growing areas of the world. It was brought to America by the colonists and has been one of the principal apple pests for more than 200 years.

It became a serious problem in the Midwest shortly after the Civil War and continued to be a problem until about 1900, when use of arsenicals became widespread. From this time to the early 1930s, commercial orchardists generally controlled it effectively, though some losses began to occur about 1925. These control failures were due largely to the codling moth's development of resistance to lead arsenate.

Increasing losses were experienced until 1946, when DDT came into use. The insect was well controlled for the next 10 years. DDT then began to lose its effectiveness, but with new insecticides such as Sevin and Guthion, injury by this pest was very light from 1959 to 1961. In certain periods, it was undoubtedly a major insect pest of apples, but at other times it was relatively unimportant. Even with the new effective spray chemicals of today, the codling moth must still be considered an ever-present threat. Recently, resistance to organophosphate insecticides has become a problem in some areas of Washington and Oregon.

■ Life Stages

Egg: The egg is very small, flattened, almost transparent and elliptical, measuring 1 to 1.2 mm in diameter.

Larva: Just-hatched larvae are very small — about 2 mm long and 0.5 mm in diameter. At this stage, the head is almost twice as wide as the body. When the larvae are young and boring into the fruit, they are pale yellow. The mature larva is white, usually tinged with pink; its head is brown, and it measures approximately 13 mm. The full-grown larva can be distinguished from Oriental fruit moth and lesser appleworm larvae found in fruit by the absence of the chitinous protuberance on the end of the abdomen called the anal comb. There are five instars.

Pupa: The brown pupae vary from 10 to 12 mm in length with a width of 3 mm. The pupae of females are usually longer and wider than the pupae of males. Immediately after the transformation of the larva into the pupa, the color of the pupa is the same as that of the larva. Later it changes, gradually becoming brown. Pupae that will develop into males can be identified by the presence of two clearly marked little circles — the future gonads — on the ventral surface of the sixth abdominal segment.

Adult: The moth averages about 19 mm across the expanded wings and 9 mm long with the wings folded. It is gray-brown, crisscrossed with fine alternating gray and white bands. Near the tips of the forewings are

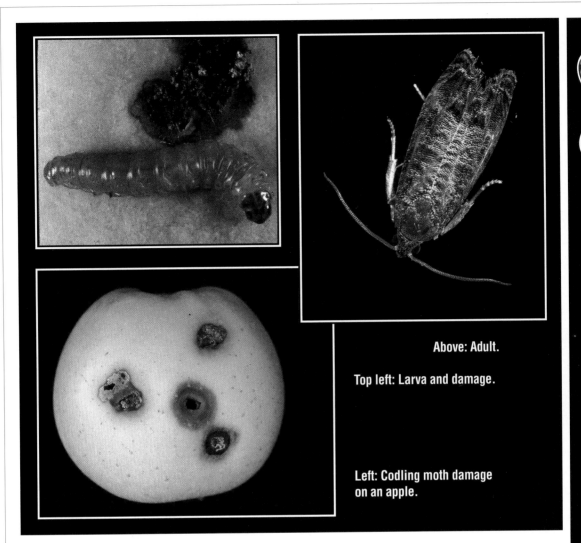

Above: Adult.

Top left: Larva and damage.

Left: Codling moth damage on an apple.

bronzed areas characteristic of the codling moth.

Host Range

The codling moth is a pest of apples and pears and a pest of walnuts on the West Coast. It is present in all fruit-growing areas of the United States and Canada. It was an apricot pest in the past and is found in quince, peach, plum and cherry.

Injury or Damage

The codling moth causes two types of injury to the fruit: deep entries and stings. Deep entries are caused by larvae that eat through the skin into the side or from the calyx end. Sting entries occur where the larvae died before gaining entry or where they began tunneling, stopped and then began other feeding entrances elsewhere on the fruit. Second-generation larvae cause most of the damage.

Factors Affecting Abundance

In all seasons, climatic conditions influence the activities of the codling moth. Temperature is the most important of the climatic factors, but humidity, rainfall and winds are also important. If high temperatures prevail during the season, adult codling moths

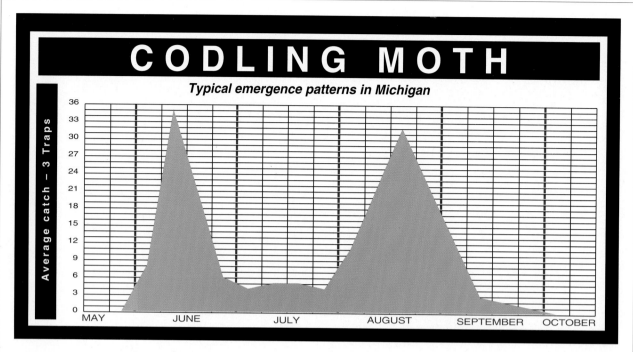

CODLING MOTH
Typical emergence patterns in Michigan

will emerge earlier in the spring and deposit more eggs. These will hatch earlier in the season and in greater numbers and, in turn, more of these larvae will succeed in finding and entering fruit. In the fruit, they feed more voraciously than they would in cool weather and mature earlier. They leave the fruit to find cocooning quarters and the moths again emerge earlier.

A warm, early spring may result in accelerated development of the first and second generations, sometimes resulting in a partial third "suicide" generation. The young larvae of this partial third generation will not survive overwintering.

Rainfall and moisture are needed to hasten the development of pupae and the emergence of moths. Low humidity, on the other hand, seems to help the larvae enter the fruit. Heavy winds will cause the moths to cling to protected hiding places, while light breezes will aid in their flight and distribution.

■ *Life History*

Codling moths overwinter as mature larvae in tightly constructed silken cocoons located principally under loose bark on the tree trunk and larger limbs. Cocoons may also be found in other places in the orchard, such as piles of wood, brush, posts and occasionally in coarse mulch, such as weed stalks and corn cobs. In addition, larvae overwinter in stored baskets or crates that have held cull fruit and in the walls of packing sheds and other buildings adjacent to the orchard.

The overwintering larvae start to transform to pupae inside the cocoon about the time that the first blossoms show color. The bulk of pupation usually occurs during bloom, but some larvae may not transform until a month later. Prior to pupation, the larva cuts a circular opening in one end of the cocoon and the pupa thrusts its way out through this aperture just before the moth emerges.

The first moth of the season usually appears as the last petals fall from the apple blossoms. Peak emergence may occur within four or five days after the first moth emerges. Weather conditions such as low temperatures may delay it as much as 10 or 12 days. The last moths of the first brood may not appear until six or seven weeks after petal fall. Moths emerge usually during the morning hours and begin laying eggs within two or three days if the evening temperatures are favorable, i.e., above 62 degrees F. Few eggs are laid at this low point, but when temperatures approach 70 degrees F, egg deposition increases greatly, and above this point even more will be laid.

Eggs are laid on the fruit or on nearby leaves. A female may lay up to 100 eggs. Eggs hatch in six to 14 days, depending on the prevailing temperatures. The newly hatched larva is white with a black head and is large enough to be seen with the naked eye. Those hatching on leaves wander about seeking the fruits, which many of them fail to find. On the fruit, larvae may wander about seeking a rough area such as the calyx or a scab spot, which aids them in making an entrance. The silken threads against which they brace themselves while digging in are more securely anchored to rough areas on the apple's surface.

If successful in entering, they feed inside the apple for about three weeks, after which they leave it to seek a cocooning site on the trunk or larger branches of the tree. If the apple has fallen to the ground, the emerging larva will travel in circles until it comes to the tree trunk or another solid object where it will find cocooning quarters.

The time spent in the cocoon depends on temperature and rainfall but is usually 14 to 21 days. Many larvae do not transform to pupae during this time, however, but continue as larvae until the next spring. Those that will emerge as moths of the second brood pupate in the cocoon as already described and start emerging as early as July. Second-brood moths will lay eggs over about two months. Mature larvae of the second brood start leaving the apples in mid-August and continue until apples are removed from the orchard or until very cold weather arrives. These larvae, together with those of the first brood that did not pupate, will overwinter and start the cycle again the next spring.

■ Monitoring

At full bloom, use one pheromone trap per 10 acres of orchard. Set the traps in the foliage at eye level on the north side of the tree. Place the traps in the portion of the orchard most likely to be entered by moths from wild hosts or abandoned or poorly sprayed orchards. Traps should be checked once a week. If the total moth counts in the commercial orchard are 14 or more per trap per week, sprays are needed. Traps and caps should be replaced about mid-July. When problems exist, apple maggot sprays will dictate the timing of codling moth sprays that are required in the latter part of July and mid-August.

Check for first-generation damage in mid-July by searching for apples with frass. This will help determine the potential of the second generation.

Using 50 degrees F as a base, degree-days (DD) for codling moth activity* are:

    150 DD ... first adult emergence.
    250 DD ... first eggs laid.
    500 DD ... peak adult emergence.
    550 DD ... peak egg laying.
  1,150 DD ... first emergence of
               second-generation adults.
  1,600 DD ... peak emergence of
               second-generation adults.
  1,700 DD ... peak egg laying by
               second-generation adults.

■ Control

Codling moth control requires careful monitoring and timing of insecticide applications to coincide with the hatching of larvae. If insecticides are applied too late, larvae will have tunneled into the fruit, where the insecticides can not affect them.

The first spray to control the first-generation codling moth is applied at 500 to 550 DD accumulated after April 1, or 250 DD after the first sustained catch in the

*Data from MSU PETE model.

pheromone traps. A second application can be made two to three weeks later, if needed. Growers who don't want to make routine applications can use an action threshold of five moths per trap per week. If the number of moths trapped exceeds this number, an insecticide application should be made in seven to 10 days. Repeat applications should be made only if the moths exceed this threshold 14 days after the insecticide application.

Sprays for the second generation are applied at 1,400 to 1,600 DD, before peak adult emergence and before the eggs start to hatch.

Common Name—
Lesser Appleworm

Scientific Name—
Grapholitha prunivora (Walsh)

Family—
Tortricidae

THE LESSER APPLEWORM IS A MINOR PEST of apple. The larvae are fruit feeders that resemble codling moth larvae. This pest is native to the eastern United States.

Life Stages

Egg: The eggs are laid singly on leaves and fruit and appear white at first. With further development, a yellow mass appears in the center of the egg. This is the newly formed larva. Just before hatching, the head capsule of the larva can be seen as a black spot in the yellow mass. The egg is 0.6 mm wide and 0.75 mm long.

Larva: The newly hatched larva is 1 to 1.5 mm long. The fully mature larva is about 9 mm long and has a characteristic pink tinge to its abdomen. This helps distinguish it from most other lepidopterous larvae that may infest the same host. Like lesser appleworm larvae, however, Oriental fruit moth larvae infest apples and they, too, are pinkish. Both the lesser appleworm and Oriental fruit moth have an anal comb. The only certain way to distinguish lesser appleworm larvae from Oriental fruit moth larvae is to rear them to adults. The head capsule of the lesser appleworm is dark brown. The last instar larva spins a loose cocoon before it pupates.

Pupa: The pupa is about 5 mm long and is found in the orchard debris or under loose pieces of bark.

Adult: The adult is a small (6 mm long), dark-colored moth with a few gold scales scattered over the forewings. Two larger gold areas occur in the middle of both wings and on top of the head. When the wings are folded in the resting position, these areas form a gold band stretching across the back. The wing span measures 10 to 12 mm.

Host Range

Apples, plums and cherries are the preferred hosts of the lesser appleworm. It has also been reported infesting apricots, pears, peaches, crabapples and wild rose hips. It can be found in all apple-growing areas of the United States and Canada.

Injury or Damage

The lesser appleworm larva can be distinguished from that of the codling moth by its feeding habits. The codling moth larva feeds through the fruit skin and burrows toward the core, leaving dark brown castings at the entrance hole. The lesser appleworm larva does not leave a definite entrance hole.

Though the calyx end is the preferred entry point, entrance through the side is very common. The appleworm

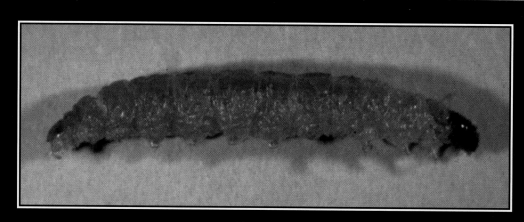

Above: Larva.

Above: Adult.

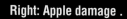

Right: Apple damage .

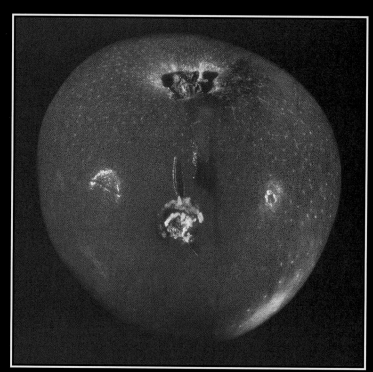

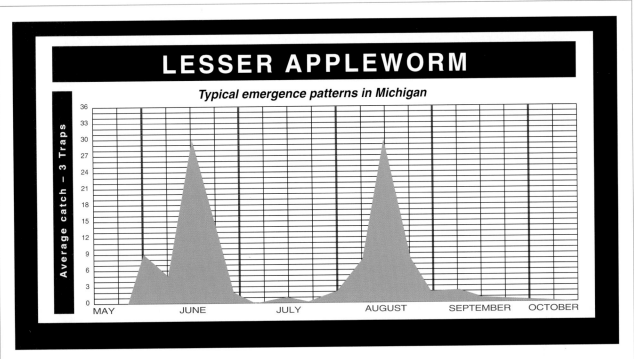

LESSER APPLEWORM

Typical emergence patterns in Michigan

can cause twig injury on apples similar to that caused by the Oriental fruit moth on peaches. This occurs early in the season when the terminal parts of rapidly growing apple twigs are succulent. The larvae enter from the terminal and consume the central parts of twigs as they work their way down the shoot for 3 to 6 inches. Twigs infested by larvae will exhibit wilted leaves, which later die and turn a conspicuous brown.

■ *Factors Affecting Abundance*

The lesser appleworm is a native pest whose original hosts were crabapple, wild rose and hawthorn. The presence of these wild hosts in a fruit tree area can be a source of lesser appleworm infestations.

■ *Life History*

The lesser appleworm overwinters as a full-grown larva in a cocoon on the tree, in litter or under the loose bark scales of the host tree. Many times, the pupa will be found in the hollow stems of dead weeds or attached to twigs or other suitable objects. During the spring — beginning at the pre-

bloom stage and continuing for about three weeks — the larva changes into a pupa. The first moths appear in the field around petal fall, with the majority appearing around first cover spray. Shortly after emergence, mating occurs and eggs are deposited on fruits or upper leaf surfaces.

Larvae appear in early June. The tiny larva immediately searches for fruit on which to feed. On occasion, it will bore into terminals and cause twig injury. On apples, the larva mines immediately under the outer skin, making a twisted tunnel that is visible through the outer skin of the fruit. The larvae are shallow feeders, producing a blotchy mine below the skin that is rarely deeper than ¼ inch.

When it matures, the larva bores to the outside of the fruit through the skin and drops to the ground. The fully mature larva has a pinkish skin. This is not a distinguishing characteristic, however, because both codling moth and Oriental fruit moth larvae can be pink.

By late July, most larvae are mature. Pupation occurs inside silken cocoons spun in sheltered places on the bark or in the fruit. First-generation adults begin emerging the first week in August. Second-generation larvae are found in fruit from mid-August through early October. When fully grown, these larvae seek sites for overwintering as mature larvae in cocoons.

■ *Monitoring*

Place pheromone traps in the orchard around full-pink stage. Replace traps and caps the latter part of July. Note that commercial lesser appleworm pheromone lures often catch significant numbers of Oriental fruit moth males because of the similarity in the pheromones of these closely related moths. Lesser appleworm males are attracted to a lesser degree to Oriental fruit moth lures. If the number of moths trapped in the first

(May–June) or second (August–September) emergence indicates a problem that the regular sprays will not control, spray one week after a steady, continuous moth catch during both the spring and late summer emergence. Note that the adult emergence overlaps that of codling moth.

■ *Control*

Spray applications should be directed at the adults before they lay their eggs and also at the newly hatched larvae before they enter the fruit. Timing of sprays is of great importance, and pheromone trapping of males is helpful. Codling moth sprays will control the lesser appleworm because both species emerge at the same time.

Common Name—
Apple Maggot

Scientific Name—
Rhagoletis pomonella (Walsh)

Family—
Tephritidae

As EARLY AS 1865, APPLE MAGGOTS seriously damaged the apple crop of New England. The apple maggot is a native pest that fed on the fruit of hawthorn and juneberries. On apples, this pest was known as "railroad worm."

■ Life Stages

Egg: The eggs are 0.90 mm long and 0.25 mm wide, elliptical, semi-opaque and creamy white.

Larva: When full grown, larvae are 8 mm long and 2 mm wide. They are usually cream-colored. The exact color depends on the contents of the alimentary tract, which may have a greenish to brownish tinge. The larva is a footless maggot. The head end can be distinguished by its pointed shape and the presence of the dark, hook-shaped, chitinous jaws that dig the tunnels and soften the pulp about the larva.

Pupa: The pupa is pale yellowish brown and oval shaped. It measures about 4.5 mm long and is about half as broad.

Adult: The female fly is about 5.8 mm long with a wing expanse of 12 mm. The thorax is black and marked with a dorsal white spot. The wings are broad and clear at the base. Four dark cross-bands traverse each wing. The abdomen of the female is black and

Wing banding patterns of deciduous fruit flies

Cherry fruit fly

Black cherry fruit fly

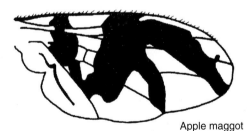

Apple maggot

striped with four white transverse bands. The ovipositor is sharply pointed and somewhat curved at the end; the tip of the abdomen is rounded. The male is smaller than the female. The male's abdomen has only three white bands on it.

■ Host Range

Apple maggots infest apples, pears, plums, apricots, hawthorns and crab-

Above: Larvae and interior damage.

Right : Apple maggot damage on an apple.

Left: Female.
Right: Male.

apples. They are a major problem in the midwestern and eastern United States and eastern Canada. The apple maggot is also found in California, Oregon and Washington.

■ *Injury or Damage*

The apple maggot causes two forms of injury. The flesh surrounding a puncture where eggs are deposited in immature fruit often fails to grow with the rest of the apple and becomes a sunken, dimplelike spot in the surface. When the larvae feed and move through the fruit, they leave a characteristic brown trail through the flesh of the apple that can readily be seen when the fruit is cut open. When several maggots are in a fruit, the interior tissues may break down and depressions and discoloration may be visible from the outside. Injured apples usually drop prematurely.

■ *Factors Affecting Abundance*

The maggot will build up large populations in unsprayed orchards.

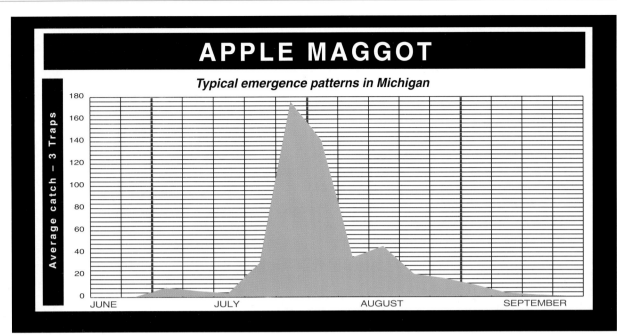

APPLE MAGGOT

Typical emergence patterns in Michigan

Life History

The apple maggot passes the winter in the pupal stage in the top 2 or 3 inches of soil. In the summer, these pupae give rise to flies, which emerge from the soil from late June through early September.

The flies do not begin to lay eggs until eight to 10 days after emergence. During this period, called the preoviposition period, both the males and the females rest and feed in the general area in which they emerged. They move readily from tree to tree but normally only for short distances, usually no more than 200 or 300 yards. The flies are not particularly attracted to apple fruits during this period and may be found in unfruited trees and shrubs in and around the orchard.

At the end of the preoviposition period and after mating, the female flies seek out the fruits. They place the eggs just under the skin through a puncture made by the sharp, needlelike ovipositor. Females may lay eggs over an extended period of time. Eggs usually hatch in less than a week. Maggots hatching from these eggs tunnel through the apple, causing a breakdown and discoloration of the pulp. The mature maggots leave the fruit and enter the soil, where they transform to the pupal stage.

Most pupae remain in the soil until the following summer. A few individuals do not emerge until the second season; i.e., they remain in the pupal stage during the first winter, all the next season and the following winter. They emerge at the normal time during the second summer. These are not of much significance to growers who maintain good control every year, but they might be of importance in an orchard where the pest was allowed to become very numerous. Even after a vigorous and successful control program had been carried out for one year, there would still be some carryover for the second season.

Monitoring

Use canary-yellow, sticky baited traps and red spheres coated with bird Tanglefoot to detect adult emergence. Growers can enhance the attractiveness of traps by sprinkling one or two teaspoons of fresh ammonium acetate over each trap when it is hung.

Place four yellow traps per orchard at about eye level in the foliage on the south side of trees one to two rows in from the edge of the orchard. Change the traps every three weeks until the end of July. Then replace the yellow traps with red spheres (with volatiles available) to detect female egg-laying activity. Clean and renew the Tanglefoot every two weeks.

Using 50 degrees F as a base, degree-days (DD) for apple maggot activity* are:

   900 DD . . . first adult emergence.
1,100 DD . . . first eggs laid.
1,600 DD . . . peak adult emergence.
1,750 DD . . . peak egg laying.
2,800 DD . . . end of adult emergence.

■ *Control*

The only practical means to control the apple maggot is to kill the flies before females deposit eggs. Measures directed against any of the other stages have not proven successful. Eggs are deposited through minute punctures in the skin and cannot be killed by known ovicides. Furthermore, the skin punctures are undesirable blemishes on the fruits that should be prevented. The maggots are also protected within the fruits. The maggots go directly from the fruits to the soil, where they and the pupae into which they transform cannot be reached readily with insecticides.

At present, no practical method of treating soil to destroy this stage has been devised, although in the past, when persistent pesticides such as the cyclodienes were employed as fruit sprays, the soil in the drip areas of the trees contained high levels of these insecticides from the spray fallout. These residual pesticides in the soil were lethal to larvae leaving the fruit to pupate in the soil and greatly reduced resident populations of the pest in orchards.

Successful apple maggot control by killing the flies before egg deposition is possible and practical because of the 8- to 10-day preoviposition period. This usually allows sufficient time to kill the flies before they can infest the fruit. Theoretically, a toxic spray need not be applied until eight days after the first emergence and not again until eight days after the residual action of the spray is gone. In practice, however, a material with 10 days' residual activity must be applied at 10-day spray intervals to ensure good control. Practically, then, it is necessary to maintain a toxic residue in the orchard during most of the period of fly emergence. Adding liquid protein hydrolysate (available commercially) to the spray can greatly enhance the spray's effectiveness, because the fly actively feeds on and ingests the mixture of spray with the liquid bait. This can help compensate for inadequate coverage and reduced pesticide dosages.

Because flies move about freely in vegetation around the apple trees, particularly during the preoviposition period, it is desirable to spray interplanted and adjacent trees and shrubs. This free movement makes maggot control in backyard plantings very difficult.

Apple maggots are rarely residents of commercial orchards — they normally fly into commercial orchards from abandoned or neglected orchards. When flies enter commercial orchards varies greatly from orchard to orchard and from season to season. Monitoring will detect the first entry of flies into a commercial orchard. With careful monitoring, growers can control apple maggots with a minimum number of sprays. Studies conducted by entomologists have demonstrated that entry into an orchard by adult flies may vary from early July until mid-August. Traps should be set in the periphery of commercial orchards in locations where flies are most likely to enter. In many cases, it may be necessary to treat only the first several rows on the periphery, where flies enter the orchard. If at any time during monitoring an average of five flies per trap are caught in a week, apply an insecticide immediately. Flies caught for one to four days following the insecticide spray can be discounted.

*Data from MSU PETE model.

Common Name—
Plum Curculio

Scientific Name—
Conotrachelus nenuphar (Herbst)

Family—
Curculionidae

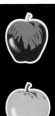

THE PLUM CURCULIO IS ONE OF THE most important insects attacking tree fruits. It is particularly destructive, and the problem is intensified where stone fruits and apples are interplanted.

■ Life Stages

Egg: The egg is 0.4 mm wide, 0.6 mm long, pearly white and elliptical. The female first constructs a cavity under the skin of the fruit to receive the egg. Then, turning around, she deposits the egg near the mouth of the cavity, forcing the egg into the cavity with her ovipositor or beak. She then cuts a crescent-shaped, oblique slit underneath the egg cavity to leave the egg in a flap of flesh. Crescent-shaped scars present on the fruit at harvest result from eggs that did not hatch or that were killed by pressures exerted by the growing fruit.

Larva: The larva is whitish and legless. When full grown, it measures about 6 to 9 mm long. The larva is slightly curved or bow-shaped and tapers slightly at each end. It has a brown head and a light brown shield behind the head. There are four larval instars.

Pupa: The pupa, which is found in the upper 1 to 2 inches of soil, is whitish or cream-colored and measures 5 to 7 mm. All of the adult structures, such as eyes, mouthparts, etc., are visible just before transformation into the adult.

Adult: The adult is a small, rough snout beetle, 4 to 6 mm long and mottled with black, gray and brown. Four pairs of ridges occur on the wing covers, but because the middle humps on each wing cover are larger, it appears to have only two humps. The sharp, biting jaws are located on the tip of a long, curved snout.

■ Host Range

The hosts of the plum curculio are apple, nectarine, plum, cherry, peach, apricot, pear and quince. The plum curculio can survive on wild plum, hawthorn and native crabapple. The plum curculio is generally distributed over the eastern states and in Canada, east of the Rocky Mountains.

■ Injury or Damage

Injury caused by the plum curculio can be grouped into four principal classes:

■ The wounds resulting from feeding and egg laying by the overwintering beetles early in the spring appear as crescent-shaped scars (oviposition injury) on the fruit, or as bumps (feeding injury) that protrude from the fruit at harvest. Badly attacked

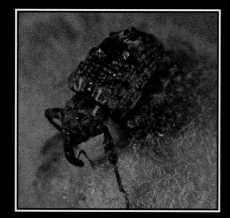

Above: Adult.

Above: Plum curculio larva and damage on apple.

Left: Egg of plum curculio in oviposition wound on plum.

Above: Oviposition scars on young apple and (right) on mature apple.

fruit may be knobby, gnarled and scarred at harvest.

- Internal injury is caused by the larvae's burrowing in the fruit. Most of the larvae-infested fruits drop to the ground during June.
- Premature dropping of the fruit during June or later in the season is a result of larval activity within the fruit or adults' feeding on the fruit.
- Feeding punctures made by the beetles in the fall just prior to hibernation are characterized by a small hole in the skin of the apple with a hollowed-out cavity in the flesh of the fruit that extends a few millimeters on each side of the opening.

Factors Affecting Abundance

Moisture and temperature regulate plum curculio activity. Moisture is necessary early in the spring to restore normal water relationships within the beetles. The exact role of water in the biology is not known, but it has been observed that beetles need water before much activity takes place. Also, beetles are more active on warm, damp, cloudy days and in thick, heavy trees that provide abundant dampness in the centers.

Temperature is the most important factor in plum curculio activity, particularly early in the spring. Several formulas have evolved to predict when beetles leave hibernation quarters and move to the trees to lay eggs or feed. They are:

- Mean temperature between 55 and 60 degrees F for three to four days.
- Mean temperature above 60 degrees F for several (three) days.
- Maximum temperature of 75 degrees F for two consecutive days.

All formulas work out about the same under field conditions. High winds, which cause considerable movement of the trees, will shake the beetles from the trees. High winds and low humidity cause beetles to leave the trees and burrow into the soil in search of moisture.

The beetles' activities are about equally distributed between day and night.

Life History

When temperature and moisture conditions are favorable in the spring, the adult beetles leave their hibernation quarters in trash on the ground, woodlots or hedgerows, and migrate to the trees. This usually occurs just about the time of bloom.

Migration continues for up to six weeks after bloom, with the largest migration occurring within the period up to 14 days after petal fall. The adults do not like strong light and prefer the dense shade of the tree's inner canopy.

After mating, the female deposits eggs into the fruit. Each female is capable of laying from 100 to 500 eggs. The incubation period for the eggs is about one week. The young larvae bore to the center of the fruit, where they feed until reaching maturity. Many infested fruits drop to the ground in June. After about 16 days in the larval stage, the full-grown larvae leave the fruit, enter the soil to a depth of about 1 inch, construct pupal cells and pupate. The length of time between larval entrance into the soil and the emergence of the new adult is about 30 days. The complete cycle from egg to adult takes about 50 to 55 days. After the adults emerge from the soil in late summer, they will feed on maturing apples until cold weather forces them into hibernation quarters.

Monitoring

During petal fall and the first cover period, tap the foliage or small limbs in early morning and catch the adults on a beating tray. Check the developing fruit for feeding and oviposition injury, especially after rain. The activity of this pest is closely related to temperature — 75 degrees F is highly favorable, and activity decreases at lower temperatures. Below 60 degrees F, activity is negligible. If temperatures reach 70 to 75 degrees F for two days before the petals fall, the beetles have opportunity to feed and mate.

■ *Control*

Petal-fall sprays and the first and second cover sprays are directed at the adult and the egg-laying period. Once the fruit is exposed, the females can lay many eggs in a short time and cause considerable damage. Under these conditions, a prompt petal-fall spray should be applied. If the weather is cool at bloom time and petal fall, the beetles may not leave hibernation quarters and move into the fruit trees until first cover. Under these conditions, a first cover application and possibly another application at second cover will be needed. Applications made at petal fall will not be fully effective under these conditions. Plum curculio is considered a difficult pest to control and requires a full dosage of an effective pesticide.

Common Name—
Apple Curculio

Scientific Name—
Tachypterellus quadrigibbus (Say)

Family—
Curculionidae

THE APPLE CURCULIO WAS FIRST described by Thomas Say in 1831. The insect is native to the eastern United States and Canada. Its original hosts seem to have been hawthorn and wild crabapple.

Life Stages

Egg: The eggs are quite uniform in size and measure 1 mm in length and 0.5 mm in diameter. They are pearly white when first laid but become yellowish within a day or two.

Larva: The larva is legless and yellowish white. Because of enlargement of some of the body segments, it has a curved form similar to that of the plum curculio larva. It passes through six larval instars.

Pupa: It averages 4.9 mm in length and 2.6 mm in width. At first the pupa is white, but it becomes darker as development progresses. It resembles the adult.

Adult: The adult apple curculio is brown with four very distinct humps on the back. The snout is longer and more slender than that of the plum curculio, being nearly as long as the insect's body. The head is small and the body enlarges toward the base of the abdomen, giving the insect a distinctly triangular outline when viewed from above.

Host Range

Apples are the major host. Cherries and plums are seldom, if ever, attacked. Females readily deposit eggs in pears, though pears do not usually offer suitable conditions for completion of the life cycle. When pears containing the eggs or grubs fall to the ground in the June drop, they dry rapidly and become shriveled and hard and unfavorable for the continued development of the pest. If the fruit containing the egg or larva continues to grow, the flesh of the pear is so firm and hard and growth is so rapid that the larva either starves or is crushed. Peaches and quinces can be hosts for the apple curculio.

In cultivated apples, some varieties are more susceptible than others. For example, more individuals can develop to maturity and emerge from Wealthy and McIntosh fruits than from fruits of such varieties as Northern Spy. However, when infested fruits fall to the ground as June drops, the insect seems to develop about equally well in all varieties. The apple curculio is found in the midwestern and eastern United States and in eastern Canada.

Injury or Damage

The larvae and adults attack apples, causing the fruit to be misshapen, knotty

Left: Relative size of plum curculio (left) and apple curculio adults.

Above: Adult and oviposition injury on apple.

and undersized. The adults eat small holes in the sides or ends of the apple, making many holes close together and causing a deadened area on the skin of the apple. Sunken pits or sharp-pointed protuberances on the apple are marked at their centers by a small puncture in the skin. On mature fruits, the injury may be distinguished from that of the plum curculio by the larger number of punctures close together through the skin, by the larger deadened areas on the fruit surface and by the absence of crescents.

Oviposition by the apple curculio does not necessarily cause the fruit to fall, but as a rule, it completely arrests growth at the point punctured. Surrounding parts continue to develop, and soon the sealed opening appears at the bottom of a more or less deep depression.

In comparing the damage done by the apple and plum curculios, it is evident that the plum curculio does the greater damage. The greatest damage to apples by the plum curculio occurs after all but the late-season feeding by the adult apple curculio has ended.

■ Factors Affecting Abundance

Closely planted, uncultivated orchards provide protection for the immature stages from the destructive heat of the sun and favorable hibernation quarters for the adults.

■ Life History

The adults begin to move about in their hibernating quarters as soon as a ground surface temperature of 60 degrees F or higher is maintained for 24 hours or longer. At first the beetles merely crawl about on the debris, frequently coming to rest on the highest objects they happen to find. If the temperature at the ground is much above 60 degrees F, some of them will fly short distances. Soon after the beetles appear in the trees, they feed on the fruit spurs, leaf petioles, blossom buds and other young, succulent growth. The beetles mate when the apples are in bloom. During bloom, they do some feeding on the blossoms and blossom stems. They attack the fruit as soon as it develops.

During oviposition, the apple curculio is much less timid than the plum curculio. When approached, it does not appear disturbed, but the plum curculio will at once seek a hiding place.

The apple curculio is not as partial to dense shade as the plum curculio — it endures strong light better and is less prone to hide. It does not have the protective instinct of folding its legs and dropping to the same extent that the plum curculio does. The apple curculio raises its beak when disturbed and takes wing more readily than the plum curculio.

Most of the damage occurs when the apples are about twice the size of a full-grown garden pea. While feeding on the fruit, the beetle eats only enough of the skin to make a tiny hole to allow its beak to pass through. The resulting cavity is as deep as the length of the snout of the beetle making it. If the beetle is disturbed, it withdraws its mouthparts and moves about for a while and then starts another cavity. The feeding cavity of the male is shallower than that of the female, which is deeper and wider at the bottom than that of the male.

When the fruits are small, many of the cavities extend to the seed. If undisturbed, the beetle may often feed from one cavity for four hours or longer. During this time, a considerable amount of excrement may be dis-charged. When the beetle has finished feeding, it may leave a deposit almost as large as itself. It is not uncommon to see as many as five or six such pellets on a single fruit.

The first eggs are laid in the apples when they are about the size of a full-grown garden pea. They are deposited in special cavities made by the feeding of the females. The puncture made through the apple skin looks similar to the regular feeding puncture. Internally, the egg cavity differs from the feeding cavity in that it is enlarged and rounded out at the bottom. Egg punctures are made on all parts of the apple — usually on the lower half of the fruit, but seldom on the calyx end. Oviposition cavities made when the fruits are small extend to the core, and the egg often comes to rest inside the young apple seed. Later in the season, when the apples are larger, the egg rests in the bottom of the cavity in the flesh of the apple. Immediately after depositing the egg, the beetle seals the cavity by forcing a pellet of greenish excrement into the puncture and carefully smoothing it with the tip of the abdomen. The egg puncture usually escapes detection until several hours later, when the plug dries and turns black.

When the fruits are small, only one egg cavity is made in each fruit. Later in the season when the apples are quite large, as many as six eggs may be deposited in a single apple. During the latter part of the oviposition period, females choose the smaller apples on the tree for oviposition. Sometimes egg-laying beetles shift from a tree with large fruits to an adjacent tree of another variety with smaller apples. A female will deposit an average of 28 eggs. The incubation period lasts an average of six days.

The newly hatched larvae begin to feed immediately. The apple curculio larvae do not tunnel around in the fruit as plum curculio larvae do, but rather feed from the side walls of the cavity made by the parent beetle. The larvae from eggs placed near the core of the apple find their favorite food, the seeds, readily available. In such cases, larvae consume the entire core before attacking the flesh. In very small fruits, everything is eaten except a thin outer layer. Larvae developing in larger fruits eat less of the core and more of the fleshy parts. Usually only one larva develops in each apple.

Larval mortality in June-drop apples is comparatively light. The chief causes of larval deaths in these fruits are exposure to sunlight and insect parasites. As with plum curculio, the death rate is considerably higher for those larvae in apples that continue to develop on the trees, particularly in apples with firm-textured flesh. Many larvae can develop in those fruits that remain on the trees, however, and after pupation, the new beetles emerge from the fruits on the trees. Larval development within June drops requires from 15 to 23 days, with an average of 19 days. Development within fruits growing on the trees takes longer.

Pupation occurs in the larval feeding cavity. The pupal period is five to nine days, with an average of 6½ days. The apple curculio develops in four main groups of apples: June drops, mummy fruits (apples that stop growing but remain on the fruit spurs, where they wither and become mummified), chemically thinned and growing fruits.

The amount of time the adult spends in the apple depends on the vigor of the individual, the prevailing temperature and the distance through which it must eat to escape. Almost invariably, the beetles from June drops make their exit holes through the uppermost portion of the apple. Most of the beetles that escape from growing apples choose the shortest distance out. Frequently, they emerge through that portion of the apple around the oviposition cavity, which is depressed as a result of limited growth.

Adults arising from pupae that have been subjected to growth pressure of the surrounding apple tissue are often deformed. Beetles begin to escape from June drops during the second and third weeks of July. Peak emergence occurs in late July or early August, but some beetles emerge in late August or early September. Emergence from thinned fruits occurs somewhat later than emergence from June drops. Beetles emerge from mummy fruits at about the same time as from June drops.

The new beetles begin to feed on the growing fruits soon after they emerge from their pupal chambers. The feeding punctures made at this time are similar to those made in the spring, but instead of being widely separated, they are usually grouped. Several punctures are usually made close together so that several of the underlying cavities coalesce. Feeding by the new beetles continues until they go into hibernation or until fruit is harvested. The beetle population in the trees at any given time during autumn does not accurately represent the infestation of the area. Many of the early-emerging beetles go into hibernation before the late-emerging ones appear in the trees.

The apple curculio passes the winter as an adult hibernating under leaves, mulch and other debris on the ground. It apparently never goes into the soil but at times may come in close contact with it. The average adult lives about 11 months.

■ *Monitoring*

Apply monitoring methods for plum curculio.

■ *Control*

Effective sprays must be applied at petal fall and first cover.

For complete information on this pest, see page 202.

ORIENTAL FRUIT MOTH IS GENERALLY CONSIDERED A PROBLEM ONLY IN STONE FRUITS. IN RECENT YEARS, IT HAS BECOME AN IMPORTANT PEST OF COMMERCIAL APPLES, YET, FOR THE MOST PART, HAS NONETHELESS GONE UNRECOGNIZED. ORIENTAL FRUIT MOTH CAN EXIST AND BECOME A PROBLEM IN APPLE ORCHARDS WHEN THERE ARE NO NEARBY STONE FRUIT ORCHARDS. PEACH ORCHARDS IN THE VICINITY WILL INCREASE THE PROBABILITY AND INTENSITY OF ORIENTAL FRUIT MOTH INFESTATIONS.

The first-generation larvae bore into apple shoots as they do into peach terminals, but in apple branches, the pests do not cause bushiness. Some apple varieties, including Red Delicious and Empire, appear to be more susceptible than other varieties to twig infestations. Investigations have shown that in some cases, the incidence of Oriental fruit moth infestations in apples is equal to or greater than the codling moth infestations.

It is possible that the Oriental fruit moth has gone unrecognized in apples because of the difficulty in separating infestations of codling moth and Oriental fruit moth. Infested apples, even when cut open and larvae are apparent, are usually considered to be infested with codling moth.

The only certain way to distinguish between Oriental fruit moth and codling moth larvae is to examine mature larvae for the presence of an anal comb. The anal comb is a hard, comb-like appendage found on the last abdominal segment (see illustration). Oriental fruit moth larvae have an anal comb; codling moth larvae do not.

(NOTE: Only mature larvae should be examined for the anal comb, because the comb is difficult to recognize in immature larvae without a powerful microscope. In mature larvae, the anal comb is visible with a hand lens and easily seen under a binocularscope.)

The most convenient way to check larvae for anal combs is to cut open infested apples and preserve the larvae in alcohol to be checked later. If you wish to examine the larvae immediately, place them in boiling water to kill them before checking.

It is very important to note that both Oriental fruit moth larvae and lesser appleworm larvae have anal combs and are similar in size and color. It is nearly impossible to distinguish the larvae of the two insects, and growers may have to wait until larvae reach the adult stage before

Special Discussion: Oriental Fruit Moth

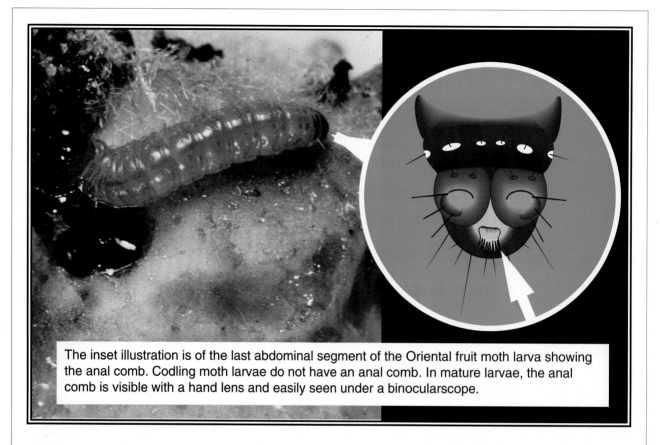

The inset illustration is of the last abdominal segment of the Oriental fruit moth larva showing the anal comb. Codling moth larvae do not have an anal comb. In mature larvae, the anal comb is visible with a hand lens and easily seen under a binocularscope.

the insect can be correctly identified. Be aware that Oriental fruit moth males are attracted to and often caught in lesser appleworm pheromone traps. Lesser appleworm males, however, are much less attracted to Oriental fruit moth pheromone lures.

Oriental fruit moth is generally considered more difficult to control than codling moth, especially with organophosphates. Emergence peaks of the two generations of codling moth occur at different times than the peaks of the three generations of Oriental fruit moth. The first generation of Oriental fruit moth, for example, usually peaks at apple's pink stage, so if spray is omitted for the fruit's pink stage, Oriental fruit moth could attack the apple terminals.

Peak emergence of the Oriental fruit moth's second generation generally occurs at the third cover spray of apples and can continue until the fourth apple cover spray. Unfortunately, since many growers apply codling moth sprays at second cover, they may omit the third cover spray. The Oriental fruit moth has a chance to cause further damage if the fourth cover spray is delayed until apple maggot appears, usually mid- to late July.

The third generation of Oriental fruit moth usually peaks about two weeks later than the second generation of codling moth. Thus, sprays applied for this generation of codling moth may not help control the third generation of Oriental fruit moth. Growers who wonder why they are having trouble controlling codling moth during this time may be surprised to learn that what they thought was poor timing or ineffectiveness of sprays was instead mismanaged infestations of the Oriental fruit moth.

The presence and emergence of Oriental fruit moth generations in apple orchards can be detected by using Oriental fruit moth pheromones in the same manner as that described for peaches on page 207. Braconids — especially those from the genus *Macrocentrus* — are important parasites of Oriental fruit moth larvae.

Chapter 2

Pests that suck sap from leaves, buds, twigs, branches, trunks or fruits

THESE ARTHROPODS ARE CONSIDERED INDIRECT PESTS. THOUGH THEY DO NOT attack the fruit directly, they affect the tree's condition and vigor by removing sap, ultimately lowering the quality of the fruit. Some cause abnormal development of fruit or stop growth. Others reduce the fruit's marketability by causing blemishes, or are vectors of disease that attack the fruit or the tree.

Because of their ability to develop tolerance to miticides quickly, mites are currently considered the most difficult pest of apples to control. Under certain environmental conditions, many generations of mites can develop in a single season. Multiple generations in a single season contribute to the mites' ability to develop tolerance to miticides quickly.

Integrated pest management is important in managing mites. This form of control uses biological control and pesticides that are less toxic to predators than to mites. Sprays are applied only when economic thresholds indicate the necessity.

Aphids can quickly develop into large, damaging populations because of parthenogenesis. This is the process by which females may give birth to living young without mating. Weather, parasites and predators greatly influence the abundance of aphids.

Some scale insects, such as the San Jose scale, have tremendous biotic potential. These scales' ability to multiply quickly from a single pair of pests into hundreds of millions of scales in a single season make them a potentially dangerous fruit tree pest. Scales are considered a difficult pest to control because of their numbers, their small size and location (which makes coverage difficult), and their ability to develop tolerance to pesticides. Superior oil, an innocuous pesticide to which scales have not yet been able to develop a resistance, has been used as a major pest management tool for these insects.

Common Name—

European Red Mite

Scientific Name—

Panonychus ulmi (Koch)

Family—

Tetranychidae

N THE ANIMAL KINGDOM, FEW OF THE LARGER orders can be mentioned about which less is known than the Acarina, popularly known as mites. The almost universal lack of knowledge of this group is undoubtedly explained by the minute size of its members, their obscure habits and the comparatively few forms that are of economic importance. The common European red mite occurs throughout the world and is probably the species of greatest economic importance among the plant-feeding mites. The European red mite began to appear in various parts of eastern North America early in the 20th century. It was reported in Ontario, Canada, in 1912 and in Geneva, N.Y., in 1915.

■ Life Stages

Egg: The egg is lenticular, flattened at the poles and distinctly grooved. A stalk about as long as the diameter of the egg arises from the center, tapering gradually from the tip, which is somewhat bent or curved. When first deposited, the egg is bright red, but it soon changes to a deep orange. Shortly before hatching, it becomes somewhat translucent, like an empty eggshell. The empty eggshells are whitish. The transverse diameter of summer eggs averages 0.132 mm. The winter eggs are very similar to the summer eggs, except that they are a deeper, richer red and somewhat larger. The transverse diameter of the winter eggs averages 0.148 mm.

Larva: The newly hatched larva is lemon-yellow to light orange, but after feeding it becomes darker, changing more or less to a reddish brown, depending on the quantity of chlorophyll it has taken with its food. The cephalothorax and the legs and palpi remain largely semi-transparent. The larva does not have the conspicuous whitish spots at the base of the dorsal bristles that occur in the adult. It has only six legs, which readily distinguish it from the other instars. The average length of larvae is about 0.15 mm.

Protonymph: The protonymph, or second instar mite, differs primarily from the larva in that it has eight legs instead of six. It is also somewhat larger and has a deeper, richer color. The size of the protonymph depends greatly on the length of time elapsing after its transformation from the larval stage. The length of protonymphs ranges from 0.20 to 0.25 mm.

Deutonymph: There is less difference between the deutonymph and the protonymph than between any of the other stages. There is so little difference that it is often difficult to distinguish these two stages. The deutonymph is slightly richer in color and somewhat larger. In the latter part of this stage, the sexes can be distinguished. The male deutonymph is smaller and more slender than the female. The length of deutonymphs is 0.25 to 0.30 mm.

Right:
Bronzing on
apple leaves
caused by
European
red mite.

Below:
Adult.

Left: Eggs; note the stalk rising
from the center of the egg.

Adult: A newly molted adult female is dark velvety brown, velvety green or brownish green, somewhat resembling the deutonymph. After a day or more, the color changes to dark velvety red or brownish red. White spots at the bases of the dorsal bristles are conspicuous. The adult male is much smaller than the female, measuring 0.26 mm long to the female's length of 0.40 mm. The abdomen is pointed, and the color is straw yellow to reddish yellow, never red.

■ *Host Range*

The European red mite is a pest of deciduous fruit worldwide — in the United States, Canada, Europe, Argentina, Uruguay, Chile, New Zealand and Australia. The favorite food plants of the European red mite are the common deciduous fruits, particularly apple, plum and pear. It has also been found on cherry, peach, grapes, raspberries and roses.

■ *Injury or Damage*

European red mite injury to deciduous fruit trees is difficult to measure and varies greatly with different varieties of fruits and different conditions. Apple, pear and plum are the most seriously affected by the mites. Cherries are affected to a lesser degree, and peaches and apricots seem to be comparatively free from attack. Among apples, thin-leaved varieties are most susceptible, but no variety has been observed to be particularly immune. Mites seem to favor Delicious, Northern Spy and Rome. Winesap is not seriously affected. No particular difference has been observed in the varieties of pears and susceptibility of plums.

The mites feed by inserting their mouthparts into the leaf cells and withdrawing the contents, including the chlorophyll. The leaves can recover if the mites are destroyed before the leaves are badly damaged. If much of the chlorophyll has been withdrawn, however, the plant seems to be unable to replace

it rapidly, and it is never entirely replaced during the life of the leaves. Apple foliage usually becomes bronzed or brown as a result of mite attacks. Bronzing over the leaf is followed by a quick decline in population. This decline is not due to debris and dust on the leaves but to two factors: the larval stylets are not long enough to penetrate to the remaining healthy cells, and an increase in the hardiness and density of the leaf cuticle and epidermal layer make it difficult for the stylets of the mite to penetrate.

In irrigated orchards, the leaves seldom drop — the abundance of moisture evidently prevents this. In non-irrigated orchards, severe mite infestations can cause partial defoliation. Pears and apples are similarly affected. The trees and fruit are also affected by infestations of mites, but these effects are not so easily seen. The mites do not feed on the fruit itself to any great extent, but the fruit is indirectly affected. Because the trees manufacture their food supply largely in their leaves, any foliage injury will reduce the vitality of the tree and, consequently, the size of the fruit, if it does not drop off. The most serious injury occurs in early summer, when trees are producing fruit and buds for the following season. Bronzing on moderately to heavily infested trees (30 mites or more per leaf) causes trees to produce fewer and less vigorous buds.

Mite injury rarely occurs early enough to affect the setting of the current year's crop. New leaves injured early in the season will not recover that season, even though mites will decrease naturally by late July or the middle of August. Growers must control mites early in the season to prevent injury.

■ *Factors Affecting Abundance*

Initial populations: The number of mites hatching from the overwintering eggs constitutes the initial population. The number of overwintering eggs is influenced by favorable or unfavorable factors of the previous season. Usually, trees that have been severely attacked by mites in midsummer will carry only a few eggs, because the population will have been depleted by predators and lack of food. This will have occurred before the season of heaviest egg deposition. Trees with foliage in good condition in late August and early September will usually carry far greater numbers of overwintering eggs.

When other factors are equal, trees with high numbers of eggs always develop larger and more damaging populations of mites at earlier dates. Data also show that it is more difficult to combat and reduce these high populations. Initial numbers, therefore, must always be considered a factor in seasonal trends.

Weather conditions: These are very important, especially during the early part of the season. Immediately after hatching, the young mites are very susceptible to low temperatures. Many instances have been observed in which threatening numbers of young mites (15 to 25 per leaf) were reduced by low temperatures to a point where they were practically harmless.

Though mites are active at somewhat lower temperatures than many insects, all their life processes are speeded up by temperatures within the general range of 70 to 90 degrees F. Temperatures above this point retard activities. Though temperature is the most important weather factor, wind plays a part in dispersing mite populations, and low humidity will reduce egg hatch. Varying degrees of light seem to influence the movements of mites within a tree.

Natural enemies: Among the predaceous mites, *Amblyseius fallacis* — a phytoseiid — and two stigmaeid mites, *Agistemus fleschneri* and *Zetzellia mali,* are most conspicuous on apples. They are a very definite factor in the control of mites on unsprayed trees, but they are not as effective in sprayed orchards unless growers take care to use broad spectrum pesticides and miticides with low toxicity to these predators. In orchards where mite populations are high, particularly after the season's spray program has ended, phytoseiid mites will frequently develop in numbers and will be a definite aid in control. Unfortunately, this almost always occurs after severe damage has occurred.

The most efficient predator among the coccinellids is *Stethorus punctum.* This is a very small, robust, black ladybird that is commonly found in connection with heavy mite infestations toward the end of the growing season. Both larvae and adults feed on the eggs and on motile mites, making the species doubly efficient. This beetle is found in numbers primarily in orchards south of Michigan because of its intolerance of extreme winter temperatures.

■ *Life History*

The European red mite passes the winter in the egg stage. Winter eggs may be found on the smaller branches and twigs of the trees. They are much more numerous on the lower sides than above, and they are most often deposited in the forks of two branches and in other roughened places. When the infestation is severe, the bright red eggs may also be found in the calyx ends of apples. At other times, a close examination will show that most of the eggs are transparent and empty because some of the insect enemies of the mites have fed on them.

The eggs start to hatch at the tight cluster stage. Fifty percent will have hatched by pink stage, and all will have hatched by the end of bloom. The first summer eggs are deposited by late petal fall or first cover.

The eggshell splits around its equator for most of its circumference, with a small portion left as a hinge. The larva lifts the upper half, or lid, and crawls out. The lid usually springs back to its original position. All the winter eggs usually hatch within a week or 10 days.

Table 1.
European red mite population potential.

| Generation | Number of mites | | Eggs/Female |
	Total	Female	
First	2	1	9
Second	9	6	43
Third	258	172	57
Fourth	9,084	6,536	33
Fifth	215,688	143,124	35
Sixth	5,009,320	3,339,546	7
Seventh	23,376,882		0

Source: New York Experiment Station, Geneva, N.Y.,

Table 2.
European red mite population on untreated Red Delicious trees.

| Generation | Number of mites | |
	Total	Female
First	90,000	60,000
Second	540,000	360,000
Third	15,480,000	3,921,600
Fourth	129, 412, 800	86, 275, 200

Source: New York Experiment Station, Geneva, N.Y.

Table 3.
European red mite population following 99 percent egg kill.

| Generation | Number of mites | |
	Total	Female
First	900	600
Second	5,400	3,600
Third	154,800	103,200
Fourth	5,882,400	3,921,600
Fifth	129,412,800	86,275,200

Source: New York Experiment Station, Geneva, N.Y.

Table 4.
The influence of temperature on the development of the European red mite.*

Avg. temperature (in degrees F)	Egg incubation (days)	Hatch to adult (days)	Total days
55	19	21	40
60	16	14	30
65	11	10	21
70	8	7	15
75	6	4	10

*It has been demonstrated that the time it takes for a European red mite egg to hatch and the mite to reach adulthood ranges from 40 days at 55 degrees F to 7 days at 80 degrees F. Note the rapid increase in the pace of mite development as the average temperature becomes higher. At 70 degrees F, development is twice as rapid as at 60 degrees F. At 75 degrees F, development is three times as fast as at 60 degrees F.

Source: New York Experiment Station, Geneva, N.Y.

Table 5.
Factors influencing mite buildup.

1 **Extremely high biotic potential of all plant-feeding mites.** In climates where the European red mite undergoes roughly eight generations a year, it has been estimated that the progeny of a single pair of mites would by the end of the season amount to 227,812,500 individuals. This is a hypothetical figure and never is met in nature.

2 **Abundance of overwintering eggs.** The extent of carryover of winter eggs is directly related to the weather of the previous season. Unless the food supply is depleted, the European red mite is incapable of producing winter eggs until mid- to late August. If the weather conditions are such that the mites are present in large numbers late in the season, you can be assured that there will be a heavy egg carryover. The opposite is true when the mites are most abundant in July.

3 **Winter egg survival.** Extreme winter temperatures will reduce the population. In 1957, unusually cold weather during January afforded the opportunity to measure the effect of winter temperatures on egg survival in New York state.

Samples of mite eggs were collected from areas where the minimum temperature ranged from –9 degrees to –34 degrees F, and the percent egg hatch was determined in the laboratory. Results showed that the winter eggs were not adjusted to survive the abnormally low temperatures that prevailed in some areas. It would appear that any temperature that falls below -22 degrees F, especially if it is sustained, could destroy an appreciable number of eggs, with mortality increasing rapidly below this figure.

4 **Weather and spray pressure during the period of egg hatch.** The period from prepink through blossoming is perhaps the most critical time in the establishment of the species. Not only are mites more susceptible to acaricidal treatments at this time, but adverse weather will also reduce the population.

5 **Summer weather.** The most important factor influencing activity is the weather. The European red mite, like most other mites, does best under hot, dry conditions.

Source: New York Experiment Station, Geneva, N.Y.

Immature stages: The small, bright red or orange larvae swarm to the young leaves and begin feeding at once. In some cases, they may travel several inches or even feet before beginning to feed. They crowd down among the unfolding leaves and are not very conspicuous. After a period of feeding during which the larva moves about to some extent, it settles down, usually on the underside of a leaf near a vein or midrib, and remains quiescent (inactive) for a time. The quiescent period lasts about as long as the feeding period. The mite remains perfectly motionless and apparently takes no food. After a time, the skin becomes smooth and glossy and finally turns pearly white, indicating that it has loosened from the new skin underneath. Within a few hours, it splits transversely across the dorsum between the second and third pairs of legs, and the eight-legged protonymph pushes its way out. The molted skins usually remain stuck to the leaf. In severe infestations, these and the eggshells may be numerous enough to give the leaf a silvery appearance.

In the protonymphal stage, the feeding and quiescent periods are repeated, though each is somewhat shorter than the corresponding period in the larval stage. Then the protonymph molts and becomes a deutonymph. The sex of the deutonymph can be determined after it has fed for a time — the females become larger and more round than the males. The duration of this stage is slightly longer than the larval or the protonymphal stage. The males complete each of these stages in a fraction of a day less than the females. The total for the immature stages averages eight days for males and nine days for females.

Adult emergence and copulation: The male becomes an adult first, and it runs about over the leaves until it finds a quiescent female deutonymph. It then settles down beside the deutonymph to await the emergence of the female. As soon as the nymphal skin of the latter splits across the back, the male begins working at the posterior half of it with his forelegs and mouthparts. The female then backs out of the anterior half of the old skin and copulation takes place immediately, sometimes even before the female has had time to free herself entirely from the nymphal skin. The male crawls under the female from the rear. The female elevates the tip of her abdomen, and the male clasps his front legs about her abdomen and his second pair of legs about her hind legs, then curves the end of his abdomen upward and forward until it meets the end of the female's abdomen. The pair remain in this position for 10 or 15 minutes.

The European red mite also reproduces parthenogenetically, a process by which females can give birth to living young without mating.

Summer egg deposition and hatching: In the summer, the oviposition period averages 12 days, during which females lay an average of 19 eggs. The first summer eggs are deposited by late petal fall or first cover. The first generation requires three weeks for development from egg to adult. Summer generations require 10 to 18 days. The average life span of the adult female is 18 days.

Deposition of winter eggs: Though it has been shown that the winter eggs of the European red mite hatch within a comparatively few days, they are deposited over a rather long period. Deposition of these eggs begins about the middle of August and continues until cold weather kills the mites or causes the leaves to drop. Winter eggs may thus be deposited over a period of months. Deposition of winter eggs is triggered by diminishing food supplies, temperature and photoperiod. Individual females of the sixth, seventh and eighth broods may deposit these eggs.

Feeding: The young mites feed mostly on the lower leaf surface. The feeding periods are relatively short, and the mites usually spend the quiescent periods on the lower surface, where there is more protection. Young mites on the upper surface are usually found in the depressions of the veins. Adult mites, however, feed indiscriminately on both surfaces. Observations made on mites feeding on apple foliage in warm, sunny weather showed that about three-fourths of the adults were feeding on the upper leaf surface. In cloudy or rainy weather, most of the adults are found on the lower surface.

Effects of weather: Though the mites are most active during warm weather, they continue to be more active at lower temperatures than many insects. The mites spin very little webbing, but they are able to cling tenaciously to the leaf surfaces and, unlike the common red spider mite, are not easily washed off by rains or heavy sprays. The webbing of the latter species is very easily washed off, along with the mites and their eggs.

Dispersal: The winter eggs are present on the twigs for about six months. Because they are inconspicuous unless present in large numbers, they easily escape detection and are often carried to new localities on nursery stock. The winter eggs deposited about the calyxes of apples are also a possible means of distribution, but the chances of new infestations starting from this source would be extremely small.

During the growing season, the mites are very easily transported from one orchard to another on the clothing of orchard workers and on vehicles and farm machinery. They are also probably blown considerable distances by winds, and they may be transported by irrigation water. When populations are high, European red mites will disperse on silk strands and be carried by wind to other trees. It also is conceivable that they could be carried on birds' feet as the young of the San Jose scale are carried.

■ *Monitoring*

Select trees such as Red Delicious or Northern Spy that are susceptible to mites. Using a lens that has a 10x to 14x magnification, examine 10 sample leaves from each of 10 trees. Treat trees if you find an average of six or more mites per leaf and less than one predator mite per leaf.

■ *Control*

Use preblossom applications of superior oil or organic miticides and apply summer applications of miticides as needed. When possible, use miticides that are selective against European red mites. To protect predators, avoid the use of pesticides such as carbamates, pyrethroids and other classes of compounds that are known to be detrimental to beneficial predators.

Mite damage is a function of time — early populations of mites before bud differentiation takes place can be more damaging than the same number of mites occurring at midseason or later. This does not mean that mid- or late season mite populations cannot cause damage. High populations of mites at mid- or late season can result in egg deposition in the calyx ends of fruit. These cannot be removed and can be considered an adulteration. Mite management to keep populations below optimum numbers for reproduction is an important factor in mite control. Preventive measures that maintain low mite populations and prevent damage are far more effective than eradicative measures that may be ineffective and come too late to prevent damage.

Miticides with different modes of action should be rotated within a season or from season to season to delay the development of resistance. Once resistance to a miticide has developed through selection pressure and the miticide is no longer used, the mite population will regress from homozygous resistance to heterozygous resistance. Therefore, a miticide to which resistance was developed some years ago can often be effective again if employed only once in a season. It generally requires a few generations for the mites to regain resistance when exposed to repeated applications of the miticide. Such miticides could be effectively used in a rotation of miticides with different modes of action.

Common Name—

Twospotted Spider Mite

Scientific Name—
Tetranychus urticae (Koch)

Family—
Tetranychidae

THE TWOSPOTTED SPIDER MITE IS present worldwide. It feeds on a wide range of both wild and cultivated plants.

■ Life Stages

Egg: The spherical eggs are clear and watery when first deposited and become opaque and glassy as incubation progresses. Just before hatching, they become a pale straw color. The red eye spots of the embryo are plainly visible at this time.

Larva: The newly hatched larva is round, about the size of the egg, and has six legs. At this time it is colorless, except for the eyes, which are carmine. Feeding begins at once and the color changes to pale green, brownish green or very dark green, and two black spots appear, one on each side of the eye spot.

Protonymph: The protonymph is larger and more oval in outline than the larva and has four pairs of legs. The ground color is pale green to dark green, sometimes brownish green. The two spots are larger and more pronounced than in the larva.

Deutonymph: The ground color of the deutonymph is generally some shade of green. It apparently is influenced by the mite's food. The spots are larger and more distinct. Males are readily distinguished from females in this stage by their smaller bodies, pointed abdomens and small spots.

Adult: The male is much smaller and more active than the female. The male's body is narrow and the abdomen is distinctly pointed. The color is pale yellow, pale to dark green, brownish or, at times, faintly orange. An inconspicuous dark area is generally present on each side, and other dark areas are frequently seen along the middle. The body of the female is oval, about 0.42 mm long and about 0.27 mm wide. The color of females varies from light yellow or straw color to green, brown, black and various shades of orange. Newly emerged females have two large black spots, one on each side just behind the eye spot. After feeding takes place, black splotches show up in irregular patterns in other parts of the body.

■ Host Range

This mite attacks many species of wild and cultivated plants in many parts of the world. Deciduous fruit tree hosts are apple, pear, peach, nectarine, plum, apricot and cherry.

■ Injury or Damage

The injury the twospotted mite causes is similar to that caused by the

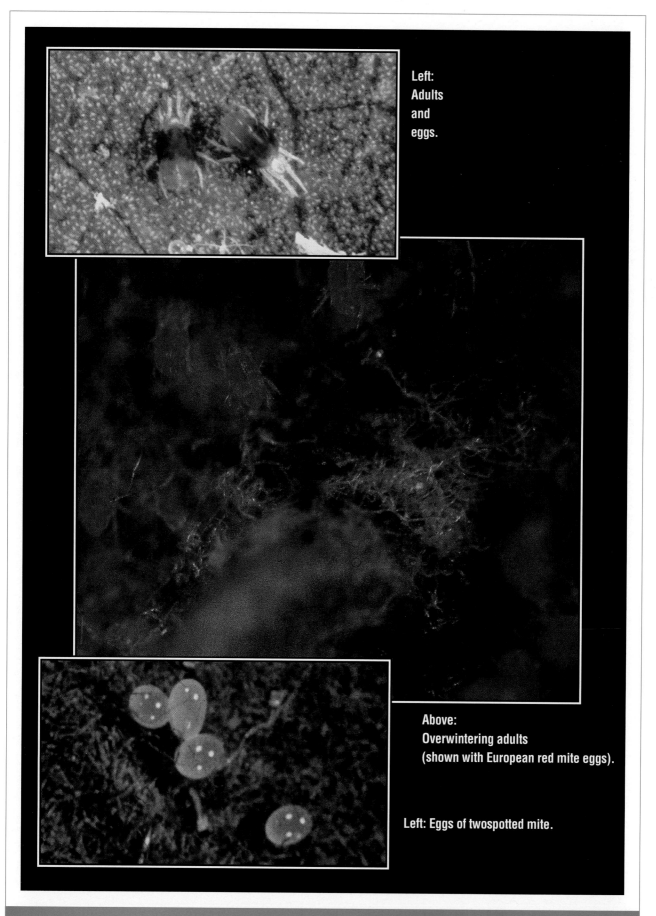

Left:
Adults
and
eggs.

Above:
Overwintering adults
(shown with European red mite eggs).

Left: Eggs of twospotted mite.

European red mite. Bronzing, however, is more gray, and there is much more webbing with twospotted spider mites than with similar populations of European red mites.

Factors Affecting Abundance

The twospotted mite has a wide range of host plants, a high biotic potential — producing multiple generations in a season — and a considerable propensity for developing resistance to miticides. Drought conditions will cause the mites to migrate from grasses to nearby orchard fruit trees.

Life History

Full-grown female mites and some immatures overwinter under bark scales on the trunk of the tree or among fallen leaves and in other protected places on the ground. With the arrival of warm weather in the spring, these mites leave their places of hibernation and start wandering about looking for food plants. Almost all of those on the tree trunk crawl down the trunk to the ground, where they feed on weeds and grasses. The first eggs can usually be found around the pink stage. In warm weather, these hatch in five to eight days. A complete generation from egg to adult may require no more than three weeks. Five to nine generations occur in the orchard each season, depending on the weather.

In mid- or late summer, when drought and other factors cause poor food conditions among weeds and grasses, mites move from the old host up the tree trunks or to low-hanging apple branches in contact with the ground vegetation. Low-hanging branches that touch grass or weeds are usually attacked first; then mites spread upward and into the interior of the tree. Once established, the population may develop into a serious infestation and cause injury. Injury to the leaves resembles that of the European red mite, except that a more grayish cast is prevalent. As indicated previously, these mites also spin a fine silken web over many infested leaves.

In the fall, the adults leave the trees and hibernate among weeds or leaves or in the soil, although some may overwinter on the trees.

Monitoring

Begin checking in early summer and continue until fall. Select 10 leaves from the lower shoots and water sprouts along the trunk from each of 10 trees in an orchard. If the ground cover touches the lower limbs, pick an additional 100 leaves from the limbs touching the weeds. Treatment is recommended if the counts average six or more twospotted mites per leaf and the predators average less than one per leaf.

Control

Control these mites with summer applications of miticides.

Common Name—
Brown Mite

Scientific Name—
Bryobia rubrioculus (Scheuten)

Family—
Tetranychidae

THE BROWN MITE, WHICH IS OFTEN CONfused with the clover mite — *B. praetiosa* (Koch) — is usually the only tetranychid mite found in unsprayed orchards. Though it is generally not a problem in treated commercial orchards, it is capable of causing damage when not controlled.

The clover mite is not a pest of orchard trees. It feeds on clover, grasses and low-growing herbaceous plants. The clover mite is a common household pest.

■ Life Stages

Egg: Brown mite eggs are bright red, spherical and slightly larger than the overwintering eggs of the European red mite. Brown mite eggs have a smooth surface and lack the stalk found on European red mite eggs.

Immature stages: Similar to those of the European red mite.

Adult: Adults are a dull reddish or greenish red. They have a flattened, saucerlike back and very long front legs.

■ Host Range

The brown mite is present mainly between latitudes 20 and 60 degrees in both the northern and southern hemispheres. It has many hosts, including herbaceous plants and deciduous and coniferous trees. On deciduous fruits, it has been found on apple,

apricot, cherry, nectarine, peach, pear and plum.

■ Injury or Damage

Foliage injury caused by the brown mite on apples is very noticeable in the ½-inch green stage of leaf development. At that time, large numbers of larvae feeding on the primary leaves may cause extensive damage. Damage to the leaves and flower buds may hinder the opening of the flowers. In the summer, the foliage damage resembles that caused by the European red mite, except that the injury at first appears as discrete off-color areas rather than a uniform discoloration of the leaf. As injury progresses, the foliage becomes pale green, then yellow and finally bronze. Badly damaged leaves are thin and feel leathery. Premature leaf drop may occur.

■ Factors Affecting Abundance

Populations of the brown mite build up in abandoned orchards. In the spring, newly hatched mites are very susceptible to low temperatures.

■ Life History

The brown mite overwinters in the egg stage. Winter eggs begin to hatch in the late delayed dormant to ½-inch green stage of leaf development of McIntosh and Delicious apples. The eggs hatch two to three weeks

Adult brown mite.

earlier than those of the European red mite, which usually start to hatch in the early pink stage. The period of hatch is relatively long. After hatching, the larvae move from the twigs to the ½-inch green stage leaves and flower buds to feed. During the initial feeding period, their color changes from scarlet to greenish brown.

Under cool conditions in spring, the larval stage may last for more than a week. When feeding is completed, practically all the larvae return to the rough bark of the twigs and fruit spurs to enter the first quiescent stage. During the spring generation, the nymphal and sec-

ond and third quiescent stages average four to five days each, so it takes about a month to reach the adult stage.

After the third quiescent stage and a comparatively short feeding period of one to two days, the adults deposit summer eggs. Eggs are found on both leaves and twigs shortly after the first adults appear. Initially, the majority are deposited on the twigs, but as egg laying progresses, the percentage laid on the leaves increases. One to three eggs per day are deposited singly. The incubation period at this time of year is two to three weeks, so the second generation begins in the first part of June. During the spring generation, practically all the larvae move back to the twigs to molt. Most of the nymphs spend the second and third quiescent stages on the twigs. Most of the mites of the first summer generation molt on the leaves.

Summer and fall generations: In the north central states, the mite usually has four generations on apples, though at times it has been known to have five generations. Though the duration of the spring generation is well defined, the summer and fall generations overlap. The incubation period during the summer is about 10 to 15 days, so the first eggs hatch before the females have completed oviposition. The fourth generation of active and quiescent mites is comparatively small because the majority of eggs laid during August and September do not hatch until the next spring. Activity continues to decrease until the first frost in the fall.

The mites spend as much time on the twigs as on the leaves. The only movement of importance occurs in the adult stage when the mites crawl to the twigs to lay winter eggs. This is not a mass migration — the deposition of winter eggs continues throughout the summer and fall. The adults do not move down to the trunk or the ground.

Winter stage: The mite passes the winter entirely in the egg stage. The bright red, spherical eggs are normally deposited on the lower sides of small twigs and fruit spurs. When the mites are numerous, the eggs are often found on the sides of the twigs and spurs, on small limbs and on the calyx ends of apples. The lower surfaces of limbs appear reddish brown when they are covered with masses of winter eggs. More eggs are deposited near the top of the tree than on the lower limbs, particularly in heavy infestations. This mite does not deposit winter eggs on the tree trunk. It was thought until recently that the brown mite started to lay winter eggs about the same time as the European red mite — in the first part of August. It has been shown, however, that a progressive buildup of brown mite eggs starts in the early part of summer. By the first week of July, about 85 percent of the eggs on the twigs and fruit spurs are winter eggs.

■ *Monitoring*

Apply monitoring methods for European red mite.

■ *Control*

Apply prebloom miticides or superior oil and, if necessary, summer applications.

Common Name—
Apple Rust Mite

Scientific Name—
Aculus schlechtendali (Nalepa)

Family—
Eriophyidae

THE LIFE HISTORY AND HABITS OF THE apple rust mite are not well known. The pest was first reported on apples in the Pacific Northwest in 1910.

■ Life Stages

Egg: The circular egg is flat and colorless and approximately 50 microns in diameter.

Nymph: Nymphs resemble the adults.

Adult: During development, adults show deuterogony, which is the occurrence of two types of females.

■ Host Range

The apple rust mite is found in all apple-growing areas of North America.

■ Injury or Damage

The mites feed on leaves, mainly on the ventral surface, causing the undersides of the leaves to become brown or bronzed while the upper surfaces remain green. Under prolonged, heavy infestations (200 or more mites per leaf), leaves become leathery and take on a silvery appearance.

■ Factors Affecting Abundance

Red Delicious varieties are more susceptible than other apple varieties to the apple rust mite.

■ Life History

The mites overwinter under bud scales or in bark crevices as deutogynes — primary (protogyne) and secondary (deutogyne) females. The protogynes have a male counterpart; the secondary females do not. Hence, deutogynes lay eggs following winter hibernation rather than during the year they grow up.

Overwintering deutogynes lay eggs in the spring on upper and lower leaf surfaces. The eggs are attached to leaf surfaces with an adhesive. By late spring, the deutogynes leave the leaves. The eggs develop into first-generation protogynes. These protogynes then lay eggs that develop into second-generation protogynes. Protogynes are found on leaves during most of the summer.

In late summer, deutogynes reappear on the leaves for a short time before moving to bud scales or bud crevices to overwinter. There are three to five generations, depending on geographic location.

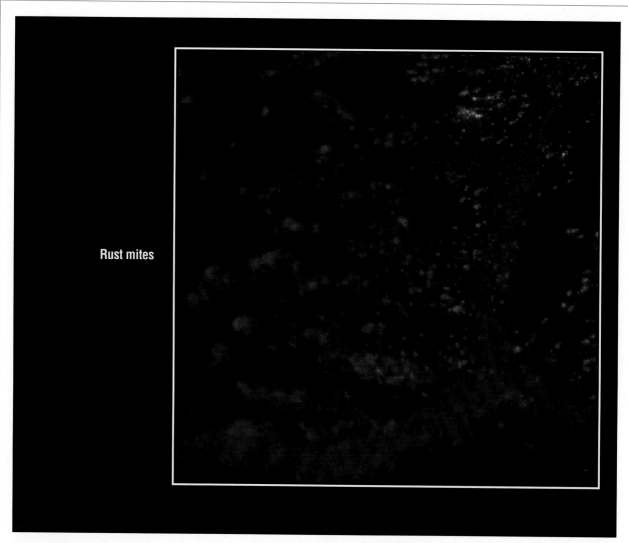

Rust mites

■ *Monitoring*

The apple rust mite rarely causes damage in the midwestern and eastern apple-growing regions. Monitoring should begin before the petal-fall stage and continue to harvest. Collect 10 leaves from each of 10 trees randomly selected across an orchard block. Select leaves from the inside to the outside of the tree. If mite populations exceed an average of 200 mites per leaf, treatment may be required to prevent damage. Before applying sprays, determine whether the predator population can develop quickly enough to control apple rust mites before they cause damage.

■ *Control*

In most areas, apple rust mite is seldom a problem and is often considered beneficial in providing a food supply for mite predators early in the season before other mite populations develop. Prebloom or summer applications of an effective miticide may be necessary if this mite becomes a problem.

			Table 6.		
			Identifying characteristics and habits of mite pests on tree fruits.		
Mite	**Crop attacked**	**Over-wintering stage**	**Mite color and shape**	**Number of genera-tions**	**Presence and location**
European red mite	Apple, pear, peach, cherry, plum	Eggs	Red, ovoid with distinct large bristles on back	6-8	Eggs hatch in pink bud stage; on foliage rest of the year
Twospotted mite	Apple, pear, plum, cherry, peach, nectarine, apricot	Female, on cover crop	Pale to dark green, ovoid with two black spots on abdomen	Variable (5-9)	All stages on cover crop until drying in June to August, then move into tree; may remain in tree rest of season
Brown mite	Apple, plum, peach, pear, cherry, nectarine, apricot	Eggs	Dull red to greenish, flat back and long front legs	4	Eggs hatch at ¼-inch green tip; on foliage rest of the year
Apple rust mite	Apple	Female, under bud scales	Very small, cream to light brown, wedge-shaped	6-10	Females move to leaves as soon as leaves open in spring and remain on foliage throughout the year
Pear rust mite	Pear	Female, under bud scales	Same as apple rust mite	6-10	Same as apple rust mite

Common Name—
Rosy Apple Aphid

Scientific Name—
Dysaphis plantaginea (Passerini)

Family—
Aphidae

THIS IS AN OLD EUROPEAN SPECIES INTRO-duced into the United States about 1870. It became a major pest of apples near the end of the 19th century. To thrive, this species must have an abundance of its summer host plant, the narrow-leaved plantain. A remarkable parallelism exists between the introduction and spread of rosy apple aphid and the narrow-leaved plantain. This aphid occurs throughout the fruit-growing areas of the United States.

■ Life Stages

Egg: The egg is oval and slightly flat-tened on the side next to the bark. The length varies from 0.49 to 0.56 mm. When first laid, it is bright yellow and covered with a gluti-nous substance that hardens with age. The color gradually changes to greenish yellow and finally to a shiny jet black. The time required for this change in color varies under normal outdoor conditions from about nine days to more than two weeks.

Nymph: The individuals that hatch from the eggs are all viviparous wingless females. There are five instars. The last is the mature stem mother, which, shortly after the fourth instar, begins to produce living young parthenogenetically. She produces an average of five to six young per day. The nymphs of the second generation, all of which are females, reach maturity in two to three weeks. The great majority of the nymphs

begin to reproduce on apple, though a few may develop wings and migrate to the plantain.

The third generation is produced in June and early July. The majority of this generation develop wings and migrate to the narrow-leaved plantain. In some seasons, wingless females of the third generation produce a fourth generation on apple. In recent years, it has been observed in some areas that damag-ing populations of rosy apple aphid have per-sisted in orchards until midsummer or later. It is not known whether this change is due to the selection process, changes of habit or lack of need for an alternative host.

Adult: The adult varies considerably in color markings. The general color is rosy brown, with a pinkish cast due to a pow-dery covering. Some of the older adults are almost purple, while the younger adults are decidedly reddish pink.

■ Host Range

Apple is the preferred host, but the aphid also feeds on pear and hawthorn. Cortland, Golden Delicious, Rhode Island Greening and Ida Red are all particularly sus-ceptible apple varieties. The aphid is found in all fruit-growing areas of the United States and Canada.

■ Injury or Damage

Rosy apple aphid feeding often causes apple leaves to curl, starting at petal fall.

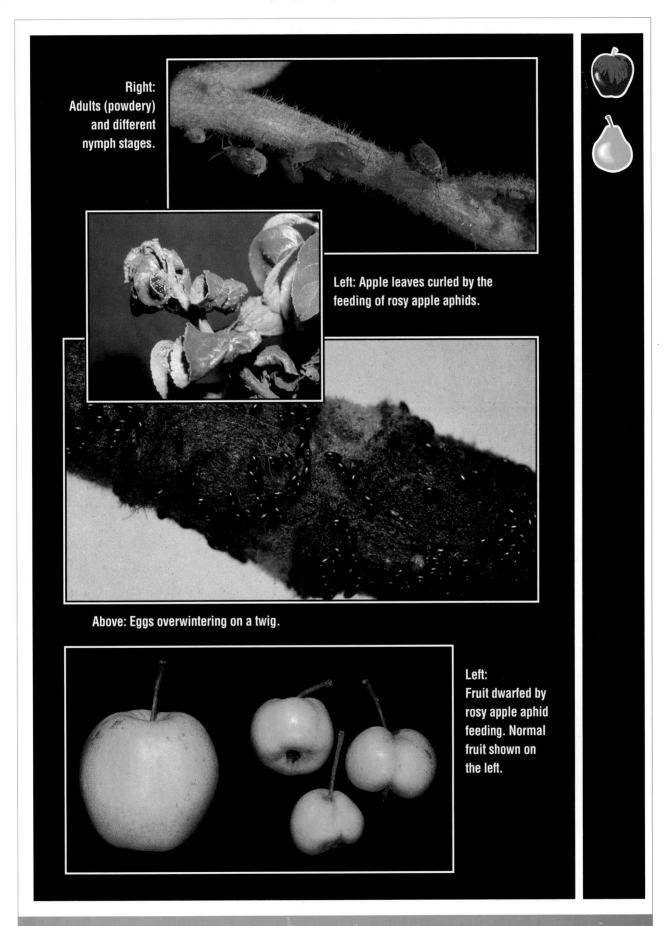

Right:
Adults (powdery) and different nymph stages.

Left: Apple leaves curled by the feeding of rosy apple aphids.

Above: Eggs overwintering on a twig.

Left:
Fruit dwarfed by rosy apple aphid feeding. Normal fruit shown on the left.

These leaves may later turn bright red. Feeding on the leaves around fruit clusters often results in the bunching, stunting and malformation of the developing fruit. These abnormalities become worse as fruit develops and can eventually render the fruit unsalable.

Large aphid populations may produce large amounts of honeydew as waste from the sap on which they feed. Honeydew excreted onto fruit will serve as a growing ground for sooty mold fungus, which will affect the finish of the apple. Toxins in the aphids' saliva also serve as a "stop drop," preventing the fruits' abscission (natural separation from the tree) at normal harvest.

■ Factors Affecting Abundance

Untrimmed trees render favorable conditions for the aphids and greatly handicap methods of control. A cool, wet spring favors aphid development because it provides conditions unfavorable for aphid parasites and predators. A large proportion of the overwintering eggs do not hatch. Mortality can be caused by temperature (either low temperature or sudden changes during the winter or during the hatching period); moisture (cold rains at or just before hatching time, causing young aphids to die before leaving the eggs); predaceous insects and birds that destroy large numbers of eggs during late fall, winter and early spring; and non-fertilization of eggs.

Males are scarce and make up only a small portion of the total population. Many females deposit eggs before mating, and these eggs do not hatch in the spring.

■ Life History

The aphid passes the winter in the egg stage. Hatching occurs early in the spring, about a week to 10 days later than the apple grain aphid and at about the same time as the apple aphid. The eggs hatch when the buds start opening in the spring, over a period of two weeks. As soon as they hatch, the young seek out the opening buds of the apple; they seem to prefer the fruit buds. They feed on the outside of the leaf bud and fruit bud clusters until the leaves begin to unfold. Then they work their way down inside the clusters and begin sucking the sap from the stems and newly formed fruits.

Their feeding causes the leaves to curl, protecting the aphids from sprays and some enemies. The severe curling of the foliage caused by this species is probably the most characteristic feature of its work. A single stem mother located on the underside of a leaf near the midrib will cause the leaf to fold tightly. It takes only a few stem mothers to cause a severe curling of all leaves surrounding an opening flower bud, providing ideal protection to the rapidly developing aphids. The stem mothers reach maturity when apple trees are coming into bloom.

The mature stem mothers are very inactive. They settle down and feed and produce young at a rapid rate. When disturbed, they quickly remove their beaks from plant tissues and seek out another spot in which to continue. The stem mothers mature about two weeks after hatching. The length of time depends largely on weather conditions. The production of young usually begins two or three days after the last molt and continues without interruption for more than a month.

The total production by a single female averages about 185. Normally, the period of reproduction extends from about early May to June. Usually, the maximum period of reproductive activity is around the last week of May and the first week of June, when the young fruits are beginning to set and start active growth. Rosy apple aphid is rarely found attacking the young and rapidly growing shoots. It restricts itself to the foliage, the flower stalks and the young fruits.

One of the characteristic features of this species is the congregation of the young about the mother. Each individual stem mother or group of mothers will have massed about it hundreds of young. The infested leaves may soon be covered — in some cases, by more than one layer of aphids. This habit of congregating soon kills the infested leaves and causes the forced migration of the aphids. The young move actively and hurriedly, seemingly anxious to locate a suitable feeding ground. They are frequently found during this period congregated on the forming fruits or attacking the new, succulent unfolding foliage.

The second generation requires four to 40 days to reach maturity and produce young. The majority of the second generation is wingless females. The average total production of each individual in the second generation is about 119. The habits and activities of the third generation do not differ from those of the second. The aphids congregate in immense numbers on the undersides of the foliage, causing severe curling. They also attack the setting and developing fruits, producing characteristic injuries.

The majority of this third generation acquires wings and migrates to narrow-leaved plantain, the summer host plant. A fourth generation may be produced. All of these produce wings and migrate to the narrow-leaved plantain. After the last molt, the winged adults are very tender and inactive. They remain secreted in the curled leaves for two or three days before venturing on their migratory flight. Just before flying, they become very active and nervous, running about or moving their wings up and down in anticipation of their flight.

The body of this aphid has a waxy coating and usually a slight purplish or rosy tinge, which gives it its name. Aphids are on the apples during May and, in smaller numbers, through June and July, though in recent years greater numbers appear to be staying on the apple trees and reproducing in large numbers until later in the summer. They feed and reproduce on the plantain until fall. In the fall, the winged females fly back to the apple trees. Darker than the migrants that left the trees in the spring, these females lay eggs. Males also develop from these eggs. The males mate with the females, after which the females deposit eggs that hatch the following spring. The eggs of the apple grain aphid, apple aphid and rosy apple aphid are so similar that it is not possible to distinguish one from the others.

■ *Monitoring*

Select trees such as Golden Delicious that are susceptible to aphids. From tight cluster through petal-fall stages, examine 100 fruit clusters in the center of susceptible apple blocks. Treatment is recommended if an average of one colony or more per tree is found in the susceptible varieties.

■ *Control*

Apply preblossom applications of contact or systemic aphicides. Apply foliage applications of systemic compounds in early season or summer. Early applications, when the aphids are fully exposed and before they curl the leaves, are most effective. Systemic pesticides are required once leaf curling has occurred.

Common Name—
Apple Grain Aphid

Scientific Name—
Rhopalosiphum fitchii (Sanderson)

Family—
Aphidae

THIS APHID IS CONSPICUOUS IN EARLY SPRING on the swollen buds of apples.

◼ Life Stages

Egg: The egg is similar to that of the rosy apple aphid.

Nymph: Newly emerged nymphs are dark green. The second and third instars are yellowish green. The fourth instar closely resembles the adult. The very short antennae and cornicles of the nymphs readily distinguish the apple grain aphid from the rosy apple and apple aphids.

Adult: Adults are yellowish green with a dark green line running down the middle of the back and four or five cross-lines of the same color. The males are a light greenish brown and more slender than the females.

◼ Host Range

This aphid attacks apple, pear, hawthorn, plum, quince, grasses and grains. It is present in most apple-growing regions in Canada and the United States.

◼ Injury or Damage

No control for this aphid is required because it does not attack fruit, and the feeding on the foliage causes little, if any, distor-tion. The first of the winged forms leaves the apple at petal fall and migration continues for about two weeks. At the end of that time, apple grain aphids are not found on the trees. They may injure young wheat in the fall.

◼ Factors Affecting Abundance

Cold, wet weather in the spring favors the aphids because it creates unfavorable conditions for aphid parasites and predators. Cold rains occurring when eggs are about to hatch can abort hatching.

◼ Life History

The eggs are laid in the autumn on apples, and the aphid spends the winter in the egg stage. The eggs begin hatching in the spring a week to 10 days earlier than those of the apple aphid or the rosy apple aphid. Hatching continues over a considerable period — usually about 10 days if the weather is favorable. The stem mothers become mature in early to mid-May and eggs hatch when the buds are swelling. The aphids may be found congregated at the very tips seeking entrance even before the tips show green. As the buds unfold, the aphids feed on the tender foliage but do not cause any marked curling of the leaves.

The stem mothers reach maturity about two weeks after hatching from the eggs. When abundant, as it frequently is, this

Adults of the apple grain aphid. Note the dark green line with four or five cross-lines that runs down the middle of the insect's back.

aphid may almost completely cover the buds. As soon as the buds open, the young aphids swarm over the leaves. They feed almost exclusively on the opening foliage but do not cause any curling. They never attack the tender twigs and have never been observed feeding on the water sprouts as the apple aphid commonly does.

The stem mothers become mature in early to mid-May. Deposition of young usually begins within 24 hours after the last molt. Young may be produced for about 30 days, and the total production of young averages about 75 per female. The young nymphs of a second generation feed almost exclusively on the foliage. Very seldom have they been found on the developing fruit.

The majority of this generation acquires wings and migrates to the summer host plants. A small proportion are wingless viviparous females that continue to produce young on the apple. Normally, a few third-generation individuals occur. All of these are winged and migrate to their summer host plants — grains and grasses. All offspring produced in these first three generations are parthenogenetic females. Most of them leave the apples around the petal-fall stage, though a few may stay on until July.

In the fall, winged viviparous females return to the apple tree and give birth to wingless oviparous females. The male aphids develop on grains or grasses and later fly to apples, where they find and fertilize the females before egg laying starts. After mating, the female starts depositing eggs. The shiny black eggs are laid on the bark all over the tree, but mostly on the twigs near the buds.

■ *Monitoring*

Because this is the earliest aphid found in the orchard, it is important to recognize this species. Do not treat for aphids if this is the only aphid found in damaging numbers. The apple grain aphid is not an economic pest, and it will leave the orchard shortly after petal fall.

■ *Control*

No control measures are required. However, it is important to recognize the apple grain aphid to avoid applying sprays when large colonies of this species only are present early in the season. The simplest method for field recognition is to examine adults for a dark green line running down the middle of the back with four or five dark green cross-lines.

Common Name—
Apple Aphid

Scientific Name—
Aphis pomi (De Geer)

Family—
Aphidae

THE APPLE APHID IS A EUROPEAN INSECT. It was first reported doing serious damage to young apple trees in the eastern United States in 1849.

Life Stages

Egg: The shiny black eggs vary in size but are generally about 0.50 mm long and 0.25 mm wide.

Nymph: The nymphs are all viviparous wingless females. The five instars include the last stage, which is the stem mother.

Adult: The wingless viviparous females are pear-shaped and light green, though in spring, some may have bright yellow bodies. The females have peculiar sensory pits on their hind tibia and are about two-thirds as large as the parthenogenetic wingless summer forms. The yellowish brown males, which have blackish antennae longer than their bodies, are one-third smaller and much less numerous than the females. In contrast to the well developed cornicles of the rosy apple aphid, the cornicles of the apple aphid are scarcely developed. The rosy apple aphid has longer antennae than the apple aphid.

Host Range

The apple aphid is a pest of apple, pear, quince and hawthorn. It is generally distributed in the apple-growing areas of the United States and Canada.

Injury or Damage

The apple aphid is abundant during June and July on young trees, water sprouts and vigorously growing terminals. It curls the foliage and covers it with honeydew. Black fungus that grows on the honeydew smuts both the fruits and the leaves and causes considerable discoloration, especially of early apples.

Factors Affecting Abundance

Early-season abundance is stimulated by migration from trees that harbor large numbers of aphids. In addition, lack of pruning — which promotes water sprouts and fruit and foliage in dense shade — encourages rapid expansion of aphid colonies. Foliar senescence and predator activity are important factors in lowering aphid populations.

Life History

The wingless females lay eggs mostly on the bark or on the buds in the fall. The eggs hatch in the spring about the time the buds begin to open. The

Left: Adults and nymphs.

Below: Apple dwarfing caused by apple aphid.

Left: Fruit smutting caused by apple aphid.

eggs hatch into stem mothers, which give birth to a generation of viviparous aphids, about three-quarters of which develop into winged females. The rest remain wingless. The winged forms spread the species to other parts of the tree or to other trees. About half of the second generation and some of the later generations may develop wings and migrate. Unlike the rosy apple aphid, the apple aphid lives on the apple tree all year. It reproduces continuously during the summer. In August and during the autumn months, the species is found almost exclusively on water sprouts or terminals of young trees that are still growing. The male and female sexual forms are produced there. After mating, the female lays eggs.

This species usually appears somewhat later in the spring than the more common apple grain aphid and is not as numerous on the buds because it waits until the leaves unfold. Because it reproduces on the trees during the whole season, however, it may be more injurious than the rosy apple aphid. Its damage resembles that of the rosy apple aphid — the leaves often curl very badly. Apples dwarfed by aphids look puckered at the blossom end.

■ *Monitoring*

Beginning in early June, select 10 growing shoots (not spurs) on each of five trees in a block. If an average of more than four leaves on the shoots are infested with wingless aphids, an insecticide application is recommended. If predators are active, delay treatment and check their effectiveness one week later.

■ *Control*

Apply preblossom applications of contact or systemic aphicides. Apply foliage applications of systemic compounds in early season or summer. Early applications when the aphids are fully exposed and before they curl the leaves are most effective. Systemic pesticides are required when the leaves have curled.

If aphicides appear to be ineffective, it is possible that spirea aphids are present. Spirea aphids are more difficult to control than apple aphids. Recently it has been shown that, in some states — including Virginia, West Virginia, Pennsylvania, New York and possibly Ohio and Michigan — a substantial proportion of apple aphids were in fact a different species, the spirea aphid, *Aphis spiraecola* Patch. Both species have similar life histories and feeding habits. If you suspect the presence of spirea aphids, contact a specialist familiar with these aphids for help in identifying them. They look much like apple aphids. Winged adult apple aphids have dark-colored veins in their wings; spirea aphids have wings with light-colored to transparent veins.

Common Name—
Woolly Apple Aphid

Scientific Name—
Eriosoma lanigerum (Hausmann)

Family—
Aphidae

THIS APHID HAS BEEN ONE OF THE MOST troublesome and widely distributed pests of apple. It was first described by Hausmann in Europe in 1802. It was first identified in the United States by Harris in 1842, though indications exist that it appeared in the United States long before that date. It is now a sporadic pest because of Merton Malling rootstocks from resistant Northern Spy.

■ Life Stages

Egg: The cinnamon-colored eggs are oval and measure 0.6 mm by 0.3 mm.

Nymph: The five instars include the adult. The nymphs are reddish brown and covered by white, cottony masses of waxy fibers.

Adult: The adults are purplish and nearly covered by a woolly mass of long, waxy fibers. The waxy fibers are much shorter on the root-inhabiting forms and give them a whitish, mealy appearance. The males, which are about half the size of the females, are olive-yellow.

■ Host Range

The woolly apple aphid is a pest of apple, pear, hawthorn, mountain ash and elm. It is present in all apple-growing areas of the United States and Canada.

■ Injury or Damage

White, cottony masses cover purplish aphids clustered in wounds on the trunk and branches of the tree or on large knots on the roots and underground parts of the trunk. Infested trees will often have many short, fibrous roots. Aboveground colonies develop around leaf axils on sprouts or on new growth, particularly at abrasions or cuts. They prevent injured bark from healing. Often found at the base of a tree just above the roots, they cause the roots to decay.

The underground aphids do the damage; the ones aboveground cause little damage, especially on larger trees. The injury consists of gall-like formations on the branches and swollen enlargements on the roots. These increase in size from year to year because of the feeding of the aphids. Such galls can form favorable places for fungi to attack. The foliage of infested trees takes on a yellowish appearance. Infested young trees are easily uprooted.

Woolly apple aphids can also transmit apple canker (*Pezicula malicorticis*).

■ Factors Affecting Abundance

Woolly apple aphid is generally not a problem in commercial orchards unless pyrethroids or carbamate insecticides are used repeatedly. These types of insecticides are very toxic to wasp parasitoids (especially

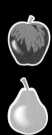

Above: Aerial forms of woolly apple aphids surrounded by cottony, waxy fibers.

Left: Damage to roots of apple tree caused by subterranean form of woolly apple aphids.

Aphelinus mali) that normally keep aphid populations under control. Some varieties, such as Northern Spy, are resistant to this pest. Elm trees in the vicinity of orchards increase the migration of the aphid to apple trees. The insect is spread by infested nursery stock.

Life History

The aphid spends the winter either in the egg stage or as an immature nymph. The nymphs hibernate underground on apple roots if elm trees are not nearby. The females lay eggs in cracks or crevices of elm tree bark in the fall. The eggs hatch in the spring into wingless, parthenogenetic, viviparous stem mothers. These feed on elm buds and leaves for two generations during May and June, causing the elm leaves to curl into rosettes. They then produce a third-generation winged form that migrates to apple, hawthorn or mountain ash. The aphids establish new colonies here, and repeated generations are produced during the summer. They feed in wounds on the trunk and branches of the tree.

In the fall, winged aphids develop in both the aerial and root colonies. They fly back to elm, where they give birth to males and females. Both males and females are wingless, have no mouthparts and do not grow after birth. A few days after mating, the female lays a single long, dark, oval, cinnamon-colored egg almost as large as her body in a crevice of the bark. These winter eggs hatch in early spring into wingless aphids.

Because of the virtual disappearance of American elm trees, the woolly apple aphid most often lives on apple trees throughout the year. Each group of aphids, small or large, is considered a colony. Aphids are present more nearly year round on the roots than on

the tops. The aerial forms are most commonly found on the twigs, water sprouts and callus tissue in wounds, cankers and scars. Wingless females in the aerial colonies may give birth to nymphs at any time in spring, summer or fall. Newborn nymphs are very important in the spread of the woolly apple aphid. They spread either through some mechanical agency or directly by crawling. Birds and insects can also transport aphids.

Any unsettling conditions will produce crawlers, though they are generally more abundant in spring and fall. Crawlers cannot work into and through the soil. In orchards, the swaying of trees in the wind, and organic matter, clods, stones and other objects may provide pathways to the roots. Crawlers begin to infest the roots early in the season. The downward movement can begin at any time when the crawlers are numerous, especially in early summer and fall. Infestations by aerial colonies are not true indications of root infestations, because trees can have aerial infestations over a season without the roots becoming infested.

Monitoring

In the petal-fall/first-cover period, examine abrasions or cuts, particularly on sprouts or on new growth, for white, cottony masses covering colonies of woolly apple aphids. If numbers warrant treatment, spray during the early season before migration to the roots occurs.

Control

Some pesticides, such as pyrethroids and carbamates, encourage outbreaks. These should be used sparingly or be combined with an aphicide. An application of a summer aphicide will control woolly apple aphids in tree tops. No control methods for underground aphids are available.

Table 7.
Characteristics of aphids commonly found attacking tree fruit crops.

Aphid	Crop attacked	Overwintering stage	Aphid color	Number of generations	Location	First nymphs present
Apple grain aphid	Apple, plum, pear	Eggs on tree	Dark green when young nymph; lighter green with dark green stripe down back when full grown	3 on apple; many on summer host plants	At tip of opening buds early; later on undersides of leaves	Green tip
Rosy apple aphid	Apple, pear	Eggs on tree	Dark purple when young nymph; purple to pinkish when full grown	3 on apple; many on summer host plants	Almost exclusively in curled leaves of spur growth	½-inch green-cluster bud
Apple aphid	Apple, pear	Eggs on tree	Dark green when young nymph; yellowish green to light green when full grown	4-6 on apple or pear	Colonies at tips of growing terminals or suckers	½-inch green-cluster bud
Woolly apple aphid	Apple, pear	Nymphs in subterranean colonies or eggs on elm trees	Reddish brown to purple; covered with white cotton-like substance	Number variable, usually 3-4 on apple	Colonies at the bases of suckers or on pruning scars	Mid-summer (variable)
Black cherry aphid	Cherry	Eggs on tree	Shiny black	2-3 on cherry; many on summer host plants	Colonies at tips of growing shoots	As leaves begin to appear in spring
Green peach aphid	Peach, nectarine	Eggs on tree	Green as young nymph, turning a straw to light green when older	3 on apple and peach; many on summer host plants	At opening buds and leaves of spurs	As leaves begin to appear in spring

Common Name—

San Jose Scale

Scientific Name—

Quadraspidiotus periciosus (Comstock)

Family—

Diaspididae

SAN JOSE SCALE WAS BROUGHT INTO California about 1870. By 1873, it had become a serious pest in the San Jose Valley; hence, the name. Marlett went to the Orient in 1901 to find the native home of the scale and found that it originated northwest of Beijing on Chinese peach. In 1886, it was brought into New Jersey on plums. The two nurseries receiving this material shipped nursery stock to all parts of the country. By 1895, it had reached all parts of the United States.

The first insect resistance to pesticides — San Jose scale's resistance to lime sulfur — was reported in the United States by Melander in Washington in 1908. Tremendous damage was done by this pest before controls were perfected. In 1922, 1,000 acres of mature apple trees were killed in southern Illinois.

■ Life Stages

Egg: The female scale does not lay eggs but gives birth to living young.

Crawler: Crawlers are minute, orange-yellow and oval, with six legs and one pair of antennae.

Adult: The females are nearly round and about 1.6 mm across with a raised nipple in the center, and they remain under their scale coverings their entire lives. The males are oval, about 1 mm long and half as broad, with a raised dot near the larger end of the scale. This waxy covering protects the male.

It emerges from the scale as a small, yellow, two-winged insect.

■ Host Range

Host plants include apple, pear, quince, plum, apricot, sweet cherries, currants, gooseberries and other woody ornamentals.

■ Injury or Damage

San Jose scale feeds on the sap of the host plant. The amount of sap that a single individual, or even several hundred individuals, could extract could not injure a healthy tree or shrub. But the species multiplies so rapidly that millions of progeny may be produced from a few scattered parents in a season or two — enough to completely cover the bark of parts or even all of the tree.

Most of our insect pests have natural enemies that restrain their multiplication so that they become destructively abundant only now and then, but the enemies of the San Jose scale are inadequate to control it. The scale may kill a young tree or shrub in two or three years; older trees withstand the attack longer, but sooner or later they are likewise destroyed. Young orchards are killed out more quickly than old ones; and where young trees are set in old infested orchards, they also become infested and die before they are old enough to fruit.

The scale does not confine its attack to the bark of the tree but infests the leaves and

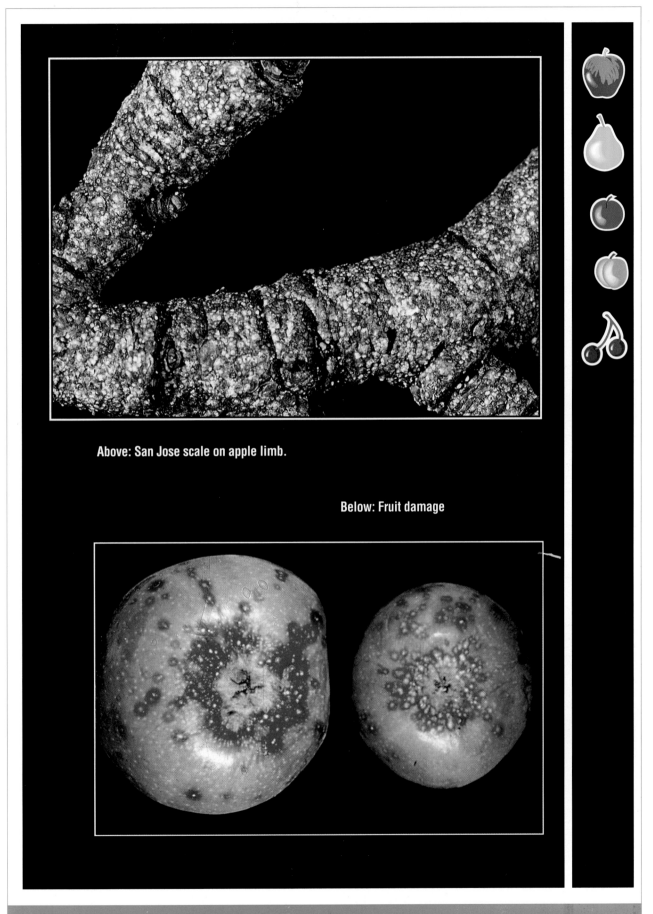

Above: San Jose scale on apple limb.

Below: Fruit damage

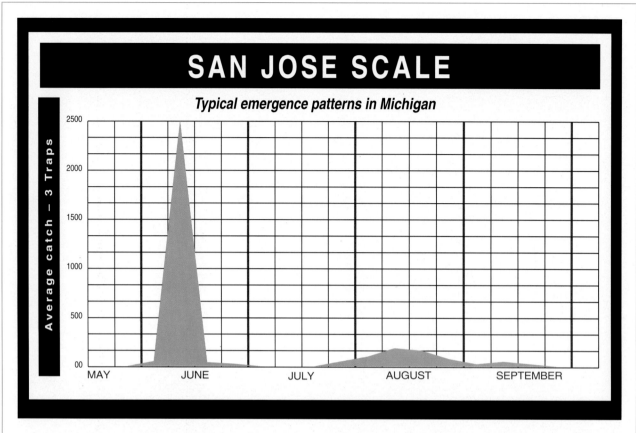

SAN JOSE SCALE

Typical emergence patterns in Michigan

fruit also. The fruits of apple, peach and pear trees frequently become as badly infested as the bark. On fruit and on young bark, the scale produces a conspicuous red spot. It is comparatively easy to prevent serious injury to the tree by using proper control measures, but it is very difficult to prevent some spotting of the fruit. Scaly fruit is unsightly and not marketable.

■ Factors Affecting Abundance

Adverse weather conditions, including winds, rains and extreme heat and cold, can cause heavy mortality. Predaceous and parasitic insects check the multiplication of this pest to a certain degree. Very low winter temperatures can cause high mortality of the early instar nymphs.

■ Life History

This insect passes the winter as partly grown scales on the tree. Up to 80 percent of the winter forms may be first-nymphal instars. The insects remain dormant, tightly fastened to the bark, until the sap starts flowing in the spring. They then begin to grow, usually becoming full grown in late May. At this time, the active males, which are tiny, two-winged insects, come out from their scales to mate with the females. (The females remain under scales throughout their lives.) The females continue to grow for a month.

After mating, the females begin to produce living young, usually at the rate of nine or 10 per day. They reproduce for about six weeks, each female bearing from 150 to 500 crawlers. Crawlers have six well developed legs and two antennae and can crawl considerable distances during their first few hours of life. They will crawl about for a few hours until they find a place attractive to them. Then they will insert their slender, threadlike mouthparts through the bark and begin sucking sap. About three weeks later, they molt and shed their skins, losing their legs and antennae with the old skin. The scales then become mere flattened, yellow sacs with waxy caps. They are attached to the bark by their sucking mouthparts.

As the insect grows, woolly secretions given off from the body are mixed with a waxy material to continue the formation of the shell. Portions of the shed skins are also incorporated into the scales after molting. The females develop through two nymphal instars to the adult. The males develop through four instars. The last two are called prepupa and pupa. Wing pads are present at the prepupa when the legs are short and thick.

This insect increases most rapidly in hot, dry weather. The descendants of a single female could number more than 300 million a year. Crawlers are spread by wind, on birds' feet, on workers' clothing and on farm implements.

There are two generations per year. Because the females bear living young over so long a period, the broods overlap and all stages may be present on the trees throughout the growing season. In the summer, each generation is completed in five to seven weeks, depending on the weather. Natural enemies include parasitic wasps and ladybird beetles.

■ Monitoring

Because of their small size, San Jose scales may go undetected until they appear on the fruit. Scales on the fruit indicate a need for control measures the following year. Place pheromone traps in the tree at the prepink stage to trap the tiny, yellowish winged males that emerge during the bloom and petal-fall periods. Then renew the cap and trap for the summer generation. In addition to monitoring male trap catch, monitor crawler populations by placing black, sticky

tape around scale-infested scaffold branches about seven to 10 days after petal fall. Crawlers will become trapped on the tape when they emerge. Check the tape often for trapped crawlers. Apply an effective pesticide for scales after you see the first crawler.

Using 51 degrees F as a base, degree-days (DD) for San Jose scale activity* are:

125 DD	first adult emergence.
225 DD	first eggs laid.
500 DD	first crawler emergence and peak egg laying.
950 DD	first emergence of second-generation adults.
1,350 DD	peak emergence of second-generation adults.
1,450 DD	first emergence of second-generation crawlers.
1,600 DD	peak egg laying by second-generation adults.

■ Control

Superior oil applied in the prebloom stage is effective. If high populations are present, an effective insecticide applied at early petal fall will control the males before they mate with the females. First-generation crawlers, which usually begin to emerge four to six weeks after adult male flight, can be controlled with thorough coverage by an effective pesticide applied immediately after capture of the first crawlers on the sticky, black tape. Check the tape often for the presence of crawlers. If it is necessary to control the second generation of scale, use pheromones to trap the second-generation males and sticky tape to trap the crawlers, and time the sprays accordingly. Degree-days listed for San Jose scale will be useful in determining the seasonal activities of this pest.

*Data from MSU PETE model.

Common Name—
European Fruit Lecanium Scale

Scientific Name—
Parthenolecanium corni (Bouché)

Family—
Coccidae

SERIOUS OUTBREAKS OCCURRED IN 1894 and 1895 in the plum orchards of New York. This scale was introduced from Europe.

■ Life Stages

Egg: A large number — more than 1,000 — of white eggs are laid under the bodies of the females during late May or June. Later, the eggs become pinkish and hatch in late June or July. The egg stage lasts two to four weeks. After the female oviposits, it dries up into a hard shell on the surface and shrinks away from the eggs that are left inside the shell until they hatch and the young crawl out. The emptied shell eventually becomes loose from weathering and drops off the tree.

Crawler: The crawlers are about 0.5 mm long, flat and yellowish, with legs, eyes and antennae. After settling and beginning to feed, they secrete a brownish scale cover, becoming spindle-shaped. The female has three instars and the male has four. Pupation lasts about one month.

Adult: The full-grown females are yellowish brown. They later turn dark brown and are covered with powdery or cottonlike material that looks like the bloom of the plum. They are oval and elevated in the shape of a spindle. Full-grown females are 3 to 5 mm long. The scales of the males are composed of delicate, almost transparent wax, with well marked ridges.

■ Host Range

Host plants include shade and forest trees. The scale will also attack fruit trees. The Northern Spy apple has been most frequently attacked. It has also been found on Wealthy and Transparent; on other fruit trees, including plum, peach and cherry; and on grapevines.

■ Injury or Damage

These scales suck the sap from leaves during late July and August and from twigs during May and June of the following year. The young scales collectively produce a great quantity of the clear, sweet liquid known as honeydew. This serves as a medium for fungus growth and gives the leaves and fruits a smutty appearance. They can cause fruit to be undersized and drop prematurely.

■ Factors Affecting Abundance

Extreme weather conditions — both heat and cold — can cause high mortality. Predators can be a factor in controlling this pest.

■ Life History

There is one brood per year. Only fertilized females overwinter, as immature small

Left: Scale on apple limb.

Below: Adult males on apple limb.

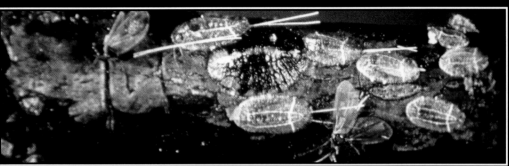

scales on the twigs. Some of the old, large, dead scales may also be present on the twigs during the winter. The over-wintering young develop in May and June to large brown scales, at which time the females have matured the eggs. The females die, leaving the scales filled with eggs that hatch in July. The young (crawlers) move to the undersides of the leaves, where they settle and feed along the main veins. Infested leaves become curled and turn yellow, the tree makes little growth, and the fruits remain undersized or drop prematurely. The crawlers migrate as far as 1 to 5 feet from the parent female and distribute them-selves in a random fashion on the leaves. After the first molt, migration back to the twigs usually begins in the late summer and continues until late fall. Reproduction is almost entirely par-thenogenetic. The distribution of this scale on the twigs is influenced by the age of the wood. There is fairly uniform distribution on one-, two- and three-year-old wood, while wood older than three years usually has bark too thick for the stylets to penetrate.

Winged males appear in late August and mate with the females, after which the males die. In the fall, the females crawl back to the undersides of the twigs for winter.

■ *Monitoring*

During the prebloom period, inspect undersides of smaller branches for brown, spindle-shaped scales. In mid- to late summer, inspect leaves and fruit for black fungus that may develop in honeydew secreted from scales. To date, there are no pheromones for this pest.

■ *Control*

Chemical sprays are directed against the newly emerged crawlers. If superior oils are used, they should be applied at the delayed dormant stage, because the European fruit lecanium scale is charac-terized by rapid growth in the spring that coincides with the development of the host plant. In the interval from delayed dormant to bloom, the scale grows from the small overwintering form to maturity. In about 10 days, the weight of the scale may increase tenfold or more. Great changes also occur in metabolic activity as the scale goes from dormancy to active growth. These metabolic changes affect the respiratory rate, which is directly related to the mode of action of the oil. Larger animals require greater dosages to produce equal mortality, so the oil becomes less effective as the season advances from delayed dormant to bloom.

Common Name—
Oystershell Scale

Scientific Name—
Lepidosaphes ulmi (Linnaeus)

Family—
Diaspididae

OYSTERSHELL SCALE WAS FIRST DESCRIBED by Linnaeus in 1785. In the United States, this pest was first described in 1796 in Massachusetts. In 1856, Fitch was one of the first in the United States to make detailed biological studies. Comstock, in 1881, made many contributions to the study of this pest, particularly in the differences of this scale on ornamentals and fruit.

■ Life Stages

Egg: The eggs are ellipsoidal and about half as wide as they are long. Some of them are a little smaller at one end than at the other.

Larva: The young nymphs are very small, six-legged and whitish.

Adult: The males are small winged insects. Females are about 0.7 mm long and cream-white in color. They are grub-like creatures without legs or antennae. The scale of the newly emerged female has a broadened and somewhat rounded posterior end.

■ Host Range

Host plants include apple, pear, mountain ash, plum, raspberry, currant, apricot and grape. This pest is found in the northern two-thirds of the United States and Canada.

■ Injury or Damage

This pest weakens the plant by its feeding and is occasionally found on the fruit so that the fruit is not salable.

■ Factors Affecting Abundance

Weather is not known to affect abundance of the oystershell scale, though temperatures of -32 degrees F have been reported to be fatal. Predators, including birds, mites and wasps, are important in the control of this scale.

■ Life History

The insect passes the winter as fertilized females. Between 40 and 150 small, grayish white eggs will be found under each female scale. The eggs hatch late in the spring, usually two to three weeks after bloom. The young nymphs are small, whitish, six-legged creatures. They crawl about on the bark for a few hours, then insert their beaks into the bark. They then begin the formation of a waxy scale coating over their bodies. A few hours after the crawler has settled, the beginnings of the first scale appear as white, waxy threads at the posterior end of the body and in spots along the sides. As the scale develops, the body of the nymph underneath flattens out consid-

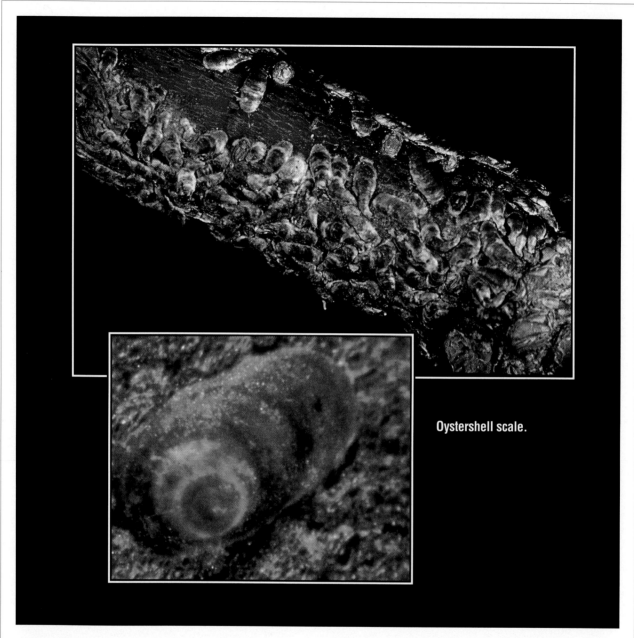

Oystershell scale.

erably, becoming about twice as long and wide as it was originally.

The first of two molts occurs two to three weeks after the eggs hatch. After a few days, the insect begins to form its second scale. The second nymphal stage lasts about three weeks. Within four to five days of the second molt, the insect begins the third, or permanent, scale. As the scale develops, the female broadens and lengthens considerably. The insect gradually works downward underneath the scale as it is formed, so that by the time the scale is completed, there is consider-able vacant space under its anterior end. It takes about three weeks for the permanent scale to be formed.

About a month after the second molt, egg laying begins and continues for about a month. As the eggs are laid, the female gradually contracts her body toward the anterior end of the scale. By the time egg laying is completed, the insect has pushed far upward in the scale so that the body gradually shrinks toward the pointed end of the scale. The females die shortly after the last eggs are laid.

■ Monitoring

During the prebloom period, examine twigs for scales in areas of trees where spray coverage is difficult. Examine fruit at harvest for blemishes made by scales.

■ Control

Cover sprays are directed at the crawler stage. Superior oil applied in the prebloom stage will provide control.

Common Name—
Forbes Scale

Scientific Name—
Quadraspidiotus forbesi (Johnson)

Family—
Diaspididae

THIS PEST HAS BEEN KNOWN IN THE MIDWEST since 1894. Originally, it was thought to be primarily a pest of cherry.

■ Life Stages

Egg: The female gives birth to living young.

Crawler: These are small and licelike, with six legs and one pair of antennae.

Adult: The adults are similar to San Jose scale, except that Forbes scales have a raised, reddish area in the center and San Jose scales have a pale yellow nipple in the center.

■ Host Range

Forbes scale is found anywhere east of the Rocky Mountains on apple, cherry, apricot, pear, plum and currant.

■ Injury or Damage

Like the San Jose scale, the Forbes scale feeds on the sap of the tree, weakening and eventually maybe killing the tree.

■ Factors Affecting Abundance

Predators and parasites are important factors in the control of this pest. Mild winters favor the Forbes scale, while severe winters cause high mortalities.

■ Life History

The scales pass winter partly grown. The males emerge in the spring and mate with the females. The nymphs appear in May and June, being produced oviparously and ovo-viviparously. In the north central states, one generation occurs per year.

■ Monitoring

This pest is much less prevalent than the San Jose scale. To distinguish between the Forbes and San Jose scales, examine the nipples of the insects. The San Jose scale has a pale yellow nipple, while that of the Forbes scale will appear as a raised, reddish area in the insect's center. In the late crawler stages, this pest is similar to the San Jose scale but is a little larger. It is also brown, compared with the San Jose scale's dull black.

■ Control

Summer applications of chemicals will control this pest.

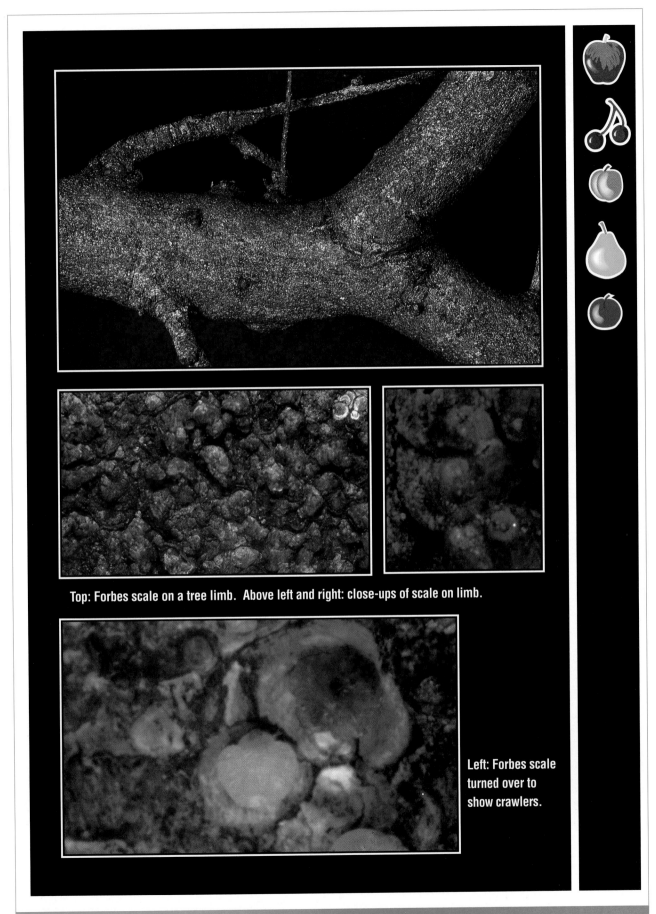

Top: Forbes scale on a tree limb. Above left and right: close-ups of scale on limb.

Left: Forbes scale turned over to show crawlers.

Common Name—
Tarnished Plant Bug

Scientific Name—
Lygus lineolaris (Palisot de Beauvois)

Family—
Miridae

THIS PEST WAS FIRST DESCRIBED IN 1746 by Linnaeus in Sweden. In America, the species was first described by Thomas Say in 1831, though there are indications that it was collected and described here as early as 1781.

■ Life Stages

Egg: The egg is elongated and slightly curved. The outer end is cut off squarely, and the lid that covers this end is usually flush with the stem. The egg is 0.95 to 1 mm long and 0.25 mm wide.

Nymphal stages: The newly hatched tarnished plant bug is a small, greenish creature less than 1 mm long. It goes through five instars, with wing pads beginning to show in the third instar.

Adult: The adult varies from 4.9 to 5.7 mm long and 2.4 to 2.8 mm wide. Generally, it is brownish mottled with various shades of yellowish and reddish brown. The bug is a flattened oval, with the small head projecting in front.

■ Host Range

This species feeds and breeds on a great variety of plants. It attacks apple, apricot, cherry, pear, peach, plum and quince. It also feeds on flowers, vegetables, field crops, small fruits, cotton and tobacco.

■ Injury or Damage

Overwintered adults begin feeding on apple buds soon after the delayed dormant bud stage. They are most abundant during the pink and blossom periods. Egg laying in the blossom buds begins as soon as the stems in the clusters start to separate and continues in the fruit until the apples are about 12.5 mm in diameter. The plant bugs then migrate to the weeds and become scarce in the trees. Common mustard weed is the preferred host.

Affected fruits may exhibit both feeding and egg-laying injuries. Feeding punctures are usually small and superficial injuries, but the oviposition punctures cause deep depressions and distortion of the fruit. Most of the injuries are inflicted in the calyx tube near the base of the sepals and petals, so the blemishes on the mature fruits appear at the calyx end. Some injuries, however, particularly those made after bloom, may occur elsewhere on the fruit surface.

Apple varieties react differently to tarnished plant bug oviposition wounds. In Red Delicious and Cortland, very deep depressions usually result. In Duchess and Greening, the depressions are less pronounced, though these blemishes may result in a lower grading for the fruit. The degree of injury depends not only on the number of insects, but also on the weather.

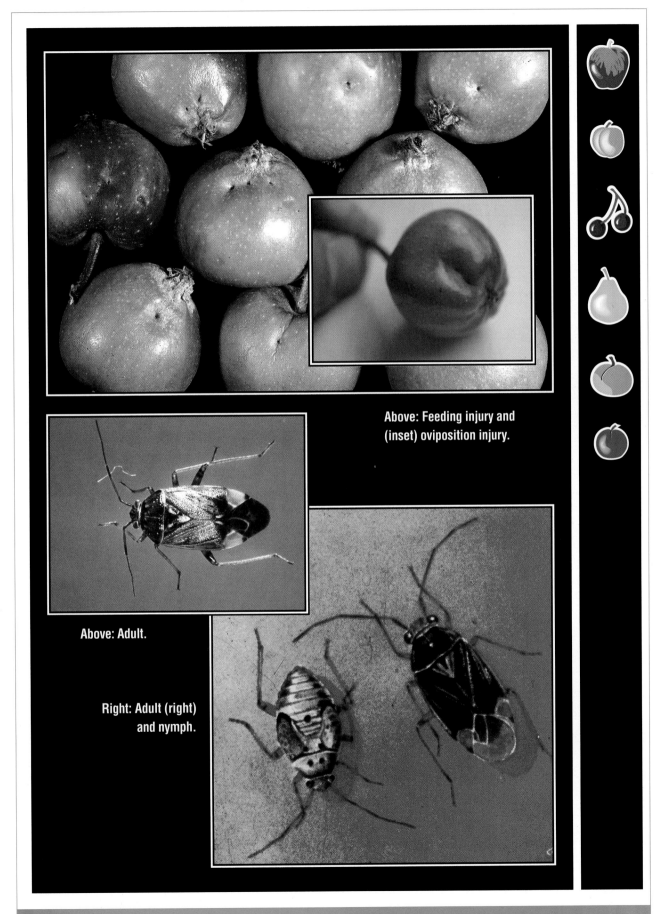

Above: Feeding injury and (inset) oviposition injury.

Above: Adult.

Right: Adult (right) and nymph.

■ Factors Affecting Abundance

Warm weather in the early season before alfalfa and other ground crops have developed will cause movement into and damage in the fruit trees. Cold, rainy or windy weather at this time will reduce or prevent feeding. Fruit trees near hedgerows, ditch banks and other hibernation locations are more seriously injured. Droughty conditions that dry up vegetation may cause plant bugs to move into trees.

■ Life History

The adult bugs hibernate under leaf mold, stones and tree bark, among the leaves of such plants as clover, alfalfa and mullein, and in many other protected places. They become active very early in spring, when they attack the buds of fruit trees, seriously injuring the terminal shoots and fruits. They do not appear to lay their eggs on these plants to any great extent, but rather migrate to various herbaceous weeds, vegetables and flowers, where the eggs are either inserted full length into the stems, petioles or midribs of leaves or into buds, or are tucked in among the florets of the flower heads.

In about 10 days, a small nymph emerges from the egg and begins feeding on the sap. It grows rapidly, molting five times. The larger nymphs gradually take on the appearance of the adult. The life cycle is completed in three or four weeks, so three to five generations probably occur each season. By late summer, the bugs can be numerous, but because of their obscure and protective coloration and shy hiding habits, they are not often noticed.

■ Monitoring

Make regular observations from tight cluster stage to first cover, particularly in orchard areas adjacent to weedy places or locations where alfalfa or other hay crops grow. Unbaited glossy, rectangular, non-reflective, white, sticky boards, hung low in the tree, are effective monitoring traps for plant bugs. Place the traps about 2 to 3 feet from the ground and monitor weekly. Use at least three traps per block, or about one trap for every 3 to 5 acres. If you find more than three plant bugs per trap by the fruit's tight cluster stage, or four bugs per trap by the fruit's pink stage, apply a prebloom pesticide. For oak and hickory bugs, hang traps in the tops of trees near the edge of the orchard when the orchard is bordered by woods.

■ Control

Crop cover management is important in preventing the tarnished plant bugs from moving into fruit trees. Plant bugs are difficult to control. Spraying weedy hedgerows and weedy areas adjacent to orchards can reduce the migration of plant bugs into the orchards. On apples, this pest should be controlled at the pink stage. Other plant bugs, such as oak and hickory bugs (*Lygocoris* spp.), can cause similar injury in orchards bordered by woods. Green stink bugs (*Acrosternum hilare*) and other stink bugs (Pentatomidae) can also cause injury, especially late in the season.

Common Name—
White Apple Leafhopper

Scientific Name—
Typhlocyba pomaria (McAtee)

Family—
Cicadellidae

UNTIL 1926, THE LEAFHOPPER attacking apple was erroneously taken for *T. rosae*. At this time, McAtee noted that there were two species of leafhopper on apple, and that *T. pomaria* was the predominant one.

■ Life Stages

Egg: The eggs are white, elongated and cylindrical. One end is slightly tapered. Dimensions are 0.80 by 0.26 mm. The first-generation or overwintering eggs are laid beneath the bark of the apple twigs in the cortex. They are laid singly and look like small blisters on the twig. Second-generation eggs are laid on the leaves, primarily on the lower surface along the main veins. They are not visible to the naked eye.

Larva: There are five instars in the development of the larva or nymph. The size varies from 1 to 2.5 mm, depending on the stage of development. The first two instars are pale white with dull red or pink eyes. The last three instars are white to yellow with white eyes.

Adult: The entire body is a faint yellow with an orange to red tinge on the thorax and head. The head is more red than the thorax. Length varies from 3 to 3.5 mm. The female is paler than the male, with little or no red tinge on the

face. The tip of the ovipositor sheath is black.

■ Host Range

The primary host is apple, but this leafhopper has also been found on peach and plum; sour, sweet and wild cherry; and hawthorn. Greening, Baldwin, Duchess and Jonathan are the most susceptible apple varieties. This pest is found in the midwestern and eastern United States and eastern Canada.

■ Injury or Damage

First-generation nymphs remove chlorophyll, and feeding sites appear as whitish spots or stippling on the upper leaf surfaces. When feeding is heavy, the entire tree may appear whitish or silvery. The loss of chlorophyll may indirectly affect both fruit quality and bud formation, especially if it occurs early in the season. The second generation is responsible for spotting and streaking on the fruit caused by accumulation of leafhopper excrement. Once dried, it is difficult to remove. The problem is most serious in dry seasons.

■ Factors Affecting Abundance

The advent of synthetic organic phosphates caused this pest to change

Above: Leaf stippling on apple caused by white apple leafhopper.

Above: Adults and nymphs.

Right: Apple damage.

Far left: Blister-like swelling on twig covering white apple leafhopper egg.
Left: Egg (exposed for photograph.)

from a minor to a major pest under certain conditions. It becomes a problem when it develops resistance to many of the commonly used pesticides.

Life History

This leafhopper has two generations in the north central states and overwinters as an egg. Eggs hatch from pink stage to petal fall. Early instar nymphs migrate to the lower surfaces of the older leaves and begin feeding. These nymphs remain on the same leaves until they reach the adult stage. The mobility of the nymphs is limited to running — only the adults can hop and fly.

First-generation adults are active during June and early July. About 10 days after first emergence, egg laying begins. These second-generation eggs are placed on the lower surfaces of the leaves, the leaf petioles, and near the midvein and larger veins. No first-generation adults are alive after mid- to late July. The second-generation eggs begin to hatch in late July, and hatching may continue into September if cool temperatures prevail. The emergence of second-generation adults may begin anytime in late August or early September. These adults lay the overwintering eggs in the bark of the apple twigs.

At times, the potato leafhopper — *Empoasco fabae* — can be mistaken for the nymphs and adults of the white apple leafhopper. To tell the difference, note the color and movement of the insects. Nymphs and adults of the potato leafhopper are pale green and move backward and forward but not sideways like the white apple leafhopper. Also, unlike the white apple leafhopper, the potato leafhopper feeds near leaf edges. These feedings show up as triangular, chlorotic areas that extend from the feeding sites to the leaf edge. A number of feeding sites on a leaf will cause the leaf to curve downward. If several leaves on a shoot are affected, shoot growth may be stunted.

Monitoring

From bloom through petal fall, examine 50 leaves selected from leaf clusters in the inside of the tree. Treatment is recommended if there is an average of 0.5 nymphs or more per leaf. For the second generation, examine 50 leaves per tree from 10 trees per orchard for nymphs from late July through August. Treatment is recommended if there is an average of one or more nymphs per leaf. An additional spray may be needed because of the extended egg hatching period.

Using 48 degrees F as a base, degree-days (DD) for white apple leafhopper activity* are:

       100 DD .... first nymph emergence.
       550 DD .... first adult emergence.
     1,100 DD .... peak adult emergence.
     1,750 DD .... peak egg laying.

Control

The white apple leafhopper has a great propensity for quickly developing resistance to chemical compounds. The insects are present on the undersides of the leaves, and thorough coverage by effective chemicals is essential for control. The first generation is best controlled at petal fall. The second generation usually requires control in early August. Second-generation control is generally more difficult than that for first-generation leafhoppers. Hatching is more uniform in the first generation, and young leafhoppers are much easier to control than adults. In addition, thorough spray coverage of upper and lower leaves is essential for leafhopper control. Because less foliage is present during first-generation emergence, growers may find it easier to cover leaves and achieve pest control at this stage.

*Data from MSU PETE model.

External chewing insects that eat holes in leaves, buds, bark or fruit

I N RECENT YEARS, LEAFROLLERS HAVE BECOME INCREASINGLY DIFFICULT TO control. Some, such as the obliquebanded leafroller, have been able to develop a tolerance to many pesticides. Timing of pesticides is important because the larvae become more difficult to control as they progress to later and larger instars.

Pheromones are available for many of the leafrollers. When properly used and interpreted, they can be very useful to predict outbreaks and time pesticide use.

Chapter 3

Common Name—
Redbanded Leafroller

Scientific Name—
Argyrotaenia velutinana (Walker)

Family—
Tortricidae

THIS IS A NATIVE PEST. REDBANDED LEAFROLLER was first reported on grapes in 1870 and on apples in 1879. It caused little or no damage to apples until about 1918.

■ Life Stages

Egg: The eggs are cemented together in patches or masses. Some egg masses contain as few as three or four eggs, while others contain as many as 145. These egg patches are usually oval in outline and vary from 1.6 to 6 mm in width. The pale yellowish or cream-colored masses resemble spots of tallow. The individual egg is a pale, flat disk about 0.8 mm in diameter. Upon close examination, the eggs will appear as overlapping scales in the mass. On apple trees, first-brood eggs are laid on the bark, chiefly on the trunk and scaffold limbs. Eggs of the second brood are laid mostly on upper leaf surfaces.

Larva: The larval stage is a pale-headed, greenish, active caterpillar that measures about 16 mm long at maturity. When newly hatched, the larva is bright yellow and about 1.6 mm long. After it has fed, the body of the new caterpillar turns green and thereafter ranges from a pale, dull yellowish green to a bright apple green, depending on the kind of food consumed. The head and thoracic shield are pale straw-colored or the same color as the body. In contrast, the larval stage of the fruit tree leafroller has a dark brown or black head capsule.

Pupa: The pupa ranges in color from light brown, sometimes with tinges of green, to deep brown, and measures from 7 to 8 mm long. The larger pupae usually produce female moths.

Adult: Moth wing spans are 12 to 18 mm. The overall color is reddish brown, relieved by lighter markings of silver-gray and orange. Though the pattern of the markings varies considerably, a fairly distinct, wide, reddish brown band extends across the forewings, giving rise to the common name of the pest. The male is usually smaller and more active than the female. Male wing spans are 12 to 15 mm, while female wing spans measure 14 to 18 mm.

■ Host Range

The redbanded leafroller is a general feeder — the larvae have been found feeding on a large number of unrelated plants, including most common fruits, vegetables, weeds, flowers, ornamentals and shrubs. Among the fruits, the leafroller shows a strong preference for apples. It is common in the apple-growing areas of the midwestern and eastern United States and eastern and western Canada. It has also damaged plums, grapes, peaches, raspberries, strawberries and cherries.

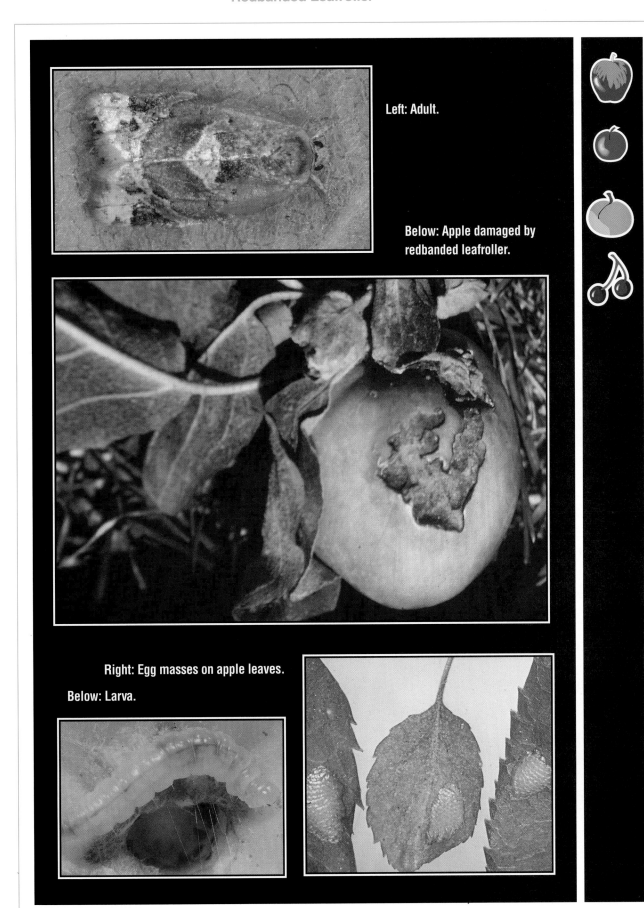

Left: Adult.

Below: Apple damaged by redbanded leafroller.

Right: Egg masses on apple leaves.

Below: Larva.

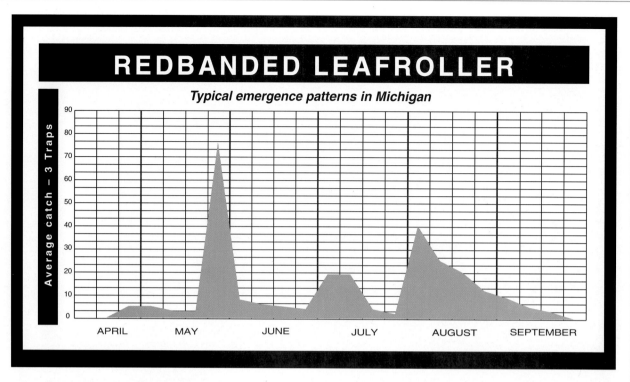

REDBANDED LEAFROLLER

Typical emergence patterns in Michigan

■ *Injury or Damage*

The redbanded leafroller injures both foliage and fruit. The injury to the foliage is of little significance except when infestations are extremely high. The larvae skeletonize leaves from the underside, folding and webbing the leaves together.

Infestations in non-bearing trees have not been heavy enough to constitute a problem. Injury to fruit is the main concern to the grower. First-brood larvae feed on apples in June and early July when the fruits are small, making irregular, shallow cavities in the fruit. Feeding may occur at the point where two or more fruits touch. A single larva may eat a considerable area. Some of these young fruits may be so severely damaged that they do not survive. The injured areas gradually cork over, and the apples usually develop into deformed or misshapen culls.

First-brood injury is distinguishable from that of the fruit tree leafroller and oblique-banded leafroller, which occurs earlier and is deeper, so that by harvest, there is a deep depression with gradually rounding edges. The injured surface is usually rough and rus-

setted. Redbanded leafroller injury is usually shallower and often is characterized by ragged edges and thick, corky tissue over the damaged area. Injury by second- and third-brood redbanded leafroller larvae occurs where a leaf is webbed to an apple or where apples are present in a cluster.

Other points favored for feeding include the depressions at the stem and calyx ends of the fruit. The larvae eat the skin and the flesh immediately beneath. Feeding areas are shallow and irregular and may be of considerable size, particularly when several larvae feed on one fruit.

Second- and third-brood injury occurs so late in the season that the fruits — except possibly hard winter varieties — are incapable of corking over the wounded tissue. Usually, however, second- and third-brood feeding areas are sources of infection for various rots and allow rapid moisture losses. Injured apples do not store well. When a high percentage of a crop is affected, it has been found impractical to sort out the uninjured apples. Consequently, whole crops have been abandoned. Injured fruits in heavy infestations tend to fall before the normal harvest time.

■ Factors Affecting Abundance

Before 1946 and the introduction of DDT, the redbanded leafroller was generally rated as a minor pest. DDT killed many of its parasites and predators, and the redbanded leafroller abruptly became a major pest. It is now an apple pest in the principal fruit-growing districts of the midwestern and eastern United States. In past years, failure to control the first generation could result in damaging numbers in the second and third generations, when coverage is more difficult because of dense foliage. Currently, redbanded leafroller is again a minor pest. It has largely been replaced by pesticide-resistant strains of obliquebanded leafroller.

■ Life History

In the north central states, the redbanded leafroller usually produces two broods, and in many years a partial third brood develops. The insect overwinters as a pupa on the ground, in the leaves and other debris under the trees. Moths emerge in the spring soon after the first green tissue shows in the buds. They may be found until after bloom, but the greatest numbers are present in the late delayed dormant to pink bud stages. Moths are commonly found resting on the trunks and main scaffold limbs of the trees. In cold, windy weather, the moths are inactive and are usually found on the sheltered side of the trees. They fly only short distances when disturbed. Moths are most active on warm days, particularly in the afternoon.

First-brood moths are found in the lower parts of the tree, while second-brood moths are found in all parts of the tree. They seem to like bright sunshine and avoid the shaded lower inside of thick trees. Moths begin laying eggs shortly after emerging, so the first eggs may appear in the delayed dormant and early preblossom period. Egg deposition may be heavy in outbreak years. First-brood egg masses are laid mostly on the bark, chiefly on the trunks and main scaffold limbs. The exact position appears to be influenced by weather conditions. Hatching usually coincides with the middle to the end of bloom for the McIntosh variety.

First-brood larvae crawl along the trunks and limbs until they reach the leaves. They feed on the undersurface along the midrib or along one of the larger veins. Each larva spins a flimsy white web that it expands as the larva grows. The clean, white webbing of redbanded leafroller larvae is easily distinguished from that of the eyespotted apple bud moth, which is active at this same time. Bud moth webbing is stained and littered with frass, and the larvae are dark brown rather than green. First-brood larvae reach maturity mostly during the first half of July, though a few mature earlier and others considerably later. When the larvae are about half grown, they may migrate to and feed on the fruit, though some individuals complete development on the leaves. The larvae pupate in a sheltered site, such as inside a rolled leaf or between leaves on which they have fed. Pupation may also take place in holes the larva had eaten earlier into the young fruit. The pupal stage lasts from 10 to 14 days.

Moths of the second brood begin to lay eggs shortly after emergence and continue until August. These eggs are laid mostly on the upper surfaces of the leaves and are difficult to find. Second-brood larvae feed on the undersides of the leaves, where they feed and make webbing until partially grown. Near the end of August, the larvae move around in the tree and may feed on the fruit or web leaves together and feed there. Damage to fruit may continue into October. Larvae pupate in the debris on the ground in October. There may be a partial third brood.

■ Monitoring

Because of a wide host range, pheromone traps, if employed as the sole indicator, are unreliable for indicating whether sprays are needed.

Using 45 degrees F as a base, degree-days (DD) for redbanded leafroller activity* are:

50 DD....	first adult emergence.
125 DD....	first eggs laid.
200 DD....	peak adult emergence.
350 DD....	peak egg laying by first-generation adults.
700 DD....	first emergence of second-generation adults.
850 DD....	first eggs laid by second-generation adults.
1,125 DD....	peak emergence of second-generation adults.
1,300 DD....	peak egg laying by second-generation adults.
1,700 DD....	first emergence of third-generation adults.
1,800 DD....	first eggs laid by third-generation adults.

■ Control

When infestations are severe, sprays applied at the delayed dormant stage will control the adults before the female lays eggs, thus greatly reducing the amount of egg laying. Normally, these eggs begin to hatch at petal fall, so broad spectrum sprays applied at petal fall will control this pest. Because the redbanded leafroller has so many host plants, pheromone traps may be useful in determining the occurrence of generations, but they have limited value in determining economic thresholds. When redbanded leafroller is a problem, it is essential to control the first generation. Large numbers of surviving first-generation redbanded leafrollers can create problem populations in the second and third generations. Inspect orchards for larvae and feeding from the first generation to determine the need for second generation sprays. Renew pheromone traps and caps to time sprays, based on trap catches, for adults of the second and a possible third generation.

*Data from MSU PETE model.

Common Name—
Variegated Leafroller

Scientific Name—
Platynota flavedana (Clemens)

Family—
Tortricidae

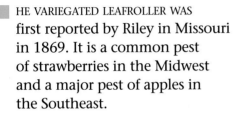

THE VARIEGATED LEAFROLLER WAS first reported by Riley in Missouri in 1869. It is a common pest of strawberries in the Midwest and a major pest of apples in the Southeast.

■ Life Stages

Egg: Eggs are elliptical and light green when first laid, but yellowish after two or three days. The eggs are normally laid in flattened egg masses of 20 to 150 eggs on the upper leaf surface. They hatch in seven to 10 days. Before hatching, the black head capsule of the developing embryo is visible through the chorion.

Larva: The newly hatched larva is about 1.2 mm long. The dorsal body is apple-green, while the ventral surface is a paler and more amber green. The head capsule is amber, and the prothoracic shield is amber to light brown. The mature larva is 13 to 21 mm long.

Pupa: The pupa is brown and about 9 mm long.

Adult: The adults of the species are dimorphic. The forewing of the male is black-brown (almost purple) except for a small part of the base next to the body and the outer portion, which is light-colored. The entire forewing of the female is reddish brown except for two darker reddish horizontal bands. The female is usually slightly larger than the male. The wing expanse ranges from 12 to 19 mm.

■ Host Range

This leafroller has been reported feeding on apples, peaches, roses, cotton, azalea, strawberries, begonia, helianthus and young maples. It is considered a general feeder. It occurs from eastern Massachusetts to southeastern New York, along the east coast to Florida, Louisiana, southeastern Texas and Arkansas to Kansas, Iowa, Illinois, Virginia, West Virginia, Pennsylvania and Michigan.

■ Injury or Damage

The variegated leafroller is a serious pest of strawberries. Injury results from the activity of the larvae, which fold and web the leaves together and feed within the protective canopy. This weakens the plants and inhibits the growth of runners. Larvae may also feed on berries.

Peaches can also be injured by larval feeding. On apples, foliage feeding is slight and of little significance. Larval feeding on fruit occurs when a dead leaf is attached to the side of the fruit or when fruits are clustered together. The larva then chews out shallow areas of the fruit. Fruit feeding by large larvae is often quite extensive. These feeding areas are separated and look like small, shallow pecking marks compared with the more

Left: Adult.

Below: Apple damaged by variegated leafroller.

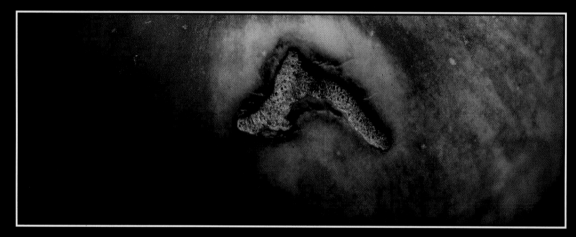

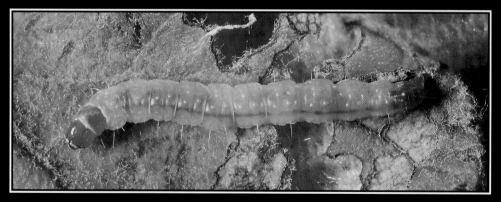

Left: Larva.

continuous feeding damage of the redbanded leafroller. Damage by variegated leafroller larvae is quite similar to that caused by tufted apple bud moth, though tufted apple bud moth shelters are unique with their cut petioles.

■ *Factors Affecting Abundance*

Because it is a general feeder, it has many host plants. Plantings of strawberries in the vicinity of orchards can contribute to orchard populations.

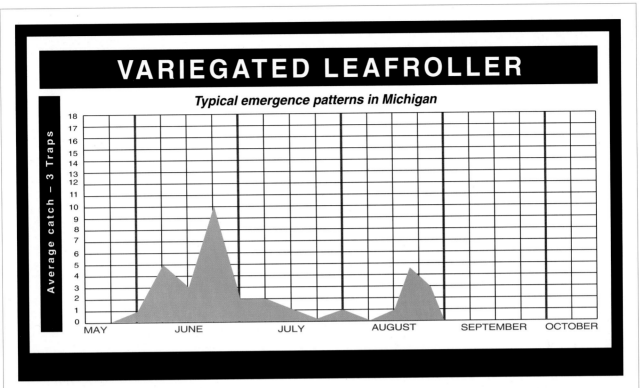

VARIEGATED LEAFROLLER

Typical emergence patterns in Michigan

Life History

In orchards, the variegated leafroller overwinters as dormant larvae in leaf litter on the apple orchard floor. In April, larvae feed on ground cover and apple root suckers. Pupation occurs in early May. The pupal stage lasts seven to 10 days. Spring moths begin emerging in early June and are present in orchards until late July. Second-generation adults emerge in late August to early September. Egg masses are laid on the upper sides of apple leaves in June and July and again in September in spherical, rectangular or oblong masses of 20 to 150 eggs.

The incubation period averages about two weeks for the first generation and about nine days for the second. The first generation has five instars, though there may be an occasional sixth. The average time for larval development is about one month. As soon as they hatch, the larvae web and construct feeding shelters on the leaves; later they fold leaves upon which they feed. The larvae will also feed on the fruit.

Like most tortricids, the larvae wiggle violently and spin to the ground when disturbed.

The larval stage lasts about two weeks. The pupal period averages about a week. Fruit is damaged in late summer and early fall by late instar larvae of the first generation and younger larvae of the second generation. Second-generation larvae continue feeding into October and overwinter in the larval stage.

Monitoring

Use pheromones to monitor brood emergences. When the larvae in the early and late summer broods begin to feed, examine 30 fruit from each of 10 trees in the orchard. Treatment is recommended if the total number of larvae for the early or late summer broods is five or more, or if there is other evidence of fresh feeding.

Control

Use pheromones to monitor the presence of adults in the orchard. Controls are most effective when directed against the early instars.

Common Name—
Obliquebanded Leafroller

Scientific Name—
Choristoneura rosaceana (Harris)

Family—
Tortricidae

THE OBLIQUEBANDED LEAFROLLER OCCURS throughout the apple-growing areas of the Northeast and Midwest. Until the 1970s, it was considered a minor problem, but since that time, it has become a major pest that has demonstrated a considerable propensity for developing resistance to pesticides.

■ Life Stages

Egg: The eggs are laid in patches that measure about 7 by 14 mm and contain up to 200 eggs. The mass is covered with a cement that, when dry, gives the mass a dull greenish yellow color. Just before hatching, the black head capsule can be seen.

Larva: The head capsule is 1.7 to 1.9 mm wide and light to dark brown or black, though color can vary considerably. All instars have dark brown or black heads, thoracic shields and legs, and yellowish green bodies. The coloration of the prothoracic shield varies considerably. Summer generation larvae have little brown pigmentation; spring larvae and overwintering larvae have more extensive and darker coloration. With bodies that range from 20 to 30 mm long, the obliquebanded leafroller larvae are the largest leafroller larvae found in commercial orchards.

Pupa: The pupae at first are light greenish brown, but they change to a deep reddish brown later. Pupae are about 11.4 to 13.5 mm long.

Adult: The adults are banded with various shades of tan to chocolate-brown scales. The female is much larger and usually more strongly colored in the forewings; in the hindwings, the distal half is yellowish. Wing span is 24 to 30 mm for females and 17 to 23 mm for males.

■ Host Range

This is a native species that occurs throughout southern Canada and the United States. It infests apple, pear, cherry, plum, peach, rose, raspberry, gooseberry, currant, strawberry and many weeds, and it is a major pest of blueberries.

■ Injury or Damage

During the prebloom period, overwintering larvae feed inside bud clusters and on various floral parts. Larvae continue to feed on the flowers during bloom and on developing fruit after petal fall. At that time, they begin to feed on both the fruit and the rapidly expanding leaves. They gouge deeply into young fruit. Numbers of overwintering larvae decrease after petal fall, but fruit damage increases as the remaining large larvae feed more on fruit as the season progresses.

Though most damaged fruits drop before harvest, some remain on the tree. Most of the severe damage to fruit caused by overwintering larvae occurs after petal fall. The larger the fruit becomes before it is damaged, the more likely it is to develop and remain on the

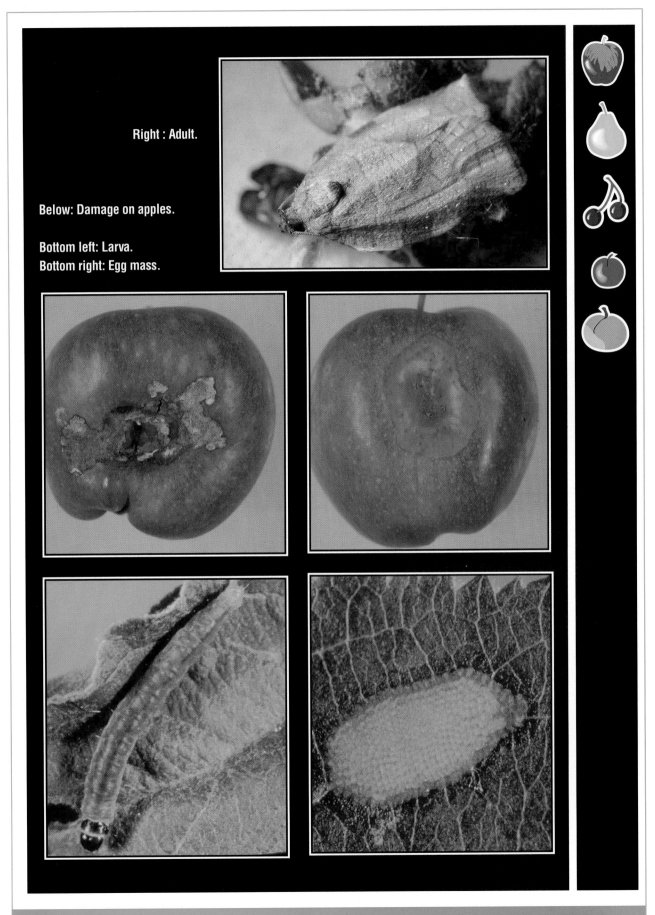

Right : Adult.

Below: Damage on apples.

Bottom left: Larva.
Bottom right: Egg mass.

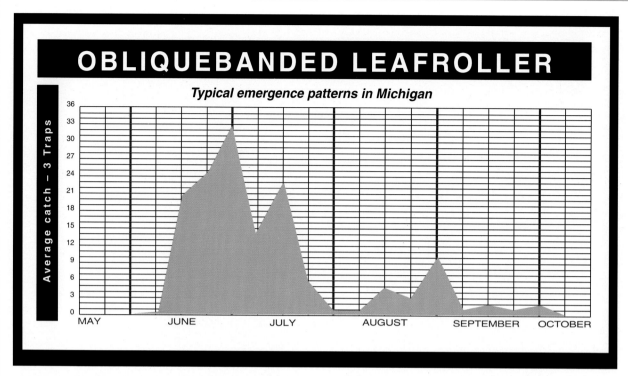

OBLIQUEBANDED LEAFROLLER

Typical emergence patterns in Michigan

tree until harvest. In late July, larvae of the summer generation can be found on actively growing terminals inside the canopy and on terminals and older leaves near fruit clusters.

■ Factors Affecting Abundance

The summer generation of larvae needs water sprouts for food. A shortage of water sprouts in fruit trees may limit their numbers.

■ Life History

This insect overwinters as a second- or third-instar larva within a hibernaculum. The hibernacula are found under old bud scales or fragments of the bark, within cracks or roughened areas, and in twig crotches. The exteriors of the hibernacula are covered with fecal pellets that weather to a dirty gray similar to the color of surrounding plant surfaces. Activity resumes in the spring when the larvae leave the hibernacula and bore into the opening buds. Later, when the leaves become larger, they form the leaves into tubular chambers, where they remain concealed except when feeding. When disturbed, they will desert this shelter, spinning down on a strand of silk.

Larvae of the overwintering generation may or may not feed on the new fruit. When apple fruits are attacked, the more heavily damaged ones fail to survive. Surviving apples bear corked-over scars at harvest. This injury cannot be distinguished from damage by fruittree leafroller and green fruitworm but is generally deeper and wider than that of the redbanded leafroller.

Pupation occurs within the feeding site and lasts about 10 to 12 days. Moths emerge from mid-June to mid-July. Peak activity occurs during the latter part of June. The eggs are laid on the leaves shortly after mating. The incubation period of the eggs is 10 to 12 days. A female is capable of laying up to 900 eggs in her seven- to eight-day oviposition period.

Newly hatched larvae quickly desert the leaves on which they hatched and crawl to leaves nearby or lower themselves by silk strands to other leaves. Winds can transport larvae on these threads for some distance. The larvae select an initial site for feeding on the undersurface of a leaf along the midrib or other large vein. First-generation larvae complete their development sometime between late July and late August. They feed on water sprouts and fruit. A shortage of water sprouts may limit their numbers because first-instar larvae need actively growing leaves or fruit tissue. Pupation takes place in their final feeding sites.

Adults are on the wing from mid-August to late September. The incubation period and the activity of the second-generation larvae are the same as those of the first generation. Most of the larvae will overwinter on the apple tree. Some first-instar larvae will be carried on their silken threads to other hosts. The second-generation larvae will feed until they reach the third instar. At this time, they will seek out suitable winter quarters on the tree and spin up a hibernaculum. This occurs between late August and late September.

■ Monitoring

Using a base of 43 degrees F, degree-days (DD) for obliquebanded leafroller activity* are:

      600 DD....first adult emergence.
      800 DD....first eggs laid.
  1,150 DD....peak adult emergence.
  1,250 DD....peak egg laying.
  2,050 DD....first emergence of second-
                  generation adults.
  2,300 DD....first eggs laid by second-
                  generation adults.

....

*Data from MSU PETE model.

Because of a wide host range, pheromone traps are unreliable for indicating whether sprays are needed. At the early petal-fall stage, examine 20 clusters per tree in five trees for each orchard. On each tree, look for larvae or larval feeding on six clusters on the outside of the tree, six clusters in the center of the tree and eight clusters near the treetop. Treatment is recommended if you find an average of two or more larvae or fresh feeding sites per tree. Use pheromones to determine when emergence of the summer brood starts; then each week, examine 10 fruit clusters and 10 terminals in the outside, center and top of five trees per orchard. Treatment is recommended if there is an average of three or more larvae per tree.

■ Control

Broad spectrum insecticides will control this pest in larval and adult stages. Sprays applied at pink stage or petal fall will prevent damage from the overwintering larvae. Timing of summer sprays should be based on pheromone trap catches. In some areas, this pest has become resistant to some pesticides, including organophosphates, so chemicals with a different mode of action may be required to control it.

Common Name—
Fruittree Leafroller

Scientific Name—
Archips argyrospila (Walker)

Family—
Tortricidae

THIS INSECT WAS FIRST DESCRIBED about 1870. It damaged cherries and apples in Colorado as early as 1891 and was considered a major pest in most fruit-growing regions. With the advent of modern organic pesticides, it has since dropped in status to a minor pest.

■ Life Stages

Egg: Eggs are deposited in dark-colored patches on twigs. Each patch contains approximately 60 eggs. The eggs are closely placed and covered with a heavy coating, so it is difficult to distinguish individual eggs.

Larva: The young larva is about 1 mm long and light green with a very large, black head and a wide, dark-colored prothorax. The body is sparsely covered with long, slender hairs somewhat noticeable along the sides. When full grown, the larvae measure from 15 to 25 mm; the head capsule is between 1.5 and 1.9 mm. In general, the body of the mature larva is light green, the head is black, and the thoracic shield is dark-colored, at least up to the last molt. Late-instar larvae are very similar to obliquebanded leafroller larvae. They can be distinguished in the field by their vigorous wriggling when disturbed.

Pupa: The pupa is light brown and usually about 10 mm long. It is very active and wiggles vigorously when handled. There are two transverse rows of backward-projecting hooks on the upper side of most of the abdominal segments. The last segment of the abdomen, which is considerably longer than the others, tapers and ends in six strong, chitinous hooks.

Adult: Wing span ranges from 19 to 23 mm for female moths and 14 to 19 mm for male moths. The front wings are rusty brown marked with silver-gray or pale gold, which usually forms two large patches on the front margin of each wing.

■ Host Range

This pest attacks all kinds of fruit trees and some shade and forest trees. The fruittree leafroller is most troublesome on apples and pears, but it occasionally attacks plums, cherries, peaches and apricots.

It is found in all apple-growing areas of Canada and the United States.

■ Injury or Damage

After hatching, the young larvae chew into opening buds and mine, often destroying many of them before they open. Newly emerged larvae may make their way down between the buds in the clusters and chew into tiny stems and buds. Such injuries weaken the fruit so that even if flowers are fertilized, the fruit will drop. Just before the blossoms open, larvae may make their way inside and web the petals together so that they are unable to open and fertilization cannot occur. At petal fall, the half-grown larvae chew into newly set fruit. The more seriously

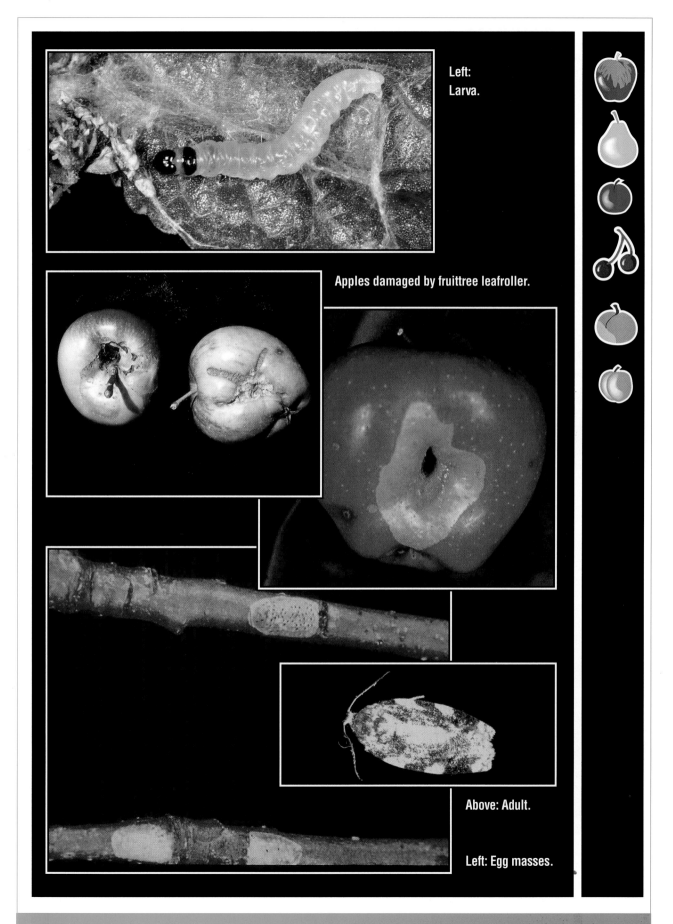

Left: Larva.

Apples damaged by fruittree leafroller.

Above: Adult.

Left: Egg masses.

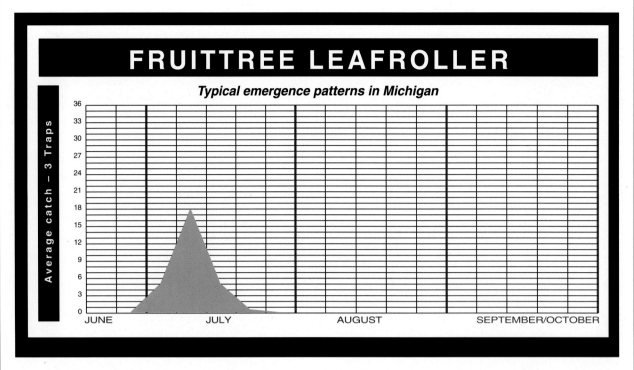

FRUITTREE LEAFROLLER

Typical emergence patterns in Michigan

Average catch – 3 Traps

JUNE   JULY   AUGUST   SEPTEMBER/OCTOBER

injured fruit will drop; those that remain on the trees to harvest heal over with depressed russet scars similar to those caused by the obliquebanded leafroller. As the season progresses, the larvae confine their feeding to the foliage and cause some degree of defoliation.

■ Factors Affecting Abundance

This pest has a wide range of host plants, including many species of wild and cultivated trees.

■ Life History

The fruittree leafroller passes winter in the egg stage. Eggs are laid in small, brown, oval clusters about 6 mm in diameter. The clusters are situated on the upper and lateral branches of the twigs and small branches. The eggs hatch in spring about the time the apple leaf buds have opened. The tiny larvae immediately work their way into the opening buds and feed on the inner parts, often retarding the opening of the leaves by fastening them together with silken threads.

They attack the fruit buds in the same way and web together and destroy the opening blossoms. On the open leaves, they fold one edge over and fasten it with silken threads, hence the name "leafrollers." The larvae hide inside the rolled leaves, sometimes feeding on the rolled leaves and sometimes coming out to feed on other leaves and on the fruit. Fruittree leafroller larvae look very similar to those of obliquebanded leafroller but are much more active when disturbed.

About the time the apples average 17 mm in diameter, most of the larvae are full grown and have begun to pupate. This takes place mostly inside the rolled leaves, though many pupae may also be found on the ground among the weeds and grass. In uncultivated or weedy orchards, many larvae drop by silken threads to the ground and complete their development on whatever succulent plants they find there.

In about two weeks, the moths begin to emerge and soon start laying eggs. The time of egg laying varies with the season, but on the average, it occurs during the latter half of June. The moths hide during the day, darting away in a zigzag manner if disturbed. They fly around late in the evening and at night. The eggs remain on the trees until the following spring. There is only one generation per year.

■ *Monitoring*

Examine buds in the tight cluster/pre-pink stage for evidence of light green larvae with large black heads chewing into opening buds and down between the buds in the fruit clusters. Pheromone traps set out in late May to mid-June will indicate the pests' relative abundance in the area.

■ *Control*

The normal cover sprays control this pest.

Common Name—

Tufted Apple Bud Moth

Scientific Name—

Platynota idaeusalis (Walker)

Family—

Tortricidae

THE TUFTED APPLE BUD MOTH WAS RECORDED feeding on black haw *(Viburnum prunifolium)* as early as 1882. Over the years, this pest has increased in abundance and distribution, and its preference for apple has become an increasing economic concern. It has caused considerable injury to apples in Pennsylvania orchards since 1918.

Since the 1970s, the tufted apple bud moth has developed resistance to organophosphates in most eastern states south of New York and is now considered a major problem.

■ *Life Stages*

Egg: The eggs are laid in masses of 100 to 125 overlapping eggs. Initially, these masses are apple-green and covered with a white, translucent envelope. About two to three days before hatching, the egg mass becomes yellowish to light brown.

Larva: Larvae are light brown to grayish tan with a chestnut-brown head capsule, a darker prothoracic shield and a dark stripe down the back of the body. This coloration distinguishes tufted apple bud moth larvae from other leafrollers. The body's last segment contains an anal comb. (See pages 43–44 for more information on the anal comb.)

Pupa: The pupa is light brown and averages about 6.5 to 7 mm long.

Adult: The adult is inconspicuously patterned with various shades of gray and brown. The moths average 12 to 15 mm in length. Both sexes are similar in appearance, though the female is slightly broader. Three main characteristics serve to identify the adult: the presence of a copper-colored patch of scales in the middle of each forewing; a longitudinally ribbed pattern on the distal end of the forewings; and a series of tufted scales in the middle of the forewings that gives the insect its common name.

■ *Host Range*

This moth is a general feeder. Host plants include apple, black haw, blackberry, Osage orange and goldenrod. It is found in Nova Scotia, Quebec, Ontario, Manitoba, British Columbia, the northern United States, the Shenandoah Valley and bordering apple-growing states.

■ *Injury or Damage*

Early Instars: Early instar larvae typically feed on the leaf undersurface. After webbing themselves in along the midrib or other large veins, they will feed to but not through the upper epidermis.

Late Instars: Late instar feeding of this pest is quite distinctive from that of other tortricid larvae. The larva chews partway through the leaf petiole so that the leaf hangs down. The larva then feeds inside a lengthwise fold fastened with an abundance of

Right: Male (left) and female tufted apple bud moths.

Below: Apples damaged by tufted apple bud moth.

Right: Egg mass on apple leaf.

Below: Larva.

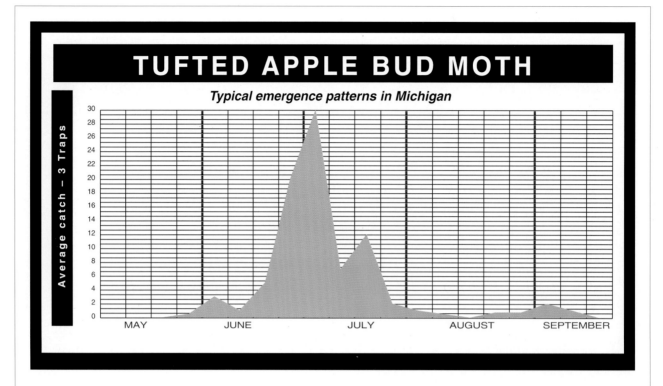

TUFTED APPLE BUD MOTH

Typical emergence patterns in Michigan

silken threads. The larva will continue to feed on a leaf even after the leaf becomes dried and withered from the petiole damage.

Fruit feeding: Only late instar larvae have been observed feeding on apples. Fruit feeding is shallow and similar to feeding by redbanded leafroller, except that areas injured by the redbanded leafroller are continuous, while feeding areas of the tufted apple bud moth are separated and appear as small, shallow pecking marks. Feeding occurs most typically where a cut leaf has fallen against an apple.

■ *Factors Affecting Abundance*

Tufted apple bud moth has many host plants, including many species of trees, shrubs, weeds and many other herbaceous plants.

■ *Life History*

This moth passes the winter as mid- to late instar larvae among the leaf litter on the orchard floor. Early in the spring, these larvae finish development on apple suckers and weeds in the ground cover. The late instar larvae mature during mid- to late May, and after a nine- to 11-day pupation period, adults will emerge. Peak emergence occurs about mid-June. The maturation and development of the early instar larvae into adults occurs about two to four weeks later, with some overlap occurring. This development of different sized larvae results in an emergence spread of about seven to 10 weeks.

Mating and egg laying occur shortly after emergence. Eggs hatch in about 10 to 14 days. Initially, the larvae are foliage feeders, but they may turn to the fruits later in the season. Some of these larvae will mature, pupate and emerge from mid-August to mid-September, thus giving rise to a second generation. This second generation will then overwinter as larvae webbed in folded dead leaves on the orchard floor.

Monitoring

Use pheromones to monitor brood emergences. When the larvae in the early and late summer broods begin to feed, examine 30 fruit from each of 10 trees in the orchard. Treatment is recommended if the total number of larvae is five or more per tree or if there is evidence of fresh feeding. Using 51 degrees F as a base, degree-days (DD) for tufted bud moth activity* are:

   125 DD....first adult emergence.
   225 DD....first eggs laid.
   375 DD....peak adult emergence.
   575 DD....peak egg laying.
1,325 DD....first emergence of second-generation adults.
1,525 DD....first eggs laid by second generation.
2,000 DD....peak adult emergence of second generation.
2,100 DD....peak egg laying by second-generation adults.

■ Control

Control measures should be aimed at the eggs and early instar larvae because later instars are difficult to control once they're webbed in folded leaves. This necessitates accurate timing, with sprays applied in late June to early July and again in early September.

Maintaining a fresh spray deposit throughout the egg hatching period is important to control this insect. The spray interval should not be extended beyond 10 days for complete applications or five to seven days for alternate-row applications during the egg hatching period.

*Data from MSU PETE model.

Table 8.
Characteristics of leafrollers commonly found attacking tree fruit crops.

Leafroller	Head capsule and thoracic shield	Body color and markings*	Mature larvae present†	Number of generations	Overwintering stage
Redbanded leafroller	Both: same color as body, light green to straw color	Light green to straw; same as head and thoracic shield	Early to mid-July	2-3	Pupa
Fruittree leafroller	Head: black; thoracic shield: dark colored	Light green	Late May to early June	1	Egg mass
Oblique-banded leafroller	Head: light to dark brown; thoracic shield: dark brown to black	Yellowish green	Late May to early June and late July to early August	2	Larva
Tufted apple bud moth	Head: chestnut brown; prothoracic shield: dark brown	Light brown to grayish tan; anal comb; dark stripe down back of body	Early to mid-May and late July to early August	2	Larva
Variegated leafroller	Both: amber to light brown	Apple green	Early to mid-May and late July to early August	2	Larva

*Based on characters of the mature larva; characters of the younger larval stages may vary.
†Average time when first mature larvae are detected in orchards.

Common Name—
Eyespotted Bud Moth

Scientific Name—
Spilonota ocellana (Denis and Schiffermuller)

Family—
Tortricidae

THE EYESPOTTED BUD MOTH IS A common pest of sour cherries and apples in the north central states. It originated in Europe, where it was first reported in 1776. It was first recorded as an economic problem there in 1840. It was discovered in the United States in 1841 in Massachusetts, where it was introduced on nursery stock. By 1892, the eyespotted bud moth was one of the most destructive pests on apple and cherry trees in Massachusetts, Michigan, New York, Pennsylvania and Nova Scotia.

■ Life Stages

Egg: Laid singly, the eggs are oval and average 0.8 mm long and 0.6 mm wide. They are creamy white at first and later turn yellow. Just before hatching, the larvae can be seen inside the eggs.

Larva: The general color is chocolate-brown; the ventral surface is paler than the dorsal. The head varies from medium brown to black. The mouthparts are brown and lighter than the head. Mature larvae are 9 to 14 mm long. In preparation for pupation, the larva shortens and becomes grayish white.

Pupa: The pupa is golden brown with deeper brown in the region of the head and wing covers. It measures 6 to 7 mm in length.

Adult: The adult is a grayish brown moth with a wing span of 12 to 16 mm. Across the middle portion of each front wing is a broad, grayish white, irregular area occupying about half of the wing. The wings are broad; their width is more than one-third of the length. The head, thorax and basal third of the forewings, as well as the outer edge and fringe, are a dark ash-gray. The middle of the forewing is creamy white with streaks of gray on the outer edge. The underside of the forewing is darker, with a series of light streaks on the outer part.

■ Host Range

This pest occurs on apples and tart cherries. It is found in all the apple-growing areas of the northern hemisphere. It will feed on all pome and stone fruits and a variety of forest trees as well.

■ Injury or Damage

On apples, the partly grown over-wintering larvae become active early in the spring and burrow into the opening flower buds, feeding on the blossoms and lessening the fruitset. As the leaves unfold, the larvae tie them together with silk and feed within the clusters thus made. Newly formed apples are often

Right: Adults.

Below: Apple damaged by eyespotted bud moth.

Above: Hibernaculum in crotch of twig.

Left: Larva.

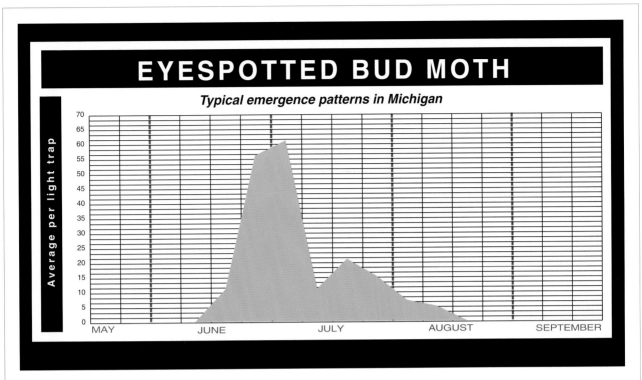

EYESPOTTED BUD MOTH

Typical emergence patterns in Michigan

Average per light trap — MAY | JUNE | JULY | AUGUST | SEPTEMBER

enclosed in such clusters. The larvae chew them, causing them to drop or to be disfigured when they mature. The larvae sometimes gnaw the fruit stems, which weakens them and causes the small fruits to drop. Often the larvae bore into the terminal shoots and cause considerable injury.

Late in the summer, the young larvae bite into the apples, making small scars. Such injury is most common when a leaf is in contact with a fruit or when two fruits hang together. This injury shows as small scars, usually in clusters. It is often lighter in color than the rest of the fruit because it has been shaded by the leaf. This is the most serious type of injury.

■ *Factors Affecting Abundance*

Eyespotted bud moth can become abundant in unsprayed orchards even if parasites are present.

■ *Life History*

On apples, the eyespotted bud moth has one generation a year after emerging from its winter quarters, which is a hibernaculum usually located at the base of a fruit spur or short twig. The larvae are similar to those of tufted apple bud moth but are much smaller and thinner and darker brown. However, unlike larvae of tufted apple bud moth, these larvae are less active and do not cut the petioles. The larva makes its way to a bud or unfolding cluster of leaves. If the bud has not opened, the larva eats into it from the outside; if the leaves are unfolding, it enters the center of the cluster. Entry of buds is indicated by the presence of frass at the bud tips. The ends of the unfolding leaves are eaten first. Then, by boring into the center of the cluster, the larva feeds on the unopened blossoms.

As the leaves unfold, the larvae tie them together with silken threads and feed within the webbed cluster. As more food is required, additional leaves are drawn into the cluster.

The pupal stage lasts about two weeks. Moths mate soon after emergence and egg laying starts in three to four days. The eggs are laid singly — mostly on the undersides of the leaves, where the larvae construct tubular shelters of silk into which they interweave hairs of the leaves. These shelters occur along the sides of the midrib or larger veins. At first, the larvae feed in their immediate vicinity. As the feeding range increases, the protecting web is enlarged. If an apple is in contact with a leaf, both may be webbed and the larva feeds on the apple.

In mid-August, the larvae start to leave the foliage and seek winter quarters — usually in a protected place at the axis of buds and fruit spurs, or in a crack in the bark, where they construct hibernacula. As the apple buds open in the spring, the larvae leave the hibernacula and attack the buds.

■ *Monitoring*

During the prebloom stage, look for clusters of leaves tied together with silk, and a brown larva whose bottom surface is lighter colored than its top surface feeding within each cluster. For the summer brood in July and August, look for leaves and apples webbed together and apples that the larvae fed upon. A pheromone is available for monitoring adult emergence.

■ *Control*

■ Apply chemicals in the prebloom or petal-fall stage to control the overwintering larvae.

■ Apply summer sprays to control the adults or larvae before they mature.

Common Name—
Fruitworms

Family—
Noctuidae

RUITWORMS ARE PESTS INTRODUCED from Europe. They are the larval stages of moths of the family Noctuidae. Several species of economic importance attack fruit. These include the white-striped fruitworm, *Lithophane antennata* (Walker); the speckled green fruitworm, *Orthosia hibisci* (Guenee); the yellow-striped fruitworm, *Lithophane unimoda* (Lentner); and the pyramidal fruitworm, *Amphipyra pyramidoides* (Guenee).

The fruitworms' name is derived from their habit of eating deep holes into the fruits of apple, peach, pear, cherry and plum trees. In the past few years, fruitworms have become a serious problem on apples, cherries and pears in the north central states. Fruitworms were first reported to be a problem on pears in Missouri and Illinois in 1970. Several species occur in the north central states.

■ Life Stages

Egg: Eggs are about 0.8 mm in diameter and 0.5 mm in height. Freshly laid eggs are white with a grayish tinge. Distinct ridges radiate from the micropilar area.

Larva: Six instars occur. The larvae are generally large and robust in various shades of green marked with yellowish or whitish longitudinal stripes. Larvae are 35 to 40 mm long.

Pupa: The pupa is about 20 to 30 mm long, about 10 mm wide, and shiny.

Adult: The adults are typical noctuid moths with considerable range in color in the forewings. The forewings are dark and the hind wings much lighter. Moths are large, with wing spans of 25 to 40 mm.

■ Host Range

Fruitworms are generally distributed throughout the United States, though the greatest numbers occur in the Northeast and Midwest. Green fruitworms attack apple, cherry, plum, pear, apricot, strawberry and quince. They also feed on a wide range of plants, including willow, birch, poplar, balsam, alder, chokecherry and maple.

■ Injury or Damage

The larvae feed on the leaves and fruits of deciduous fruit trees, usually newly formed apples, pears and cherries. Most flower buds and blossoms damaged by green fruitworm larvae abort. Most fruits damaged up to and shortly after petal fall also drop prematurely. Those that remain at harvest exhibit deep, corky scars and indentations. This injury is indistinguishable at harvest from that caused by the overwintering larvae of the obliquebanded leafroller.

Above: Speckled green
fruitworm larva
damaging young
apple.

Left: Adult.

Right: Eggs.

Above: Mature apple damaged by
speckled green fruitworm.
Left: Typical apple damage caused by fruitworms.

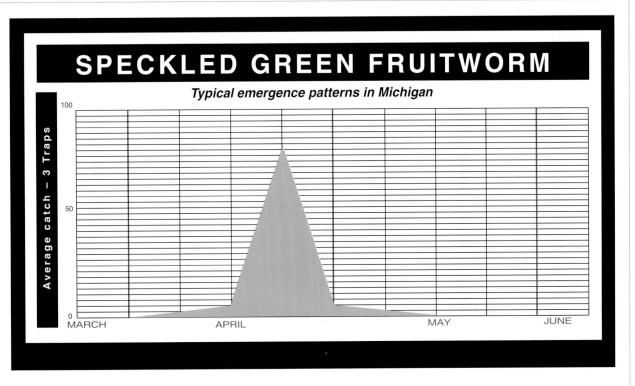

SPECKLED GREEN FRUITWORM

Typical emergence patterns in Michigan

■ *Factors Affecting Abundance*

Omitting insecticide sprays in the pre-bloom period or using ineffective pesticides in the prebloom sprays can increase the number of fruitworms. When natural adult fruitworm populations in wild habitats peak, they may move into commercial fruit orchards and cause damage.

■ *Life History*

With the exception of those of the pyramidal fruitworm, eggs are laid in the spring when new growth is appearing in the buds. (Eggs of the pyramidal fruitworm are laid in the fall and overwinter.) Adults of the *Lithophane* genus overwinter as adults and lay their eggs in the spring. The eggs of all species start to hatch when apple buds have reached the half-inch green bud stage. The young larvae feed on the unfolding leaves, and it is not uncommon to find them occupying rolled leaves in much the same manner as leaf-rollers. Feeding may or may not include the fruit. Where this does occur, fifth- and sixth-

instar larvae will be involved. These are large, robust larvae. The feeding will take place from the time the young fruits are set or when they are about 6 mm in diameter, until they measure about 18.7 mm across. About 70 percent of the fruits attacked will not survive.

The wounds on the fruits that do survive attack gradually become sealed over with corky scar tissue that makes them unsalable. Typically, a larva will feed on more than one fruit and may damage a dozen or more. With the exception of the pyramidal fruitworm, the mature larvae drop to the soil and enter to a depth of 2 to 4 inches, construct a pupal chamber and then enter the pupal stage. They remain in the pupal stage until the following spring. Only one generation occurs annually.

The pyramidal fruitworm adults are on the wing from July until November and begin to lay eggs in late September. The eggs hatch in late April when the host leaf buds begin to swell. Larvae become full grown about the middle of June, drop to the soil and form a prepupal larval stage in a cocoon made of silk and debris from the soil. The prepupal stage lasts about a week and the pupal stage that follows lasts about a month.

■ *Monitoring*

From pink stage to first cover, examine 20 fruit clusters per tree on five trees per orchard. On each tree, look for larvae or signs of fresh feeding on six fruit clusters on the outside of the tree, six clusters in the center and eight clusters near the top of the tree. Treatment is recommended if there is an average of two or more larvae per tree or evidence of fresh feeding. A commercial pheromone is available for monitoring *O. hibisci* adult emergence early in the season.

■ *Control*

Sprays must be applied in the prebloom stage to prevent injury. Temperature-dependent pesticides are of limited value in the early season. Pesticides such as pyrethroids that have a negative temperature coefficient — which are more effective in cool than warm weather — work more efficiently against fruitworms earlier than later in the season.

Common Name—
Pistol Casebearer

Scientific Name—
Coleophora malivorella (Riley)

Family—
Coleophoridae

THIS INSECT WAS FIRST REPORTED IN Pennsylvania in 1877, where it caused considerable injury to apples. In 1896, casebearers caused considerable damage to apples in New York, but they are now a minor problem.

■ Life Stages

Egg: The egg measures 1.8 mm to 0.5 mm in diameter and is shaped like an inverted cup. The shell is sculptured with ridges that run from the base to a sunken area in the top of the egg. It is brown but turns grayish as hatching time approaches.

Larva: The newly hatched larva is yellow. The color deepens to orange-yellow in the overwintering stage. It is seldom seen outside its case. The case is black to dirty gray or brown and is enlarged as the larva grows. The case-bearer more resembles a pistol as the case is enlarged. The length of the overwintering larva is about 2 mm and the case about 3 mm. The full-grown larva is about 6 mm long in a case about 9 mm long. Cases containing larvae are found attached to twigs or leaves and also on the ground beneath infested trees.

Pupa: The pupa is found within the larval case with the head facing the posterior end of the case. It averages about 6 mm long and is light brown. The color deepens to dark brown as the time of emergence approaches.

Adult: Like all the Coleophoridae, the adults are distinguished from other moths by their narrow wings bordered with wide fringes. The adult is a beautiful steel-gray moth measuring 13 mm with wings spread. The front wings are flecked with white scales on the basal half.

■ Host Range

Eggs are deposited on a variety of plants, including poison ivy, flowering dogwood, elm, oak and wild cherry. The established larvae have been observed only on pear, apple, plum, cherry, quince and wild cherry. Apple is the favored host. The insect is found in all apple-growing areas east of the Rocky Mountains.

■ Injury or Damage

Larvae attack growing buds. Later in the season, they feed on young leaves, making mines similar to those of true leafminers. They attack opening flower buds, blossoms, mature leaves and fruits. In fruit, they mine to a short distance beneath the skin, causing the fruit to become slightly deformed.

Larva and case.

■ *Factors Affecting Abundance*

Low maximum temperatures during the brief egg-laying period, lack of healthy foliage at the time of moth flight and abundance of natural enemies have an adverse effect on casebearers.

■ *Life History*

The partly grown larvae overwinter in cases attached to fruit spurs or small branches of infested trees. On the first warm days of spring, often before the buds show green, some of the larvae detach their cases and move with them to nearby buds. There they feed for a time and partly or entirely destroy leaf and fruit buds. Later feeding is continued — with less interference from cold weather — on the foliage, flower parts and small fruits.

As the larvae grow, they enlarge their cases by adding leaf tissue, excrement and cast skins bound with silk to the anterior opening and to the sides of the ventral slit. The material added at the anterior opening appears as a collar that is lighter colored than the older portion of the case. There are three instars.

About mid-June, the larvae secure their cases to twigs or leaves by spinning silk around the anterior openings. They then reverse their position within the cases and pupate.

The pupation period lasts two to three weeks at normal temperatures. The moth emerges from the ventral slit in the curved end of the case. The peak of emergence, ordinarily in early July, is usually very pronounced. The majority of moths usually emerge within a week. Most of the eggs are deposited within two to five days after the females emerge. Most are deposited on the upper surfaces of leaves among the upper branches. Eggs are placed singly over a leaf, sometimes in a semblance of rows.

Hatching occurs within 11 to 20 days. In hatching, the larva only slightly disturbs the shell, which it leaves on the leaf. It goes through the base of the egg into the leaf and emerges on the underside from one to three days after hatching with a case already partly formed of leaf tissue and silk.

For several days, the larva strengthens it into a tubelike case that may be flared at the base, after which it begins to take on a pistol shape. Feeding continues until late fall. In the fall, larvae attach themselves securely to small twigs or fruit spurs by spinning silk to fasten the forward ends of their cases to the bark. They remain in this position until spring.

■ *Monitoring*

Examine twig bark or bark scales of older trees for cases containing overwintering larvae. Later in the season, observe trees for larval cases on the leaf or for skeletonized leaves (except for the lower epidermis). A commercial pheromone has not been developed.

■ *Control*

Prebloom sprays may be directed against the overwintering larvae during the green tip to prepink period. Post-blossom sprays are directed at emerging adults or larvae.

Common Name—
Cigar Casebearer

Scientific Name—
Coleophora serratella (Linnaeus)

Family—
Coleophoridae

A T THE TURN OF THE 19TH CENTURY, this was a major pest of apples in the eastern United States and Canada.

■ Life Stages

Egg: The eggs are light lemon-yellow and quite deeply pitted over their entire surface with triangular depressions separated by narrow ridges. They are cylindrical with rounded ends. They measure 0.3 mm by 0.2 mm.

Larva: Dark orange with black heads, the larvae are about 5 mm long. They overwinter in cigar-shaped hibernacula attached to small branches. In the spring, new, larger hibernacula are constructed of leaf tissue to accommodate the growing larvae.

Pupa: The pupa is dark brown and averages 6 to 8 mm in length.

Adult: The adult is a small, steel-gray moth with the fringed wings characteristic of this group of moths.

■ Host Range

The cigar casebearer is a pest on pear, apple, plum, cherry, quince and wild cherry. It is found in all apple-growing areas east of the Rocky Mountains.

■ Injury or Damage

Larvae feed on growing buds and young leaves. On leaves, they feed as leafminers. In addition, they may damage flower buds, blossoms and fruit. The larvae injure the fruit by mining just below the skin, causing the fruit to become slightly deformed.

■ Factors Affecting Abundance

Adverse low temperatures during the egg-laying period, scarcity of foliage during the flight period and natural enemies will reduce populations.

■ Life History

The cigar casebearer spends from September to April as a small, half-grown larva in a small case attached to a twig. In the spring, the larvae feed on opening buds, expanding leaves, stems, flowers and fruits of the apple tree. In late spring, they discard the hibernacula for larger, cigar-shaped hibernacula. They feed from their hibernacula, eating through the epidermis of the leaf and mining out the inner tissue over an irregular area without leaving the hibernacula.

In late June they stop feeding and pupate. About three weeks later, the adults emerge and lay eggs. The egg stage lasts about two weeks, with larvae emerging about the middle of July. The larvae feed as leafminers for two or three weeks. In September, the lar-

Larva and case.

vae migrate to the twigs and pass the winter in newly constructed hibernacula.

■ *Monitoring*

After the growing season, look for larvae in small cases attached to twigs. In season, look for true leafminers — larvae mining out the tissue between the upper and lower epidermis. A commercial pheromone has not been developed.

■ *Control*

Prebloom sprays directed at the overwintering larvae during the green tip to prepink period or postbloom sprays for the adults or larvae will give control.

Common Name—

Japanese Beetle

Scientific Name—

Popillia japonica (Newman)

Family—

Scarabaeidae

THE JAPANESE BEETLE WAS FIRST FOUND IN the United States in 1916 in a nursery near Riverton, N.J. Before that, this pest was known to occur only in the main islands of Japan. It is a minor pest of fruit in Michigan.

■ Life Stages

Egg: The egg is elliptical and about 1.5 mm in diameter. It varies in color from translucent to creamy white. Shortly after being laid, the egg begins to swell and eventually becomes about double its original size. At that time, it is more spherical, and the developing embryo can be seen through the shell.

Larva: On hatching, the larva or grub is white and about 1.5 mm long. It has chewing mouthparts with strong, thick mandibles (lower jawbones); three thoracic segments (each bearing a pair of legs); and 10 abdominal segments. There are three instars. When full grown, the C-shaped larva is about 25 mm long.

Pupa: The pupa resembles the adult except that the legs, antennae and wings are closely folded to the body. The pupa is about 12 mm long and 6 mm wide. Initially a cream color, the body gradually becomes tan and, finally, the metallic green of the adult.

Adult: The adult is about 12 mm long and half as wide. The body is a bright metallic green and the legs are a darker green. The hard wing covers are a coppery brown and extend nearly to the tip of the abdomen. Unique distinguishing characteristics are two small tufts of white hairs just behind the wing covers and five patches along each side. Males and females have the same coloring and markings, but the males are smaller.

■ Host Range

The beetles feed on most plants, including fruits, field crops, trees and ornamentals.

■ Injury or Damage

Beetles chew leaf tissue between veins and leave a lacelike skeleton. Severely injured leaves turn brown and often drop. Fruits, including apple, cherry, peach and plum, may be attacked. The damage shows as irregular, shallow feeding areas.

■ Factors Affecting Abundance

Drought during the egg-laying period has an adverse effect on this pest because dry soil prevents larvae from developing and keeps emerging adults from breaking through the pupal surface. Wet summers are favorable to the development of eggs and larvae and are usually followed by seasons of increased numbers of beetles.

Right: Adult.

Left: Apple foliage injured by Japanese beetle.

Below: Adult (side view).

■ Life History

The beetle requires one full year to complete its life cycle. It overwinters as a larva 4 inches deep in the soil and completes its growth in early spring. Adults emerge in large numbers in midsummer and are active for about a month. They are very active on warm, sunny days. Beetles usually fly short distances from plant to plant, but they are vigorous fliers capable of flying against the wind one-half mile or more to an orchard of ripening fruit.

Adults enter the ground in early evening. During their life cycle, females lay 40 to 60 eggs, which hatch in two weeks. Larvae feed on organic matter and fine grass roots until late fall. They reach maturity in early spring, then spend three to four weeks in the pupal stage. Adults emerge in late June and early July. There is only one generation per year.

■ Monitoring

The beetles are most active on warm, clear summer days. Early in the morning they are usually resting, but when temperatures reach about 70 degrees F, they will begin to fly and collect on fruit plants to feed on the fruit and foliage. Fruits that mature before the beetles are abundant, such as cherries, may escape injury.

Ripening or diseased fruit is particularly attractive to the beetles. The fruits of apple, peach, nectarine and plum, which are mature when the beetle is abundant, can be seriously injured. Pheromone traps are available and should be hung in the orchard in early July to detect the presence of beetles in the orchard.

■ Control

Fruit and foliage may be protected from damage by spraying at intervals when the first beetles appear.

Leafmining or leaf-feeding insects

I N RECENT YEARS, LEAFMINERS HAVE BECOME A SERIOUS PROBLEM because of their ability to develop a tolerance to most pesticides. When pesticides are not used, parasites can control nearly 100 percent of these pests. In any given season, it is important for each individual grower to determine whether leafminer populations warrant the use of pesticides. Pheromones can help determine emergence patterns of generations.

Leafhoppers can also develop a tolerance to pesticides. Though pheromones are not available for this insect, visual counts can help growers determine the need for chemical control.

Chapter 4

Common Name—
Spotted Tentiform Leafminer

Scientific Name—
Phyllonorycter blancardella (Fabr.)

Family—
Gracillariidae

THIS INSECT HAS INFESTED APPLE FOLIAGE throughout the northeastern, northwestern and midwestern United States and southeastern Canada. In the United States, it was first observed on apples in New York in 1914.

■ Life Stages

Egg: The egg is oval, with the flattened surface fixed to the surface of the apple leaf on the lower epidermis. The domed upper surface of the egg is translucent, reticulated and yellow. It measures 0.25 by 0.35 mm. Eggs are laid singly and fairly randomly on the leaf.

Larva: Five larval instars and two distinct morphological forms develop during the larval stage. Instars 1 through 3 are dorsoventrally compressed, apodous (without legs), deeply segmented and plasmophagous (sap-feeding). Instars 4 and 5 are eruciform (caterpillarlike) and histophagous (tissue-feeding). Body length ranges from about 1 mm for the first instar to about 5 mm for the fifth instar.

Pupa: The pupa is cylindrical and elongated and tapered at the posterior end. Pupae are yellow to light brown during early development and gradually darken to a deep brown as development continues. Overall length is 3 to 4 mm.

Adult: The adults are small moths with a wingspan of 7 to 8 mm. They have distinctive gold, black and white wing patterns. They tend to rest on leaf undersides during the day and are extremely active at night.

■ Host Range

This insect attacks primarily apples but has also been found on various crabapples. It is found in apple-growing areas of the northern United States and Canada.

■ Injury or Damage

The larvae mine the leaves of the apple. About 4 percent of the leaf area is disrupted by each larva. When population densities are high, severe defoliation occurs. A heavy infestation can cause stunting of fruit growth, reduced terminal growth, early leaf drop, premature ripening, drop of fruit and reduced fruitset the following season. Extensive mining combined with drought conditions can worsen plant damage.

■ Factors Affecting Abundance

Parasitism under natural conditions is nearly 100 percent. Birds and predator insects reduce populations. Mortality in winter can be high, especially under conditions of alternate thawing and freezing.

■ Life History

In the north central states, this leafminer has three generations per year.

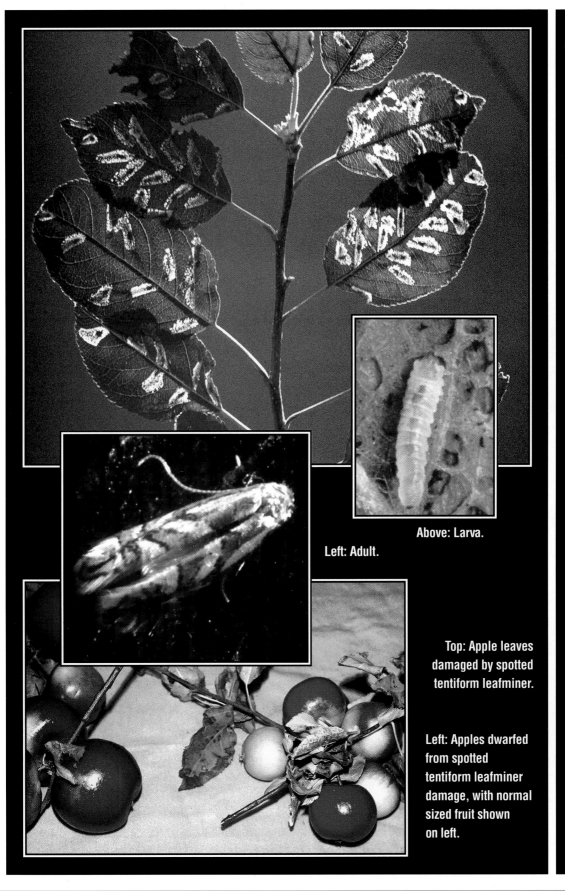

Above: Larva.

Left: Adult.

Top: Apple leaves damaged by spotted tentiform leafminer.

Left: Apples dwarfed from spotted tentiform leafminer damage, with normal sized fruit shown on left.

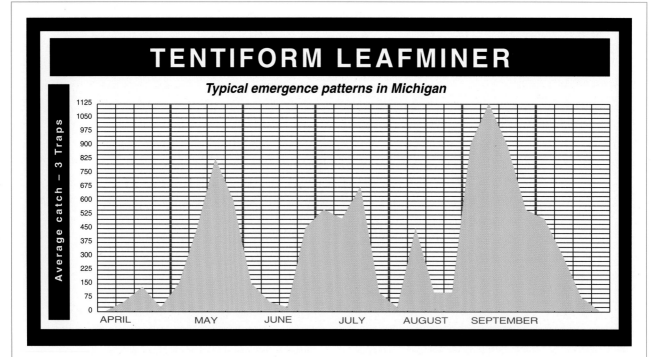

TENTIFORM LEAFMINER
Typical emergence patterns in Michigan

Spring-generation adults emerge in late April and continue flying until the middle of June. The life span of the adults in the laboratory is five to seven days. The eggs are laid soon after emergence and require less than one week to develop. The larva exits the egg through the flat surface adjacent to the leaf and enters the leaf directly. The first-instar larva begins feeding around the entry point by shearing open the spongy mesophyll cells with its specialized mouthparts. This instar and the two subsequent instars feed wholly on the protoplasm of these cells and are called sap-feeding larvae.

Instar 2 larvae form a linear mine between the lower epidermis and the spongy mesophyll tissue of the leaf. Instar 3 larvae extend the boundaries of the mine and form a blotch-shaped mine. When the third instar molts, the caterpillarlike fourth instar emerges and the feeding habit changes. Instars 4 and 5 larvae feed on whole cells of the leaf's parenchyma tissue and are called tissue-feeding larvae. The fifth instar feeds through the columnar parenchyma tissue up to the upper epidermis of the cell, causing

irregular, translucent feeding sites over the entire mined area. This gives the mine a spotted appearance, providing the insect with its common name.

The larvae pupate within the mine in a loosely knit cocoon at one end of the mine. After a three-week development period, the pupa pushes its way through the lower epidermis of the leaf and the adult emerges. The adult rests on the leaf surface for a few hours until it is ready for flight. At this time, it is very vulnerable to various predators that inhabit the leaf surface.

The time span between spring-generation adult emergence and first-generation adult emergence is about 60 to 70 days. The second generation develops like the first but, because of the warm summer temperatures, requires only 30 to 40 days to develop.

The third generation begins in mid-August and continues until the advent of cold weather, when it then pupates in the leaves. It spends the winter in the pupal stage in leaves on the ground. Adults begin to emerge the following spring in late April.

■ Monitoring

Depending on the need, there are a number of methods to monitor the tentiform leafminer.

Growers should note that, during the prebloom period, there is a correlation between numbers of adults and mines per leaf. To monitor adults, use a pheromone in a trap hung about 5 feet from the ground in the interior of the apple tree. Use one trap for every 3 to 5 acres. If the total prebloom capture from silver tip to pink stages is more than 12 adults per trap, apply a pesticide against the adults.

Sampling for first-generation eggs at the pink stage will provide information on the need for first brood control. Control at this time can help prevent damaging populations of the second generation. To sample, select four clusters from each of five trees in a block. Using a lens, count the total number of eggs on the undersides of the second, third and fourth leaves in each cluster. If the total for all clusters is more than 60, apply a treatment either after the sampling analysis or at petal fall. If the total is less than 60, no treatment against first-generation adults is required.

Another way to determine the need for spraying is to count the mines. At petal fall, randomly select five trees of the same variety and pick 10 terminal leaves per tree. Count the number of mines on the undersides of the leaves. No treatment is needed for a find of zero to one mine per leaf. For second-generation monitoring, pick younger leaves rather than terminal leaves. Count incipient mines made by the second generation. If you find two or fewer mines per tree, treatment is not needed.

Pheromones are unreliable for indicating whether sprays are needed.

■ Control

In abandoned orchards, biological control of this pest is nearly 100 percent. At present, there is no apparent biological window when chemical control could be applied without serious effects on the parasites, though some pesticides applied at the pre-pink stage for control of tentiform leafminer eggs and adults have minimal effects on parasites. Low numbers of leafminers in the first generation do not guarantee that heavy infestations will not occur in the second and third generations.

The need for control of first-generation leafminers can be determined at petal fall by counting the number of incipient mines on the undersurfaces of the leaves. The spotted tentiform leafminer has demonstrated great proclivity for developing resistance to chemicals. If effective, chemicals can be applied at the pre-pink stage as ovicides and adulticides.

Effective chemicals with translaminar activity can be applied at petal fall against the larvae. Pheromones can be employed for timing of pesticide applications as ovicides and adulticides, or as larvicides to control the second and third generations of tentiform leafminer.

Insects that bore into the trunk, branches or twigs

THE DOGWOOD BORER HAS A WIDE RANGE OF HOSTS, INCLUDING OAK, DOGWOOD, cherry, mountain ash, hickory, willow, birch, pine, elm and myrtle. In cultivated crops, it attacks pecans and blueberries. With the recent introduction of clonal rootstocks and their predisposition to produce burr knots, the dogwood borer has become an economic problem on apples.

Chapter 5

Common Name—
Dogwood Borer

Scientific Name—
Synanthedon scitula (Harr.)

Family—
Sesiidae

N THE EARLY 1960s, THE DOGWOOD BORER WAS found causing economic damage to blueberries, but it has since been only an occasional pest in them. Before this, the borer was noted only for causing occasional damage to ornamental trees and shrubs, such as dogwood. Oak and dogwood, which are especially common in the Midwest, are considered to be the borer's natural hosts.

Since the early 1980s, the dogwood borer has been a problem in the burr knots of apple varieties in Michigan, New York, New Jersey and Pennsylvania.

■ Life Stages

Egg: The egg is oval, measuring 0.5 by 0.3 mm. The egg incubation period is about nine days.

Larva: Body color ranges from near white to light pink but may appear slightly orangish when the larva is removed from the burr knot because of a covering of sap from the feeding wound. The head capsule is sclerotized and deep brown. Mature larvae measure 12 to 13 mm. There are seven instars.

Larvae of the dogwood borer and American plum borer are similar in size, but crochet location is different. Dogwood borer larvae have only one row of crochets in a line on the prolegs. Crochets on American plum borer larvae are arranged in a circle.

Pupa: The cocoon is made up of a silken thread with fragments of frass adhering to it and is rather small. It is positioned in the galleries the larva has made in the burr knot, usually close to the surface and covered by a layer of reddish frass. The pupa is about 9 mm or slightly shorter. When the adult emerges, the pupal case protrudes out of the tree slightly and will remain visible for a long time.

Adult: The adult is a typical black and yellow sesiid moth similar to adult peachtree and lesser peachtree borers, but its wingspan of 1.4 to 2 cm makes the dogwood borer adults much smaller than the average-sized adults of either of the other two borers. The female has a wide yellow band on the fourth abdominal segment; the male has a much narrower band on the same segment.

■ Host Range

The dogwood borer is a native clearwing moth found in all parts of the United States east of the Rocky Mountains. It occurs throughout the apple-growing areas of the eastern United States and Canada on a wide range of host plants, including oak and their galls, dogwood, black cherry, apple, mountain ash, hickory, willow, birch, American chestnut, beech, pine, elm and myrtle. It may also become a pest in pecans in the South and is an occasional pest of blueberries. On apple, the borer was not an economic problem until the introduction of clonal rootstocks, which are much more prone to produce burr knots than conventional rootstocks.

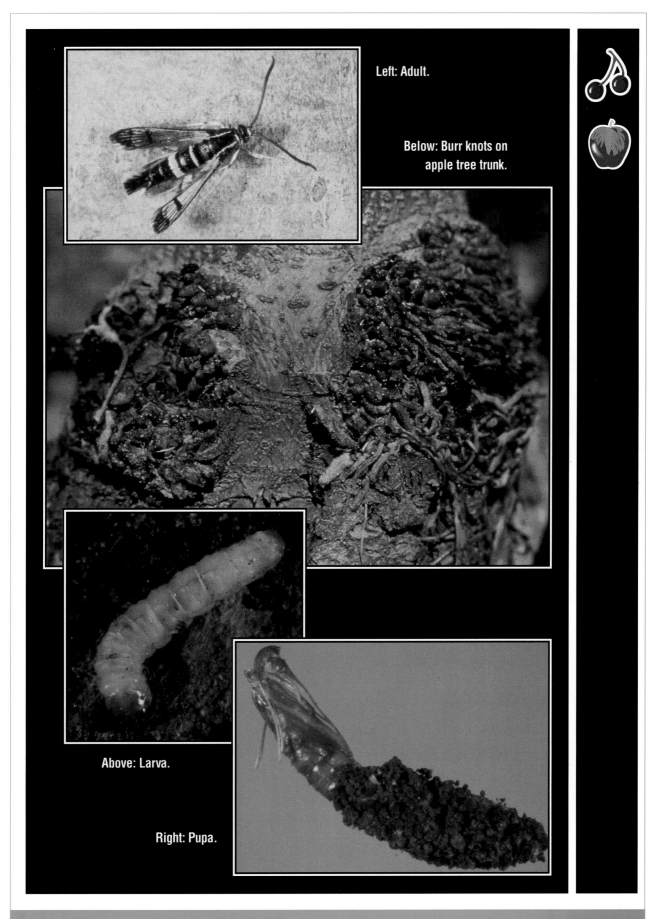

Left: Adult.

Below: Burr knots on apple tree trunk.

Above: Larva.

Right: Pupa.

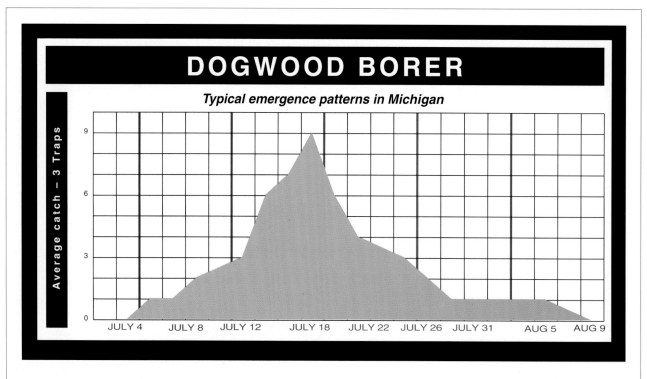

DOGWOOD BORER

Typical emergence patterns in Michigan

Average catch – 3 Traps

JULY 4 | JULY 8 | JULY 12 | JULY 18 | JULY 22 | JULY 26 | JULY 31 | AUG 5 | AUG 9

■ *Injury or Damage*

On apple, dogwood borer larvae feed inside burr knots, which can develop on the aboveground portion of clonal rootstocks. All commercial dwarfing and semi-dwarfing rootstocks tend to develop burr knots. This tendency can be enhanced by low light conditions around the trunk due to shading by weeds, low limbs, suckers, opaque mouse guards and shallow planting. Burr knots are aggregations of partially developed root initials that usually occur in clusters at or below the graft union. Reddish frass on the surface of a burr knot indicates an active infestation. The tunnels in newly infested burr knots are irregular, not well defined and usually quite shallow.

Feeding is initially confined to the burr knot but sometimes spreads to healthy bark outside it. Feeding in the burr knot itself does little or no damage to the tree, but feeding below the bark is much more destructive and may eventually girdle the tree. Tree kills attributable to dogwood borer usually take several consecutive years of infestation, even though several dozen larvae may be found on a single tree at one time. Persistent infestations over several years can contribute to a slow decline of the tree and reduce yields. Infestations probably also increase the chances of disease introduction.

■ *Factors Affecting Abundance*

Dogwood borers are very attracted to the grafting of new scion wood onto older trees. Populations of the insect build up quickly under these conditions, and the larvae can soon girdle the graft union area. Adults are attracted by dark tape and grafting wax. Opaque mouseguards provide oviposition sites for females.

■ *Life History*

In the fall, the larvae enter a hibernaculum stage. The hibernaculum is generally found in a gallery the larva has made in or around the burr knot on the tree. The larva emerges from the hibernaculum in May and pupates in early June for about 25 days. After emergence, the empty pupal cases often protrude from beneath the bark and remain visible for up to a year. The adults emerge over a period of about two months beginning in early June and continuing until the end of July, peaking in late June to early July.

The moths, whose life span is six to eight days, are most active at dawn and twilight. Mating and egg laying occur within a few days of emergence. The female lays eggs on or near burr knots. Trees that are already infested and that have large numbers of burr knots are particularly attractive. The larvae hatch after eight to nine days and seek entry into the plant. The burr knots consist primarily of meristematic, non-lignified root tissue that larvae can easily penetrate and feed on. On apples, they almost never enter healthy bark or pruning wounds to feed. In October and early November, the larva constructs a hibernaculum and overwinters in the larval stage in this structure.

■ *Monitoring*

Look for reddish frass on the surface of burr knots. Use pheromone traps placed in trees in mid-June to detect the presence of adults and peak emergence.

■ *Control*

Dogwood borers can be controlled with diluted trunk applications of residual insecticides. Thorough coverage of the lower trunk and burr knots is necessary for good control. A single spray timed to the first or peak egg hatch will give effective control.

Evidence from New York and Michigan seems to indicate that the timing of trunk sprays may not be as crucial for dogwood borer control as it is for other borer control on fruit trees. Some sprays that were applied

to full-grown larvae even before the larvae pupated in Michigan and after peak egg hatch in New York still gave good control. This is possibly because the spray can penetrate into the spongy burr knot tissue and be taken up by the relatively shallow feeding of the larvae.

NAA applied to the burr knots will destroy the knots but will not discourage attack by the dogwood borer. Killing the burr knot tissue with NAA is not desirable because it forces the larvae to feed at the edges of the burr knot in the healthy cambium. In addition, other borers such as the American plum borer may establish in the dead burr knots. New York studies on M.9, M.9/MM.106 and MM.111 rootstocks showed some difference in varietal susceptibility, but only MM.111 rootstocks had a considerably lower infestation level. The Empire variety seems to be the most heavily infested, possibly because it tends to have more burr knots per tree.

Planting deep and avoiding rootstock exposure will eliminate the burr knot problem. In already planted trees, place soil around the trunk up to the graft union to prevent borer access to the burr knots. This can be practical where the graft union is not too high off the ground. Burr knots and borers, however, have been found on Empires above the graft union and as high as 5 feet above the ground, so this may not always be possible.

Place the soil around the trunk in a wide mound rather than a narrow cone to avoid winter injury to the covered portion of the trunk. The additional root growth from the buried burr knots should improve anchorage and increase tree vigor.

Common Name—
Periodical Cicada

Scientific Name—
Magicicada septendecim (Linnaeus)

Family—
Cicadidae

THE PERIODICAL CICADA IS A SPECIES NATIVE to North America. Studies pertaining to this pest date back to 1666. It is not found north of Lansing, Mich.

Life Stages

Egg: Eggs are laid in the wood of several small branches.

Nymph: The nymph resembles the adult but does not have an adult's wings.

Adult: The adult is about 38 mm long and black. It has red eyes and other reddish markings. The wings are large and clear except for orange-red veins. Males are capable of making a high-pitched whine to attract females for mating. The females make no sound.

Several species of annual cicada adults with one- to three-year life cycles may also be found in orchards (particularly cherry and peach orchards). The activity of these adult cicadas is limited mainly to feeding, and they rarely cause any damage. They are black, about 50 mm long and have greenish rather than reddish markings, and their veins are red and green instead of orange-red.

Host Range

The periodical cicada is found in the eastern and midwestern parts of Canada and the United States. This pest will deposit eggs in almost any deciduous tree or shrub, and sometimes in evergreens or herbaceous plants.

Injury or Damage

Injury is caused by the female cicada depositing her eggs into twigs with a strong, chisel-like ovipositor. The oviposition slits weaken the twigs so that the branches may break off in the wind. In severe infestations, many of the tree's branch tips may be killed. Since most of the branches in larger trees are thicker than those that the female cicada prefers for egg laying, loss of these branch tips may not severely damage the tree. The preferred branches are those from fruit trees four years old or younger. These branches are generally about the width of a pencil (about 12 mm) or a little larger in diameter.

Under severe infestations, young trees can be severely damaged or killed. The loss of potential scaffold limbs can affect the productivity of a tree for the rest of its life. When nymphs enter the ground, they attach themselves to the roots of the fruit tree. They feed on the plant by inserting their needlelike mouthparts into the roots. Loss of nutrients can affect the tree's vigor, particularly since

Above: Peach tree branch showing cicada damage.

Above: Adult, viewed from top and from side.

Below:
Adult and nymph.

Left: Peach tree damaged by cicada.

feeding will continue during the pest's 17-year life span.

■ Factors Affecting Abundance

In orchards, trees adjacent to woodlots are more subject to attack from cicadas, and some varieties appear to be more subject to attack than others. Cicadas are more active in trees receiving sunlight than in those in shaded areas.

■ Life History

Adult cicadas usually start emerging from the soil in late May and continue activity for about six weeks. The mature nymphs dig themselves out of the ground, then crawl to the nearest tree trunk or other upright plant and climb up several inches. The nymphs molt, and the winged, sexually mature adults emerge. Egg laying begins about two weeks after emergence. Each female may deposit 400 to 500 eggs. Eggs are laid in twigs in pockets of 15 or more, so a single female may deposit 25 to 35 pockets.

To lay eggs, a female slices into the wood of the branch with her ovipositor and places the egg into the wood. Egg laying takes place for about a month. The eggs hatch in about six to seven weeks into small white nymphs. The nymphs fall to the ground and burrow into the soil to feed on grass roots and, eventually, tree roots for the next 17 years.

■ Monitoring

Many broods of cicada emerge periodically over the years. It is difficult to predict whether a particular orchard will be severely affected. The best strategy is to be alert for the high-pitched sounds of the males, which are caused by the vibration of a membrane on the first abdominal segment beneath the wings. Scout the orchards intensely a week later to look for egg-laying females, which do not sing but locate males for mating by the males' singing. To reduce adult populations, time spray applications during the preoviposition period to prevent damage caused by the egg-laying slits or punctures made by the female. Because of the month-long emergence period, you may find it necessary to make multiple applications of sprays to control the cicadas during the egg-laying period.

■ Control

Plantings can be delayed to avoid cicada emergence. To decrease the damage to future scaffold limbs, the winter pruning of trees younger than four years old should be delayed. Summer pruning should be done within a four- to six-week period after eggs are laid (but before the nymphs fall to the ground) and the prunings then burned to prevent the nymphs from going into the ground. During the emergence period, apply pesticide sprays, particularly to trees younger than four years old. Examine the orchard twice a week during the egg-laying period to check on the effectiveness of the pesticide.

Pear Pests

Pear
Pests

From pear psylla to mites, a variety of pests attack pears. The pear psylla causes major problems because of its considerable tendency to quickly develop resistance to pesticides. To date, biological control methods are limited as well. Hence, it is possible that, in the future, control of pear psylla may become very difficult.

Chapter 6

Common Name—
Pear Psylla

Scientific Name—
Cacopsylla pyricola (Foerster)

Family—
Psyllidae

PEAR PSYLLA WAS INTRODUCED INTO Connecticut from Europe about 1832. It spread to the Northwest in 1939. Now it is common wherever pears are grown.

■ Life Stages

Egg: The eggs are yellowish orange and about 0.3 mm long. They are deposited in the creases of the bark, in old leaf scars and about the bases of the terminal buds. They are elongated and pear-shaped and have a smooth, shiny surface. A short stalk at the larger end attaches the egg to the bark, and a long, thread-like process projects from the smaller end.

Nymph: Small, yellow, wingless nymphs are about 3 mm long when newly hatched. There are five immature stages. The fifth-instar nymph acquires wing pads.

Adult: Adults are dark reddish brown and have four wings.

■ Host Range

The pear psylla is a pest of only pears and is present in all pear-growing areas of Canada and the United States.

■ Injury or Damage

The pear psylla secretes honeydew, which serves as a substratum for the growth of a black fungus that gives the tree a smoky, sooty appearance. Foliage may wilt and drop to the ground. Trees that are heavily infested for a long time produce little growth and set fewer fruit buds. Fruit remains undersized, fails to mature and may fall off the tree when only partly grown. The tree shows symptoms from "psylla shock" caused by the toxin the psylla have injected into it. Prolonged infestations may kill the tree outright.

■ Factors Affecting Abundance

The pear psylla has an unusual ability to develop resistance to chemical compounds.

■ Life History

The adults hibernate on the trunks, in crevices and under bark. When they are very abundant, they may collect under leaves and trash. On bright, sunny days near the end of March or in April, if the temperature is above 50 degrees F, the adults emerge from winter quarters. Most of the eggs are laid before the buds open. Eggs hatch in 11 to 30 days, depending on the temperature. Most of the eggs will have hatched by petal fall.

The nymphs migrate immediately to the axils of the leaf petioles and stems. If these places become crowded, they will scatter out to the undersides of the leaves and leaf petioles. They use their sucking mouthparts to feed on sap. The sap is changed in the body to honeydew and the honeydew is given off as droplets. Each nymph surrounds itself with a small puddle or smear of honeydew, which reflects light and flickers in the sunlight.

Above: Healthy pear tree on the right and pear tree injured by pear psylla.

Left: Sooty mold on pear fruit caused by pear psylla.

Below left: Adult.

Below right: Nymph.

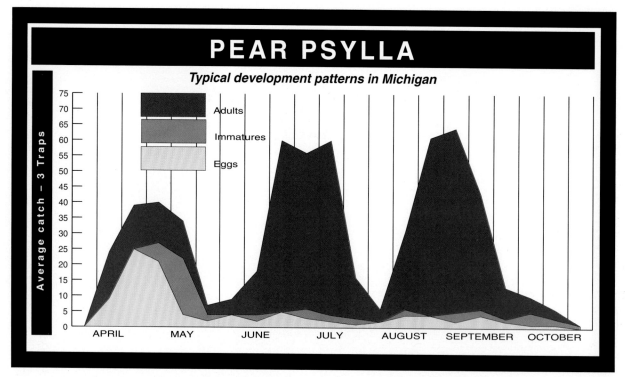

PEAR PSYLLA
Typical development patterns in Michigan

Average catch – 3 Traps

Adults
Immatures
Eggs

APRIL MAY JUNE JULY AUGUST SEPTEMBER OCTOBER

There are five immature stages. Nymphs get wing pads at the fifth molt. Three generations occur per year. The second and third generations of adults are smaller and lighter colored than those of the first generation. The females of later generations do not lay eggs on bark but deposit them along the midrib on the leaf undersides or place them in the notches at the edges of the leaves. Overwintering adults are produced in the fall.

■ Monitoring

In the prebloom period, use a beating tray early in the morning to sample adults. Construct trays from aluminum screening, making an 18-inch square frame covered with white cloth. You can dislodge and collect adult pear psylla by tapping a limb with a rubber hose and holding the tray underneath the limb. Yellow, sticky traps used for monitoring apple maggot and cherry fruit fly can also be used to monitor overwintering pear psylla adults very early in the spring.

■ Control

Pear psylla can develop resistance to chemicals quickly. The prognosis for contin-

ued chemical control of this pest is uncertain because the limited size of the crop does not warrant large expenditures to develop a pesticide to control this insect. Because pears are the only host of pear psylla, the entire population in an orchard is treated with each spray. The pear psylla population is thus subjected to great selection pressure with little chance of dilution of the gene pool. This hastens the development of resistance.

Because they tend to fly considerable distances, a few scattered infestations can become a general infestation in a short time. Few parasites and predators exist, so control depends almost entirely on insecticides. Timing is important because the hard shell makes the adult stage and the fifth instar hard to control. The chances of reinfestation are very great because overwintering adults fly considerable distances in the fall and spring.

Pruning water sprouts around mid-July can greatly reduce populations because nymphs find it difficult to feed on old, hardened-off leaves.

Common Name—
Pear Rust Mite

Scientific Name—
Epitrimerus pyri (Nalepa)

Family—
Eriophyidae

THE PEAR RUST MITE IS AN ERIOPHYID mite that is restricted to pears.

Life Stages

Egg: Eggs are spherical and about .05 mm long. When first laid, they are clear. They later turn white.

Nymph: The nymphs, which resemble the adults, have two instars.

Adult: The adult is about .05 mm long and wedge-shaped, with the widest part at the head end. The color varies from dull white to light brown.

Host Range

The pear rust mite is restricted to pears.

Injury or Damage

Mite feeding on leaves causes leaves to turn brown or bronze. This injury may stunt the growth of young trees. On older trees, mites feeding on leaves cause minor damage compared with the greater effect of mite feeding on the fruit. Extreme russetting of the fruit surface can occur, leaving the entire pear surface rough and brown. This injury renders the fruit unsalable for the fresh and processing markets.

Early in the season, rust mites tend to feed at either the calyx or the stem end and cause a localized russetting in those areas. Feeding and russetting may spread over the fruit if the mites go unchecked. Late season feeding tends to be scattered more uniformly over the fruit surface, with the intensity of russetting determined by the number of mites and the length of their feeding period.

Factors Affecting Abundance

Hot, dry weather favors a rapid buildup of this pest.

Life History

The mite overwinters as an adult female under leaf scars or bud scales or in small cracks on twigs. With the advent of warm weather, even before the buds break, these mites are feeding and laying eggs under the bud scales. As the blossom cluster expands to throw off the outer scales, the exposed mites start to migrate toward the developing bloom, resulting in a concentration of active stages in the calyx end of the nearly developed fruit. The young mites from the hatched eggs also feed on the flower stems just prior to bloom. By petal fall, they are feeding vigorously on leaves and at the calyx end of the devel-

Left: Rust mite.

Below: Pear rust mite damage on pears.

oping fruit. Later they spread over the tree, also feeding on leaves.

Damaged areas of fruit gradually russet or turn brown. In June, the first russetting shows mainly at the calyx end of the fruit, and most russetted fruit is usually on the sunny south or east side of the tree. Once the mites spread out over the tree in large numbers, succeeding generations (several during the season) move onto the fruit from the stem ends and, if not controlled, will gradually russet whole fruits. In July, some females begin to hibernate for the winter, but if the weather is hot and dry for long periods, the mites will go on feeding into August until cool weather occurs, at which time they will seek shelter and overwinter under leaf scars or bud scales.

■ *Monitoring*

In winter or very early spring, collect and open pear buds to determine the relative density and distribution of pear rust mites in the orchard. Later in spring, sample 25 fruit clusters in an orchard. Treatment is recommended if pear rust mites are found in five or more clusters. When examining clusters, use a hand lens with a magnification of 10x or higher, and make sure the area is well lit.

■ *Control*

Prebloom and petal-fall sprays are essential to control this pest. Trees must be sprayed dilute from both sides and should be monitored for pear rust mite until harvest.

Common Name—
Pear Sawfly
(Pear Slug)

Scientific Name—
Caliroa cerasi (Linnaeus)

Family—
Tenthredinidae

THE PEAR SAWFLY, ALSO COMMONLY known as the pear slug, was common in Massachusetts in 1796. It was first recorded in Europe in 1740.

■ Life Stages

Egg: The egg is oval in outline, sometimes slightly flattened at one side, and measures 0.9 by 0.5 mm. It is pale to almost colorless, appearing light green through the leaf tissue.

Larva: When first hatched, the larva measures 1.2 mm long and 0.5 mm wide at the thorax — the broadest portion. The body is pale and free from slime; the head is light brown. As soon as the small slug begins to eat, the particles of green leaf tissue show through its body. The slug secretes a coat of slime soon after hatching and then appears dark olive-green, with a dark brown head. The slugs grow very rapidly at first. As the slugs grow, they become lighter colored. They are orange-yellow when fully mature.

Pupa: The pupa is 5.8 mm long, 2.4 mm wide and lemon-yellow.

Adult: The adult is a sawfly. It is black and yellow, about 5 mm long — a little larger than the common housefly — and it has four wings.

■ Host Range

The pear sawfly is a pest of cherry, pear and plum. It is generally found in all pear-growing regions in Canada and the United States.

■ Injury or Damage

The larvae feed on the surface of the leaves and skeletonize them, leaving only a framework of veins.

■ Factors Affecting Abundance

Biological control is a factor — this pest has a number of parasites and predators that attack it. The pear sawfly can increase rapidly in neglected or unsprayed pear trees.

■ Life History

The pear sawfly passes the winter in a cocoon formed in an earthen cell 2 or 3 inches below the surface of the ground. In the late spring, shortly after the cherries have come into full leaf, the adults emerge from these cocoons. After mating, the female inserts her eggs in the leaves. The eggs hatch in seven to 11 days. The young larvae emerge from the eggs to the upper surface of the leaf and cut semicircular holes in the epidermis. The young slugs begin to eat out small pieces of the leaf, first taking only the

Larvae of pear sawfly feeding on pear leaf.

epidermis in patches, later eating deeper in large areas into the parenchyma to the veins. The feeding period varies from two to three weeks. They then crawl or drop to the ground, burrow into it and change to the pupal stage.

Adults emerge during late July and August and lay eggs for the second generation of slugs. This generation usually causes the greater amount of injury, especially on young trees, which they may completely defoliate. When this second generation of larvae becomes fully grown, they go into the ground and remain as larvae until the following spring, when they pupate.

■ Monitoring

In spring, shortly after pears or cherries have come into full leaf, examine leaves for olive-green, sluglike larvae covered with slime that are eating out small pieces of the leaf. Re-inspect in late July or August for the summer generation.

■ Control

No special sprays are needed — the cover sprays applied for the common pests of pears will control it.

Common Name—
Grape Mealybug

Scientific Name—
Pseudococcus maritimus (Ehrhorn)

Family—
Pseudococcidae

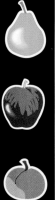

THE GRAPE MEALYBUG HAS BEEN A serious pest of pears in California for many years. In recent years, it has become a problem in the pear-growing areas of Washington and Oregon.

■ Life Stages

Egg: Eggs are yellowish or orange and are laid in cottony egg sacs under rough bark scales on the trunk and main scaffold limbs of pear.

Nymph: The nymphs are pale yellow. Nymphs go through four to five instars, depending on the sex, with each instar larger than the one preceding it.

Adult: Males have one pair of wings. They have no mouthparts and die soon after emergence. Mature females are about 4.8 mm long.

■ Host Range

The grape mealybug has a wide range of hosts, including apple, pear, peach and grape. It is a common pest in all pear-growing regions of the West Coast and an occasional pest of pears in the midwestern and eastern United States and eastern Canada.

■ Injury or Damage

The most obvious damage caused by the mealybugs is a honeydew secretion that drips to the foliage, twigs and fruit. A black fungus grows in the honeydew and gives the foliage and fruit a sooty appearance. Honeydew droplets can cause a type of russetting that makes the pears unsuitable for fresh shipping. The feeding of mealybugs within the calyx end of the fruit can cause a breakdown of the cells and softening in the end of the fruit when the pear starts to ripen. Present washing practices will not remove these insects from the calyx end, so the mealybugs remain on the fruit after it is packed. Infested fruit is rejected by both cannery and fresh market outlets.

■ Factors Affecting Abundance

Grape mealybugs tend to build up in older orchards that provide better overwintering sites than younger pear orchards.

■ Life History

The grape mealybug overwinters as newly hatched first-instar nymphs in egg sacs composed of waxy filaments. These are located under bark scales on larger limbs or trunks or in trash at the bases of pear trees. Most crawlers will stay in the nest until the weather warms enough in the spring to make them active.

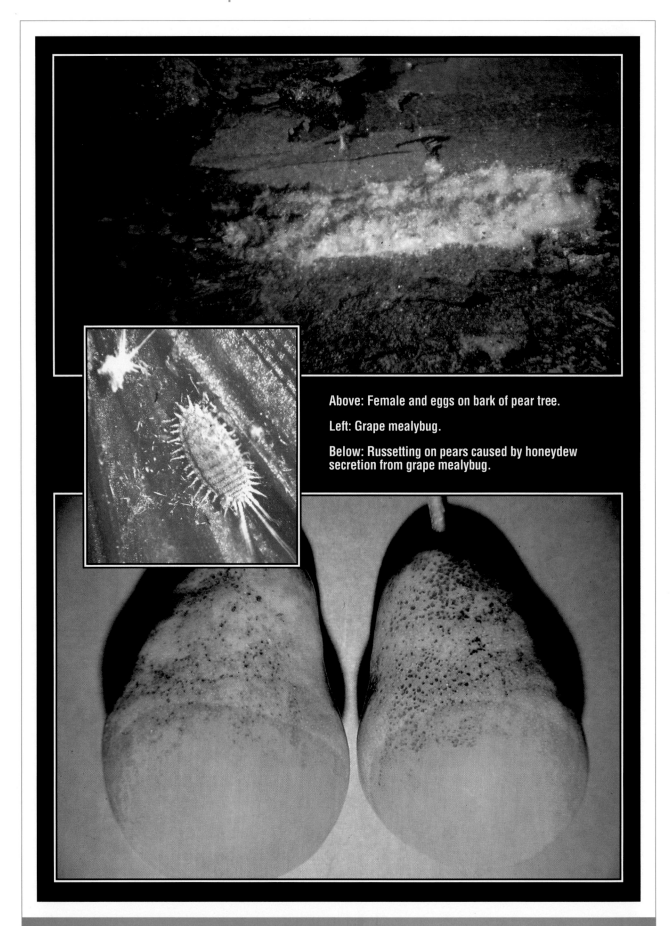

Above: Female and eggs on bark of pear tree.

Left: Grape mealybug.

Below: Russetting on pears caused by honeydew secretion from grape mealybug.

The crawlers begin migrating from the egg sacs to the buds in April, as soon as the buds begin to swell. The first crawlers to emerge begin feeding at the bases of the buds. These are often located near water sprouts, so these areas should be inspected for early detection of this pest. When the buds open, the crawlers go directly to the new shoots and leaves. The nymphs will settle and feed in clusters at the bases of shoots or in leaf axils of the current season's growth.

Shortly after feeding begins, crawlers begin to produce the wax that gives them their characteristic appearance and makes them more difficult to control with chemicals. The nymphs will go through four to five instars, depending on whether they are male or female. The adults begin to appear in late June, and the males appear about 10 days earlier than the females. The male adults have one pair of wings and are capable of flight.

The males possess no mouthparts and die shortly after mating. The females begin to emerge about mid-July. After they mate, they search for rough bark or older wood for egg-laying sites. Eggs are laid in late summer. Some eggs may hatch, but the majority remain in the egg sacs as first-instar larvae until the following spring.

■ *Monitoring*

In late summer, examine rough bark or older wood in pear trees for females and egg sacs. Infestations found at this time indicate that a problem exists and that treatment will be required the following year.

■ *Control*

Normally, mealybug populations will go undetected until late summer when females and egg sacs become visible. At this time it is generally too late for control measures. Identifying the infestation can alert you that a problem exists and that control measures should be applied the following year. The best control strategy is to control the migrating crawlers before they settle down and develop their protective covering. Early in the growing season when the crawlers are migrating, there is less foliage on the trees so that spray coverage of the bark on the trunks and limbs is more nearly complete. Control of the nymphs before they reproduce will reduce the damage from this pest.

Common Name—
Pear Leaf Blister Mite

Scientific Name—
Phytoptus pyri (Pagenstecher)

Family—
Eriophyidae

THE PEAR LEAF BLISTER MITE IS AN ERIOPHYID mite. It came from Europe about 1870 and became a pest about 1902 in the United States.

■ Life Stages

Egg: The egg of the blister mite is dull white, oval and about 0.05 mm long.

Nymph: The immature stages resemble the full-grown mite, except in size.

Adult: The adult is white or light red and ranges from 0.16 to 0.25 mm long. The body is long and tapering to the rear. The front end bears the head with the mouthparts. Two pairs of legs are attached just behind the head. There are long hairs, or setae, on the legs and five pairs on the sides of the body. The covering of the mite is annulated so that it looks like about 80 narrow rings.

■ Host Range

This mite is a pest of pear, apple and European mountain ash. It is a problem in all of the pear-growing areas of Canada and the United States.

■ Injury or Damage

Two distinct types of damage occur: fruit spots and blistered leaves. These mites cause brownish blisters on the undersides of pear and apple leaves. On pear, the blisters appear as small, greenish pimples that soon take on a reddish color and later turn brownish. On apple, the first stages are pale yellowish and the blisters never become as red as on pear. The blisters, about 3 mm wide, may be massed together to nearly cover the underside of the leaf surface. If you look at these with a hand lens, you will see many small mites. Heavy infestations cause blistering of leaves that can seriously impair leaf function.

Early feeding of the mites on the developing fruit causes depressed russet spots, which can be the most serious aspect of blister mite attack. The fruit is often deformed and misshapen. The presence of these oval russet spots, usually depressed with a halo of clear tissue surrounding each spot, is a characteristic symptom of blister mite attack. The Bartlett pear is very susceptible to fruit damage.

■ Factors Affecting Abundance

Failure to apply effective prebloom sprays with thorough coverage can result in a buildup of pear blister mite populations.

■ Life History

The adult mites typically enter the second or third bud scale in August or September and spend the winter there. When foliage comes out in the spring, they become active, migrate to the tender leaves, burrow beneath

Above: Pear damage.

Below: Early (left) and late stages of pear leaf blister mite damage.

the epidermis of the undersurface and start feeding. The resulting irritation produces a thickening of the leaf tissue — a gall. The eggs are laid in the gall and the young remain in the gall until they mature. Adults leave the gall through a minute opening in the underside. They migrate to new leaves and start new blisters. Reproduction is continuous and new galls are formed throughout the growing season. In late summer and early fall, the adult mites seek shelter for the winter beneath the outer bud scales.

■ *Monitoring*

When the foliage comes out in the spring, inspect the undersides of pear leaves for incipient blisters. The blisters will appear as small, greenish pimples that take on a reddish color and later turn brown.

■ *Control*

Effective cover sprays are necessary, especially in the prebloom stage, if there is a serious problem.

Codling Moth

For more complete information on this pest, see page 22.

Control of the first generation of codling moth is often not necessary for pears grown in the Midwest and East because the growing pear may be too hard for larvae to enter successfully. However, first-generation codling moth has been known to damage pears, and Oriental pears may be more attractive to this pest than other pears because they are softer.

The second generation of codling moth can be a problem because larvae can readily enter the more mature, softer pear. Larvae may enter through the sides, the stem end or the calyx end of the pear. Entries through the calyx end are difficult to detect, and a pear that appears sound may actually harbor larvae. Larvae often penetrate a short distance into the fruit, where they may die, either from insecticides or natural causes.

To control the second generation, apply sprays at 1,400 to 1,600 degree-days (DD). This timing will coincide with peak adult emergence and egg hatching.

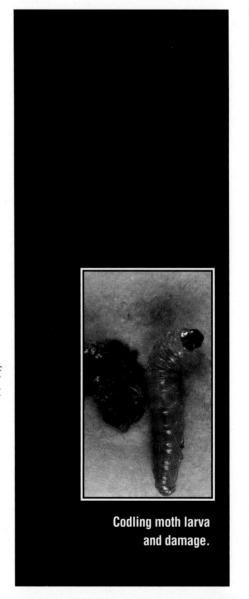

Codling moth larva and damage.

ARTHROPOD PESTS
OF
STONE FRUITS

- *Cherry Pests*

- *Peach, Plum, Nectarine & Apricot Pests*

Section II

PEACH BUD DEVELOPMENT STAGES

1. Dormant

2. Silver tip

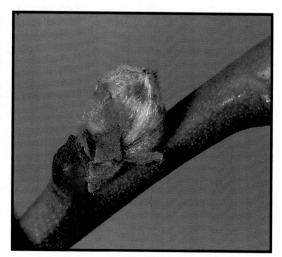

3. Green tip

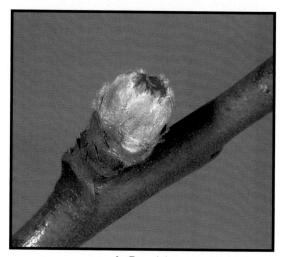

4. Pre-pink

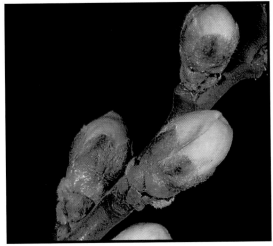

5. Full pink

6. First blossom open

7. Full bloom

8. Petal fall

9. Shuck-split

10. Shuck-off

Cherry Pests

Insects that burrow into or feed inside the fruit

Growers must take great care to control cherry fruit flies because there is a zero tolerance for cherry fruit fly larvae in processed cherries. Because there are a number of flies with dark-banded wings, it is very important to be able to recognize and identify the various species of fruit flies from the banding on their wings.

Unlike the larvae of other pests, cherry fruit fly larvae sink when cherries are placed in containers filled with water. This increases the risk of cherry fruit fly larvae getting into processed cherries. Cherries infested with plum curculio larvae and the larvae themselves tend to float in water.

Common Name—
Cherry Fruit Fly

Scientific Name—
Rhagoletis cingulata (Loew)

Common Name—
Black Cherry Fruit Fly

Scientific Name—
Rhagoletis fausta (O.S.)

Family—
Tephritidae

THREE SPECIES OF PICTURE-WINGED FRUIT flies attack stone fruits in the north central states. Two species, the cherry fruit fly and the black cherry fruit fly, attack sweet and tart cherries and wild species of cherries. The apple maggot fruit fly is primarily a pest of apples but will attack plums and prunes late in the season.

■ Life Stages

Egg: The egg is whitish, oval and 1 mm long.

Larva: Full-grown larvae or maggots measure 7 mm long. Larvae are glossy white or yellowish and legless, and they taper toward the head end. Under magnification, two mouth hooks may be seen at the head end.

Pupa: The puparium is golden brown to dark brown, resembling a grain of wheat, and is approximately 4 mm long.

Adult: The adult flies are blackish with yellowish heads and legs. They measure about 4.5 mm long, about two-thirds the size of the housefly. Near the center of the back is a small cream or yellow dot. The two species of flies are distinguished by prominent dusky bands or markings on the wings (see illustration, p. 31) and by markings on the body. The body of the black cherry fruit fly is entirely black, while the abdomen of the cherry fruit fly is black with white transverse bands across it, four bands on the female and three on the male. The cherry fruit fly is usually by far the more abundant species.

■ Host Range

In addition to cultivated sweet and tart cherries, one or both species have been found in wild black cherry, pin cherry, mahaleb cherry and chokecherry. Cherry fruit flies have been reported from all sections of the north central states where cherries are grown. Normally, pin cherry is the wild host for the black cherry fruit fly, and wild black cherry is the host for the cherry fruit fly.

Right: Male cherry fruit fly.
Below: Male black cherry fruit fly.

Above: Larvae.

Left: Pupae.

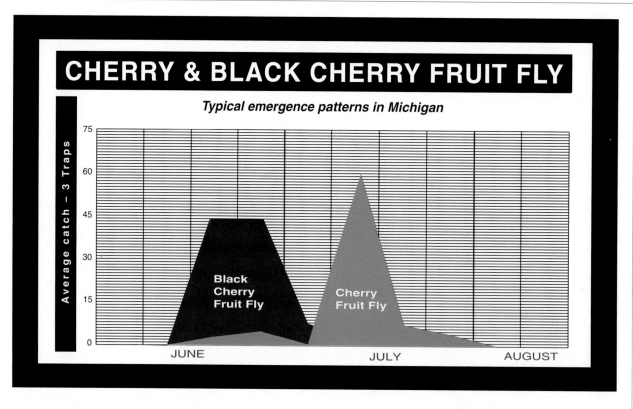

CHERRY & BLACK CHERRY FRUIT FLY

Typical emergence patterns in Michigan

Average catch – 3 Traps

Black Cherry Fruit Fly

Cherry Fruit Fly

JUNE　　JULY　　AUGUST

■ Injury or Damage

Damage to the fruit occurs in two ways: feeding by the adults and feeding by the maggots. Oviposition injury by the adult may occur from egg laying. Punctures made by the female's ovipositor are usually made near the bottom of the fruit. Up to 40 eggs have been reported as being deposited in a single fruit. Normally, only one maggot develops in each fruit, even though many eggs may have been deposited in that fruit. Primary damage results from the feeding of the larva within the fruit. Infested fruits appear normal until the maggot is nearly full grown, at which time sunken spots appear. Maggots and their frass within the fruit render the product unsalable. Infested fruit is more susceptible to brown rot and other diseases, so materials used to inoculate for disease in the orchard should be increased.

■ Factors Affecting Abundance

The time of adult emergence varies with the season and appears to be early or late in direct relation to the temperature and rainfall, especially during late May and early June. Seasons with an even distribution of rainfall and moderate temperatures appear very favorable for the development of the species. Normally, a rainfall sufficient to wet the upper inch of soil is required before flies will emerge from the soil. Conversely, extended drought periods are unfavorable for emergence, and during such periods, fly emergence is likely to be irregular. Extremely hard-baked soil at the time the maggots are entering the soil will reduce the population significantly.

Mechanical harvesting of cherries leaves some cherries on most trees. Because these cherries hang on the trees for some weeks, any pesticide that was present on the fruit at harvest degrades or is washed off the remaining fruit. Fruit flies from wild hosts, particularly wild black cherry, emerge for some time after cherry harvest. These flies are able to infest cherries left on the trees. The larvae complete their development, pupate in the soil and infest the orchard the following year.

■ *Life History*

For all practical purposes, the two species of fruit flies can be considered as one because the life cycles and control measures for them are almost identical.

The cherry fruit fly spends about 10 months of the year in the soil beneath the trees in a puparium resembling a grain of wheat. In late May, the pupae transform to the adult flies and, depending on location, start emerging from the ground. Peak emergence for the black cherry fruit fly is about mid-June; that of the cherry fruit fly, about harvest time (mid- to late July). Normally, the black cherry fruit fly will emerge 10 days to two weeks earlier than the cherry fruit fly. The adult flies spend about 10 days feeding in the tree (this is the preoviposition feeding period) before they lay eggs. The adult flies are active on warm, bright days, feeding on the surface of the leaves or fruit on drops of dew, plant juices or honeydew secretions from aphids, or from feeding punctures in the fruit. The feeding habits of these insects, and the fact that there is a preoviposition feeding and mating period, present a means of control; i.e., the application of insecticides to kill the adult flies before they can lay eggs.

The female inserts eggs beneath the skin of the fruit through a needle-shaped ovipositor. Eggs are most frequently inserted on the sides of the fruit. Each female is capable of laying 300 to 400 eggs during the three to four weeks she is active. The eggs hatch in five to seven days, and the legless maggots start to feed around the pit and later in the pulp of the cherry. Maggots feed for approximately two weeks. When fully grown, they drop to the ground and burrow into the soil. They usually burrow 1 to 2 inches beneath the soil surface but have been found at depths up to 5 inches.

The maggot constructs a puparium in the soil and overwinters. Only one generation of cherry fruit flies occurs each year, though some of the puparia may remain in the soil for two years.

■ *Monitoring*

In June, hang canary-yellow, sticky traps in the foliage of cherry trees. Cherry fruit flies respond to high concentrations of ammonia, so add a teaspoonful of ammonium acetate or ammonium hydroxide to the trap before hanging. Identify each species and its abundance by examining the banding on the wings (see illustration, p. 31). The black cherry fruit fly will emerge 10 to 14 days earlier than the cherry fruit fly. Treat within five to six days after the first catch.

■ *Control*

The flies must be controlled with effective chemicals in the eight-day preoviposition period before the female matures and she can lay eggs. Bait traps that are colored canary-yellow, coated with a sticky material, and baited with a feeding attractant such as ammonium acetate or protein hydrolysate should be employed for monitoring the emergence of the fruit flies.

Common Name—
Mineola Moth
(Destructive Prune Worm)

Scientific Name—
Acrobasis tricolorella (Grote)

Family—
Pyralidae

THE MINEOLA MOTH WAS FIRST DISCOVERED and described by Hulst in Colorado in 1900. Found on apples in Washington in 1919, it was first reported as an economic pest in Idaho in 1925 when it was found attacking prunes. In 1965, this pest caused severe losses of tart cherries in Michigan.

■ Life Stages

Egg: The eggs are spherical to oblong and average 1.6 by 2.1 mm. They are light yellow to reddish orange. The surface is pitted — the depressions are light yellow and the raised edges are reddish orange. The eggs turn gradually darker as hatching time approaches.

Larva: The newly hatched larva is about 1 to 2 mm long. The body is yellow and the head brown. The body is covered with many short spines. The larva becomes dark brown as it grows. The mature larva is slightly more than 13 mm long, dark brown on the dorsal side and lighter, reddish brown on the ventral, with a distinct juncture about midway on the side of the body where the two colors join. There are five instars.

Pupa: The pupa is brown and about 9 mm long. The anterior portion is large and the posterior end tapers rapidly.

Adult: The adult is a bluish gray moth about 9 to 12.5 mm long. It is distinctly wedge-shaped when at rest. The antennae lie straight over the body. There is a broad transverse white stripe about midway on the forewings. This stripe is bordered posteriorly by a smaller, reddish brown stripe. A similar white and red band, though much narrower and more irregular, occurs near the posterior edge of the forewings. It is similar in size and appearance to the closely related American plum borer.

■ Host Range

The mineola moth has been found on cherries, apples, wild plums and chokecherries. Plums and tart cherry trees are preferred hosts. It can be found in all cherry-growing areas.

■ Injury or Damage

The overwintering larvae feed on fruit buds and developing flower parts. The insides of the buds are often entirely consumed, and a single larva may destroy several buds. When the fruit buds develop into the blossom stage, the larvae feed externally on the opening petals and developing leaf clusters. Nests are formed in the leaf terminals, and the larvae continue to feed on the expanding leaves from these shelters. The most serious damage is caused by larvae from the moths that emerge in June. These larvae attack the cherries, entering the fruit from the side or by the stem end. These larvae may be present in the cherries at harvest.

Clockwise from top left: Adult; larva feeding on cherry blossom; hibernacula; cherries damaged by larvae.

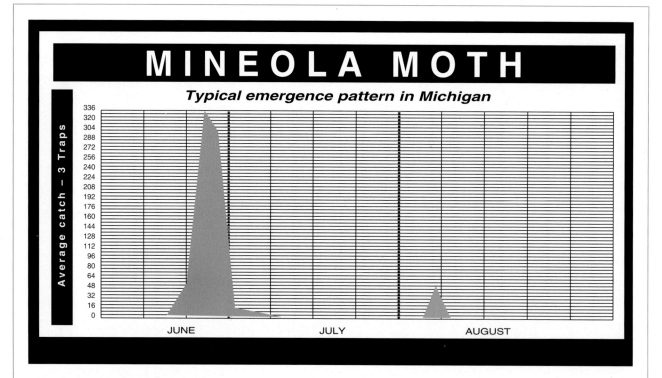

MINEOLA MOTH

Typical emergence pattern in Michigan

Average catch – 3 Traps

JUNE   JULY   AUGUST

■ *Factors Affecting Abundance*

A small percentage of larvae mature instead of forming hibernacula. These larvae pupate in the soil, and a partial second generation of adults emerges in about one month and deposits eggs. The larvae that hatch from these eggs overwinter in hibernacula after harvest when pesticides have degraded or have been washed off the trees. Hence, these larvae can be a source of infestation the following year.

■ *Life History*

In the north central states, the mineola moth has one complete and a partial second generation. It overwinters as a partly grown second-instar larva in a hibernaculum. The hibernacula are small, silken nests with bits of bark and frass embedded in them. They are usually found on the smaller branches, in the crotches of buds and twigs, and in bark depressions. The overwintering larvae migrate from the hibernacula to the buds in the latter part of April.

After emergence from the hibernaculum, the larva crawls along the twig to a cluster of buds, where it constructs a tubular nest in and around the bud cluster. The nest is lined with silk and is concealed by bits of bark and frass. The larva forages from its nest, entering the base of the bud and eating the bud contents. Injured fruit buds are marked by protruding light brown frass and webbing at the entrance to the feeding site. The insides of the buds are often entirely consumed, leaving only the outer scales. One larva may destroy several buds. Superficial damage in the form of a small hole in the bud scale may be found on a leaf bud that is just opening.

Larvae will often move out into the expanding leaves and web them together. This results in the characteristic clumping of leaves meshed in silk and frass. The larva then rolls another leaf and constructs another silken nest. As the leaf withers and dies, the larva pulls together more leaves and repeats the process. Many buds and leaves are destroyed in this manner. When the fruit buds develop into the blossom stage, the larvae feed externally on the opening petals and developing leaf clusters. The blossoms may open before they have been completely destroyed, but they will not set.

At full bloom, the larva will often move to a new bud cluster. It may form webbing and a tubular nest again or it may feed on many of the blossoms by entering from the tops without first forming a nest. In either case, some webbing is found lightly holding the petals together, and large quantities of frass are present.

The larvae feed primarily on the flower parts and only occasionally on the petals. By petal fall, most of the larvae are full grown and leave the leaf nests to pupate in the soil. The spring larval feeding period from bud break to petal fall is usually about four to five weeks.

The larvae drop to the ground during the full bloom/shuck-split period and pupate in the orchard litter. The adults of the first generation begin to emerge 19 to 20 days after full bloom and continue to emerge for another 22 to 27 days. Both sexes emerge with equal frequency. Females contain an average of 138 eggs, of which about 65 percent are oviposited on protected areas of the fruit spurs and on the undersides of leaves. Eggs are laid four to six days after adult emergence and hatch in seven to nine days.

Immature larvae enter near the stems of the cherries and burrow irregularly toward the pits. They continue to feed around the pits and form small pockets in the tissues of the cherries. The majority of the larvae feed in the ripening cherries for 11 to 14 days before leaving to form hibernacula in the crotches of the fruit spurs. The two periods of greatest summer mortality occur when larvae migrate to feed in the cherries and to form hibernacula. Larvae overwinter in the second and third instars.

From 1 to 5 percent of larvae do not form hibernacula but continue to feed in the cherries until they are mature. These larvae drop to the ground to pupate and initiate a second generation. The larvae from eggs laid by these moths feed on leaves in nests constructed adjacent to the leaf midribs. Larvae form hibernacula that cannot be distinguished from those formed by first-generation larvae. This generation is important because it occurs in the orchard after harvest and contributes to the following year's insect population.

■ *Monitoring*

In the prebloom stage, examine fruit buds for larvae feeding. In the blossom stage, look for later feeding on petals. Look for nests formed in the leaf terminals. In mid-June, use black light traps to catch emerging adults. A commercial pheromone has not been developed for this pest.

■ *Control*

Chemical controls should be applied, depending on the severity of the outbreak, at one or both of the following stages: to overwintering larvae when they leave the hibernacula to feed on the developing buds, and at the beginning and again at the peak of emergence of the first brood of moths.

Spray directed at the overwintering larvae should be applied between the green tip and popcorn stages. It is important that rows be sprayed from both sides at each application. Spraying rows from only one side does not provide adequate coverage to control overwintering larvae.

Sprays applied at the initial and peak emergence of adults should be applied from both sides at each application. This provides sufficient coverage to kill adults or larvae emerging from eggs.

Common Name—

Cherry Fruitworm

Scientific Name—
Grapholitha packardi (Zeller)

Family—
Tortricidae

THE CHERRY FRUITWORM WAS FIRST REPORTED in Texas by Zeller in 1876. It was reported as a pest of apples in Missouri in 1891 and as a pest of apples, peaches and roses in New York by Forbes in 1923. In 1939, it was reported as a pest of blueberries in New Jersey. It was first reported as a pest of tart cherries in 1929 in British Columbia. In 1939, cherry fruitworms caused heavy losses of tart cherries in Washington. In 1949, it was first noted as a pest of tart cherries in Wisconsin and Michigan. In 1985, it caused severe damage to blueberries in Michigan.

■ Life Stages

Egg: The eggs are whitish yellow and circular to elliptical. They are difficult to detect because they are the same color as the fruit when they are laid. As development proceeds, the contents of the egg turn grayish white. Shortly before they hatch, the larval head capsules are readily visible.

Larva: Newly hatched larvae are very similar to those of lesser appleworm. They are whitish gray with black heads and are 1.4 mm long. The head capsule measures 0.9 mm. As the larvae mature, their skin gradually becomes pink-tinted. When full grown, they are about 9 mm long and have an anal comb. The hibernaculum in which a larva overwinters has a light gray-silver cover. Under the cover are two more layers, which are very black, quite tough and brittle.

Pupa: The pupae are slender, yellowish brown and 6 mm long.

Adult: The adults are small, grayish black moths with a wingspread of 9 to 10 mm.

■ Host Range

The cherry fruitworm is a pest of tart cherries, blueberries, apples and peaches. It is found in all fruit areas in Canada and the United States. It has three generations on apples in New York.

■ Injury or Damage

The cherry fruitworm causes its injury by boring into the fruit. The larvae bore through the epidermis shortly after they hatch. This early injury can be detected in a few days. The entrance holes made by the young larvae can be seen as small, brown trails caused by their tunneling. The larvae may feed extensively just below the surface. This will be indicated by sunken, rough, brownish areas. A maturing larva may damage more than one fruit. Mature fruits are roughened, blackish and generally distorted. Larval frass may be present on the surface of the cherry. The inside of the cherry, next to the pit, is completely eaten away. The cherry fruitworm has also been found boring into the tips of young apple shoots.

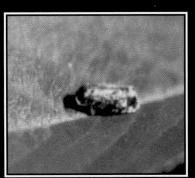

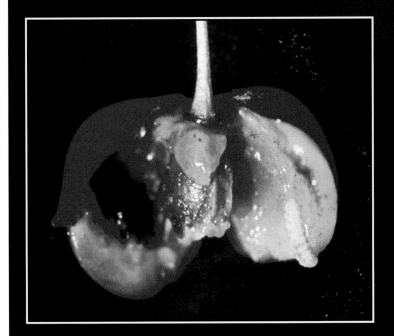

Top left: Larva.

Top right: Adult.

Above and left: Cherries infested by cherry fruitworm.

■ *Factors Affecting Abundance*

Severe winters can cause high mortality in overwintering larvae. Inclement weather at the time of adult emergence can restrict activity and reduce oviposition. The overwintering population will be reduced if larval development is not complete before the fruit is harvested.

■ *Life History*

The cherry fruitworm has one generation a year on cherries and blueberries.

It overwinters as mature larvae in hibernacula on the tree. The hibernacula may be found under loose pieces of bark, in roughened stubs of broken branches or in holes bored into the stubs of pruned branches. The hibernacula are extremely well hidden.

The larvae pupate in their hibernacula in the spring. The pupae may project from the hibernacula just prior to and after emergence. The average length of the pupal stage is 29 days. The appearance of the first adults will vary with seasonal conditions. The moth flight commences two to four weeks after petal fall and extends for two to three weeks. The moths are most active during dusk and late evening. If the weather is cool, humid and cloudy, they begin flying about 4 p.m. On sunny days, they will not fly unless disturbed.

The adult moths mate immediately after emergence, after which the female is ready to lay eggs. The eggs are laid on the unripe fruit, usually next to the suture at the base of the petiole or at the calyx end next to the pistil scar. Generally, a roughened area on the cherry is preferred. The incubation period is 10 days.

Larvae bore through the epidermis of the cherry shortly after they hatch. The entrance holes may be near the petiole, on the side or at the pistil scar. At first the larvae tunnel just beneath the epidermis, but gradually they work toward the pit. Some of the larvae may attack several fruits before their development is complete. They mature in about three weeks, then leave the fruit. The larvae usually leave the fruit before harvest, though mature larvae can be present in the fruit during harvest. After leaving the fruit, the mature larvae spin nests under loose pieces of bark, in roughened stubs of broken branches or twigs, in the ends of pruned twigs, or underneath the bark on the trunk and limbs of the cherry tree.

■ *Monitoring*

On the cherry's surface, look for frass and an entrance hole leading to small, brown trails just below the surface. A commercial pheromone has not been developed.

■ *Control*

Chemicals must be applied and timed according to the emergence of the adults. Insecticides should be applied at 10 and 20 days after petal fall.

For more complete information about fruitworms, see page 123.

Green fruitworms can cause considerable damage to cherries. In Michigan, the speckled green fruitworm *(Orthosia hibisci)* is responsible for most of the fruitworm damage to cherries. Injury occurs when the insect feeds on and destroys large numbers of blossoms, and later feeds on small, developing fruit. This later feeding causes cherries to abort and drop from the tree.

Small larvae are difficult to see because they blend with their surroundings. To monitor, shake cherry tree limbs and jar the larvae from the tree to a ground sheet or beating tray.

Pesticides applied at the petal-fall stage will prevent fruitworm feeding on the fruit. To prevent blossom damage, apply sprays at the popcorn stage. When cool weather prevails at this stage — especially in northern cherry-growing areas — avoid using temperature-dependent pesticides. Pesticides with a negative temperature coefficient (those that work better at cooler temperatures, such as pyrethroids) have provided good control.

Peak emergence of the speckled green fruitworm occurs between the white-bud and petal-fall stages. A pheromone is available to help control the timing of sprays for this fruitworm.

Speckled green fruitworm larva damaging young apple.

Pests that suck sap from leaves or are leafminers

THESE ARE SPORADIC PESTS THAT CAN OCCASIONALLY CAUSE DAMAGE. Though they are not generally a problem, it is helpful to be able to recognize them when they occur so that remedial methods can be used to control them.

Chapter 8

Common Name—
Plum Rust Mite
(Plum Nursery Mite)

Scientific Name—
Aculus fockeui (Nal. & Trt.)

Family—
Eriophyidae

A T TIMES, THE PLUM RUST MITE CAN BE A serious problem on cherry, plum and nursery stock.

■ Life Stages

Egg: The egg is flattened and elliptical and glued closely to the leaf. It is translucent when first laid but becomes whitish just before hatching. It is microscopic in size, measuring about 52 microns long and 49 microns wide.

Immature stages: Two immature stages occur — the larva and the nymph — and both resemble the adult. The larva is whitish and somewhat translucent, and measures about 67 microns long and 25 microns wide. The nymph is pale yellowish white and closely resembles the adult. It varies from 105 to 130 microns long and 37 to 42 microns wide. (Note: a micron is 1/1000 of a millimeter.)

Adult: The adult mites are minute, wormlike creatures with two pairs of legs. They are barely visible to the unaided eye when placed on a black background and quite invisible on foliage. The females measure about 157 microns long and 52 microns wide; males are slightly smaller. Newly matured adults are pale yellowish and become brownish yellow with age. This species is arrhenotokously parthenogenetic,

meaning that unfertilized females produce only males.

■ Host Range

In the United States and Canada, this mite has been reported on sweet and tart cherries, European plum and myrobalan plum. The plum varieties Fellenberg, Stanley and Abundance grow poorly when infested with this mite.

■ Injury or Damage

The mites live on both the upper and lower surfaces of the leaves along the midribs. They feed extensively on only young foliage, so injury is confined chiefly to terminal growth. Though the mite is common on mature trees, particularly on water sprouts and terminal shoots, serious injury has been noticed particularly on nursery stock. Feeding causes the leaves to roll upward longitudinally and turn brown. Symptoms may be present over the entire tree. Early injury to the leaf may cause dwarfing of the foliage and a brown or bronze scurfy condition on the lower leaf surface. On plums, individual leaves may exhibit a condition known as "chlorotic fleck."

Symptoms of chlorotic fleck are more or less well defined chlorotic areas (abnormally yellow color of plant tissue resulting from partial failure to develop chlorophyll) that range in size from mere spots to 1 to 2 mm in diameter. The number of flecks on a single

Above: Dead and dying cherry tree leaves caused by plum rust mite damage.

Left: Cherry limbs denuded of leaves by plum rust mite damage.

leaf may vary from one to more than 50. If sufficiently numerous flecks are present, the leaf may become twisted. Severely infested shoots are rosetted, and many leaves do not expand to normal size. Symptoms may occur on the bark of plum shoots in the form of ovoid spots. In cherries, partial defoliation will occur under severe infestations.

■ Factors Affecting Abundance

Temperature and rainfall are the major factors affecting abundance. Warm temperatures shorten the time to complete a generation. Egg incubation requires 15 days in April but only 3.3 days in August; larvae and nymphs require 12.8 days to develop in May but only 3.3 in August. The length of a generation is 18.7 days in May, 11.4 in June, 8.3 in July, 9.0 in August and 14.2 in September.

Normally, the highest mite population occurs in the latter part of July. When heavy midsummer rains prolong the season, however, the mites may be destructively abundant well into September. Dry weather may reduce mite populations by checking tree growth and hastening maturity of the foliage. Only a small percentage of mites survive the winter. This is especially true of those in more exposed situations, such as beneath the bud scales.

■ Life History

Female mites overwinter chiefly in the cavities of dead or shrunken buds, where they may occur in clusters of 20 or more, and to some extent in crevices of twigs and bark.

Some enter healthy buds, usually just within the margins of the outer scales. Many of these die by the following spring. Mites begin to leave the buds and migrate to the expanding foliage as the buds open. They scatter over the leaves and feed for a few days before starting to lay eggs. Necrotic flecking that results from this feeding may be observed within 14 days after a population has become established. At peak populations, which usually occur in late July, several hundred mites may be present on each leaf. The greatest injury occurs during July but may not be evident until later in the season.

Overwintering females start to be produced in August. All the males die in the fall. Males are produced the following spring by the unfertilized females. As many as 15 generations may occur per year, depending on the temperature.

■ Monitoring

In the prebloom stage, examine the cavities of dead or shrunken buds under a binocularscope for overwintering plum rust mites. In midsummer, examine young foliage in terminal growth under a binocularscope for mites.

■ Control

Apply effective materials to control plum rust mites when it appears that they are becoming a problem. In cherries, the plum rust mite often becomes a problem after harvest. If necessary, take chemical control measures after harvest to ensure tree vigor for the winter.

Common Name—
Black Cherry Aphid

Scientific Name—
Myzus cerasi (Fabricius)

Family—
Aphidae

THE BLACK CHERRY APHID FREQUENTLY causes serious injury to sweet cherries and may occasionally be a serious pest on tart cherries. This insect has been reported occurring wherever cherries are grown.

■ Life Stages

Egg: The shiny black winter eggs are oval and less than 1 mm long. The eggs are deposited among the buds or attached to the bark of smaller branches.

Nymph: Nymphs look like the adults but are smaller. Like the adults, the nymphs have piercing-sucking mouthparts that they insert into the leaves to feed.

Adult: The adult black cherry aphid is soft-bodied and black, and measures about 3 mm long. Adult aphids may be winged or wingless. Wingless forms occur during most of the season.

■ Host Range

The black cherry aphid has shown a preference for sweet cherries but will infest and feed on tart cherries. Black Tartarian, Napoleon, Schmidt and Windsor suffer great damage by this insect. Dikeman and Yellow Spanish are not seriously injured. Tart cherry varieties such as Early Richmond, Montmorency and English Morello are attacked less frequently and, when attacked, are injured only slightly. The aphid is found in all cherry-growing areas in Canada and the United States.

■ Injury or Damage

Two types of injury occur on the tree. Curling, twisting and stunting of the leaves are caused by the aphids' feeding on the leaves. Severe infestations may kill young trees and reduce the quantity and quality of the crop on mature trees. Honeydew secreted by the aphids spots foliage and fruits. Later, a fungus grows in the honeydew, causing it to turn black and leaving fruit and foliage smutted and black.

■ Factors Affecting Abundance

High temperatures, combined with adequate moisture, are favorable for aphid development. Individual aphids may reach maturity in one week under favorable conditions. In parthenogenetic insects, this can result in a rapid multiplication of pests.

■ Life History

The shiny black eggs overwinter on buds or bark of smaller branches and start to hatch about the time the buds open.

The stem mothers hatching from the overwintering eggs rapidly establish colonies on the new growth by giving

Above: Curled cherry leaves resulting from infestations of black cherry aphids.

Left: Cherry leaf infested with black cherry aphids.

birth to wingless females. The process is called parthenogenetic ovoviviparous reproduction. Within a few weeks, the tips of the new leaves are curled and the undersides of leaves are covered by aphids and the honeydew they secrete. Several generations are produced in a short time, depending primarily on temperature.

Winged adults develop in the middle of the summer and migrate to other hosts, usually plants of the mustard family, though a few aphids can still be found on the cherry tree. A later generation of male and female winged adults migrates back to the cherry, usually in September and October, and pro-

duces wingless individuals that lay the overwintering eggs. Males appear only in the fall.

■ *Monitoring*

During the prebloom period, look for shiny black eggs on the buds or bark of smaller branches. In postbloom, look for colonies on the undersides of leaves in the growing terminals.

■ *Control*

Contact or systemic aphicides are directed against the stem mothers early in the spring.

Common Name*—

Cherry Leafminer

Scientific Name—
Nepticula slingerlandella (Kft.)

Family—
Nepticulidae

THE CHERRY LEAFMINER WAS FIRST reported by Slingerland in 1909 and Crosby in 1911 near Rochester, N.Y. Braun reported finding it in Ohio in 1917. From 1964 to 1968, this pest was a problem in some tart cherry orchards in Michigan.

■ Life Stages

Egg: The egg is about 0.2 mm by 0.3 mm., oval in outline, dome-shaped in profile and flattened where it attaches to the leaf.

Larva: The larva is a small, cylindrical, oblong, annulated caterpillar. The early instars are transparent; later instars become a more opaque greenish white. The full-grown larva is about 4 to 5 mm long and about 0.4 mm wide. There are four larval instars.

Pupa: The pupa is enclosed in a small, tan-brown cocoon measuring 2 by 2.5 mm. It is broadly oval in outline and domed in profile. It has a thin flange on its anterior third formed by the upper and lower halves of the pupal case closely pressed together. The adult emerges by forcing this flange apart.

Adult: The adult is a small moth with a wing expanse ranging from 3.5 to 5 mm. The forewings are a bronzy black with a shiny band at the outer third. The hind wings are light gray.

■ Host Range

The insect attacks tart cherries, sweet cherries, plums, prunes, wild cherries and wild plums. It has been reported as a pest of Montmorency cherries in Michigan, New York and Ohio. It caused considerable damage to Montmorency cherries in southwestern and west central Michigan in 1967 and 1968.

■ Injury or Damage

The larva is a leafminer. It has caused severe defoliation in cherry orchards that resulted in reduced yield and tree growth.

■ Factors Affecting Abundance

Because pin cherry and plum are the cherry leafminer's favorite hosts, an abundance of these plants in a cherry-growing area could be the source of infestations in commercial cherry orchards.

■ Life History

This pest overwinters in orchard litter in the pupal stage. Adults emerge from late May to mid-June. Peak emergence occurs about two weeks after the

---

* Though referred to as *cherry leafminer* for the purposes of this text, this insect actually has no common name that is approved by the Entomological Society of America (ESA).

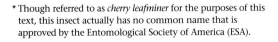

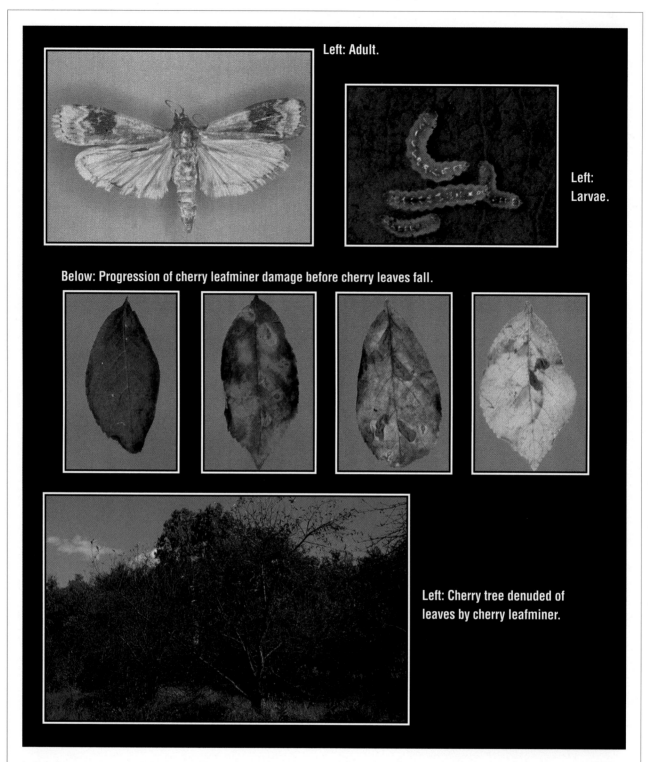

Left: Adult.

Left: Larvae.

Below: Progression of cherry leafminer damage before cherry leaves fall.

Left: Cherry tree denuded of leaves by cherry leafminer.

initial emergence. Mating takes place shortly after emergence. The adults are most active at twilight and rest during the day on or under rough bark. The eggs are laid on the undersides of the leaves. Oviposition begins within one or two days of emergence, with most of the egg laying occurring four to seven days after emergence. The females lay an average of 15 to 20 eggs, though some can deposit as many as 80 eggs. The incubation period is about three weeks.

The larva hatches from the egg through a minute, round hole made in the upper side of the shell, then bores directly into the

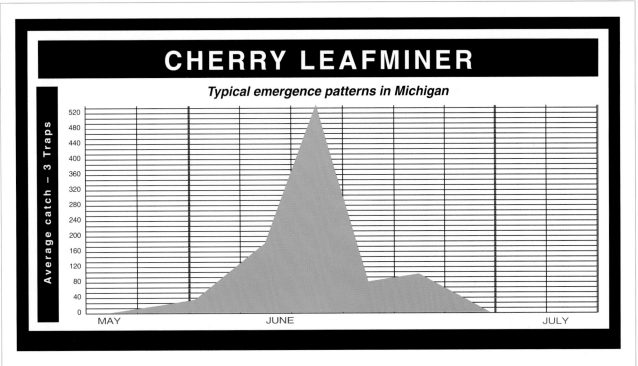

CHERRY LEAFMINER

Typical emergence patterns in Michigan

Average catch – 3 Traps

520
480
440
400
360
320
280
240
200
160
120
80
40
0

MAY   JUNE   JULY

underside of the leaf, so it is not exposed to the outside environment. On hatching, the larvae move immediately to the upper epidermis of the leaf and mine the tissue directly below it. As the larvae grow, they mine a greater percentage of the leaf profile, including a portion of the spongy parenchyma cells. The lower epidermis, however, remains much greener than the upper, which becomes almost transparent.

In the early stages, the mine is tartarous, light-colored and filled with frass. It is difficult to detect, though it can be more readily seen on the upper surface of the leaf. As the larva grows, the mine becomes more extensive. It often makes a 180-degree turn, then widens abruptly to an egg-shaped blotch measuring about ⅛ by ½ inch when completed. The frass in this blotch occurs in an irregular zigzag pattern that never extends entirely to the end.

In this final stage, the larva is visible through the upper cuticle of the leaf. Its head moves slowly from side to side as it mines, while its posterior remains relatively stationary. When mature, the larva cuts a small, semicircular slit through the upper leaf epi-

dermis at the end of the blotch, then drops to the floor of the orchard to pupate. The complete mining cycle is completed in about two weeks.

After dropping to the soil, the larvae spin small, light tan cocoons in the litter that are often attached to bits of partially decayed organic matter. The larvae begin to transform into pupae immediately. They overwinter in the pupal stage. Only one generation occurs per year.

■ Monitoring

About mid-May, use black light traps to catch emerging adults. In summer, look for progressive discoloration of leaves from mining, followed by defoliation. No pheromone is available for this pest.

■ Control

Chemical control should be directed at the adults before the eggs are laid. Two applications — the first at initial emergence and the second two weeks later — can control this pest. Black light traps can be used to time emergence because adults are attracted to them.

Insects that bore into the trunk or branches

IN RECENT YEARS, THE AMERICAN PLUM BORER HAS BECOME A MAJOR PEST IN commercial cherry orchards. The American plum borer attacks a wide variety of forest, ornamental and fruit trees in the United States and Canada. It has been found in commercial plantings of apple, apricot, peach, pear, plum, nectarine, and sweet and tart cherry.

The advent of mechanical harvesting of cherries and resulting injury to the bark have been responsible for this insect's transformation from a minor to a major pest of cherries.

Chapter 9

Common Name—
American Plum Borer

Scientific Name—
Euzophera semifuneralis (Walker)

Family—
Pyralidae

I N RECENT YEARS, THE AMERICAN PLUM BORER has become a major pest of commercial cherry orchards. The American plum borer is often found in close association with the lesser peachtree borer beneath the bark of wounded cherry trees. The damage caused by both of these insects is similar.

■ Life Stages

Egg: The eggs are ovoid with a strongly reticulated surface of triangular facets. They average 0.35 mm wide by 0.60 mm long. Immediately after oviposition the eggs are white, but they change to a tin hue to pink and eventually to a deep pink-red as they develop. They are laid singly or in small, loose clusters.

Larva: The color of the larvae varies from dusky white to grayish purple with the dorsum darker than the underside, though many specimens taken are dark lavender or dark red. The head capsule, cervical shield and anal plate vary from dark yellow to dark brown and often exhibit indefinite pigmented areas. Only long and distinct primary setae are present, giving the larva a bristly appearance. The larva is 18 to 25 mm long; its head capsule is 1.7 mm wide.

Hibernaculum: The larvae overwinter in silken cocoons that appear identical to those in which they pupate. All instars are capable of forming them for overwintering purposes. The hibernacula are most often located amidst frass accumulations, though the frass particles are not a structural component of the hibernaculum, as with the lesser peachtree borer.

Pupa: Pupae are enclosed in chitinous cases within silken cocoons beneath the bark near previous feeding sites. Female pupae average 12 mm in length; males, 11 mm. Immediately after pupation the pupae are translucent white, but they quickly change to brown and eventually near-black prior to adult emergence, which occurs in about 2 to 2½ weeks. When the adult emerges, the remaining pupal skin is usually retained within the cocoon, though occasionally it may protrude slightly.

Adult: The adult males and females are dull grayish purple with an irregular transverse band two-thirds the distance to the outer forewing. The hind wing is entirely grayish tan, and both wings have a short fringe on the outer margin. The average wingspan is between 20 and 25 mm. The female is slightly larger than the male.

■ Host Range

The American plum borer has been located in a wide variety of forest, ornamental and fruit trees across southern Canada and the United States. Infestations of this insect have been reported in commercial plantings of sweet and tart cherry, apple, apricot, peach, pear, plum and nectarine.

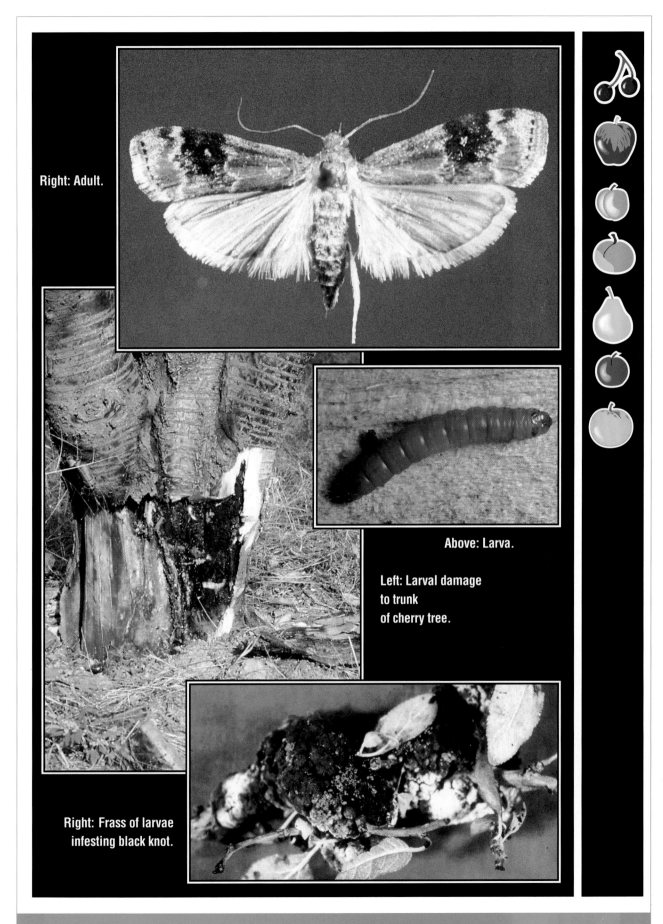

Right: Adult.

Above: Larva.

Left: Larval damage
to trunk
of cherry tree.

Right: Frass of larvae
infesting black knot.

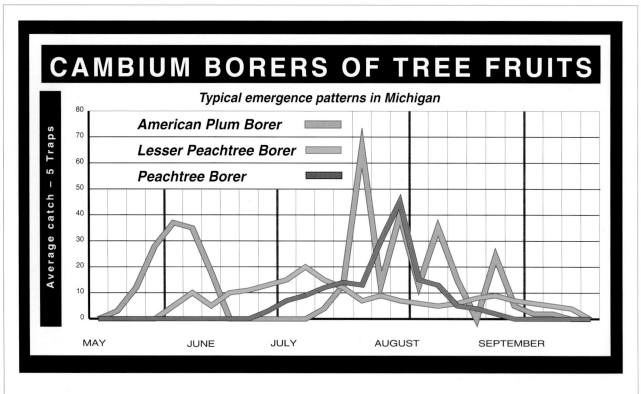

CAMBIUM BORERS OF TREE FRUITS

Typical emergence patterns in Michigan

- American Plum Borer
- Lesser Peachtree Borer
- Peachtree Borer

Average catch – 5 Traps

MAY JUNE JULY AUGUST SEPTEMBER

■ *Injury or Damage*

American plum borer larvae feed on the cambium of the tree. On apple it has been reported feeding on burr knot tissues in association with the dogwood borer. Infestation of healthy, non-wounded tissue is rare. In cherries, 90 percent of all larvae will be found in the 2- or 3-foot trunk area between the ground and the bases of the scaffold branches. They are not commonly found on the branches above the main trunk.

The larvae tend to be somewhat gregarious — for as many as 20 larvae to occur around a single wound site on a tree is not uncommon. As a result of larval feeding, wounds often do not heal properly, and tree vigor is continually diminished as more cambial tissue is consumed. The extent of larval feeding is seldom apparent because the bark directly above the immediate feeding area appears normal, even when the larvae have advanced several inches from the wounded area. With enough time, they will completely girdle the tree. A 4- to 6-inch scaffold limb can be rendered commercially unproductive

in two years. Open wounds, sap flows and frass accumulations also act as excellent nutrient reservoirs for fungi and other insects that further damage tissue.

Second-generation larvae feeding on black knot of plum have been observed leaving the black knot to feed on ripening fruit.

■ *Factors Affecting Abundance*

The advent of mechanical harvesting of cherries has been responsible for this insect changing from a minor to a major pest of cherries. The highest infestations occur in older orchards that have experienced several years of wounding, especially where mechanical harvesting is used. The larvae thrive on cambium tissue, and any wounds that expose cambium are prone to infestation. Open wounds and sap flows are very attractive to the females as oviposition sites.

Black knot on plums is extremely attractive to the American plum borer. Large populations often develop on these sites.

Life History

The insect overwinters beneath the bark as a larva within a hibernaculum formed during mid- to late October. It resumes feeding in early spring as temperatures rise. The overwintering larvae begin pupating in early to mid-April, and first-brood adults emerge in early May. These first-brood adults continue to emerge into early June, with peak emergence in mid-May at the white-bud stage. The adults generally emerge about midafternoon. They live for a maximum of two weeks. They are nocturnal in habit and, because of their cryptic coloration, are seldom seen in the field. In the resting position, they assume a twiglike posture by resting motionless, with the head and thorax held away from the twig and the abdomen pressed tightly against the bark. They fly over short distances with an erratic flutter. Egg laying occurs throughout this period, with eggs deposited singly or in small clusters in cracks near the cambium, especially in and around wounds. Each female deposits an average of 25 to 50 eggs over a period of two to three days. The eggs are laid at night. The larvae emerge in about nine days. Development time from first-instar larvae to pupae is about five weeks.

The larvae feed beneath the bark, favoring areas with available cambium and frass accumulations for protection. For this generation, pupation occurs from mid- to late June. The second-generation adults emerge from early July to mid-September, peaking in mid-July. This second emergence and egg-laying period coincides with most mechanical harvesting schedules for cherries, thus creating an ideal situation for oviposition because wounds are readily available. The following generation of larvae continues feeding until temperatures fall and trees harden off in about mid-October, at which time larvae seek overwintering sites beneath the bark and form hibernacula.

Monitoring

Examine the trunk area up to 3 feet from the ground level for frass and fresh gumming with frass. Place pheromone traps in trees at the end of April. Replace caps and traps near the end of June for the summer generation. Use three traps per block. An average of more than six adults per trap per week indicates a potential problem. Be aware that alternate host plants, especially near wooded areas, can interfere with trap catches.

Control

Apply an effective pesticide with a hydraulic gun directed at the trunk at the white-bud or petal-fall stage on tart or sweet cherries, when the first generation adults are emerging. Some pesticides will provide seasonal control of first and second generations with a single application at the white-bud or petal-fall stage.

Iɴ ᴛʜᴇ ᴘᴀsᴛ, ᴘᴇᴀᴄʜᴛʀᴇᴇ ᴀɴᴅ ʟᴇssᴇʀ ᴘᴇᴀᴄʜᴛʀᴇᴇ ʙᴏʀᴇʀs ᴡᴇʀᴇ ɢᴇɴᴇʀᴀʟʟʏ ᴄᴏɴsɪᴅᴇʀᴇᴅ ᴍɪɴᴏʀ ᴏʀ ᴏᴄᴄᴀsɪᴏɴᴀʟ ᴘᴇsᴛs ᴏғ ᴄʜᴇʀʀɪᴇs. Cʜᴀɴɢᴇs ɪɴ ʜᴀʀᴠᴇsᴛ-ɪɴɢ ᴍᴇᴛʜᴏᴅs — ɴᴀᴍᴇʟʏ, ᴛʜᴇ ᴜsᴇ ᴏғ ᴍᴇᴄʜᴀɴɪᴄᴀʟ sʜᴀᴋᴇʀs — ʜᴀs ᴄʜᴀɴɢᴇᴅ ᴛʜᴇ sᴛᴀᴛᴜs ᴏғ ʙᴏʀᴇʀs ᴀᴛᴛᴀᴄᴋɪɴɢ ᴄʜᴇʀʀʏ ᴛʀᴇᴇs ғʀᴏᴍ ᴍɪɴᴏʀ ᴛᴏ ᴍᴀᴊᴏʀ ᴘᴇsᴛs.

For complete information on the peachtree borer, see page 216. For complete information on the lesser peachtree borer, see page 219.

About 80 percent of the tart cherries in the United States are grown in Michigan. To reduce time and labor costs, mechanical equipment has been developed over the years to harvest cherries. In this process, the tree trunk and limbs are shaken so the cherries are jarred from the branches onto revolving catchers made of fabric. Mechanical shakers bruise the limbs and trunk, as well as disturb the root area near the surface of the soil.

Bruised and injured tissue on branches and trunks is particularly attractive to the female lesser peachtree borer for oviposition. Though the relationship of increased peachtree borer damage and mechanical harvesting is not as clearly known as that of lesser peachtree borer and mechanical harvesting, it appears probable that the lateral movement of the tree trunk during the shaking operation provides easier access to the base of the tree just below the ground level for peachtree borer larvae on hatching, particularly larvae emerging from eggs laid on the soil near the tree.

Since the advent of mechanical shakers, the status of borers attacking cherry trees has changed dramatically from minor to major pests. The lesser peachtree borer requires injured tissue to become established — it will not attack healthy tissue. Upon hatching, the larvae feed on the tender growing bark at the edges of injured areas. They may continue to feed until the limb is girdled and killed. Injured areas are also susceptible to attack by valsa canker fungus.

In the past, the peachtree borer rarely attacked tart cherries. Now, infestations of this pest are far more common. The injury is similar to that on peach trees — larval activity is restricted to the trunk area from a few inches above to 6 inches below the soil surface. Larval feeding may kill young trees by completely girdling the trunks. More mature trees may not be killed but are often severely injured and made more susceptible to other insects, diseases and environmental conditions. An organophosphate called chlorpyrifos is, to date, the only insecticide that will control in a single application both the lesser peachtree borer and the peachtree borer, as well as another major pest of cherries, the American plum borer. For seasonal control, a dilute application of chlorpyrifos should be applied with a hydraulic gun at the white-bud or petal-fall stage. Thorough coverage of the scaffold limbs and trunk, including the base of the tree, is essential.

Peach, Plum, Nectarine & Apricot Pests

Insects that burrow into and feed inside the fruit or suck sap from the leaves

MANY OF THE PESTS LISTED FOR APPLES ARE PROBLEMS ON STONE FRUITS as well. For example, plum curculio, mites and leafrollers may attack stone fruits.

The Oriental fruit moth is a major problem on peaches. Pheromones are useful for determining the emergence of this insect's generations.

Chapter 10

Common Name—
Oriental Fruit Moth

Scientific Name—
Grapholitha molesta (Busck)

Family—
Tortricidae

THE ORIENTAL FRUIT MOTH HAS BECOME A general pest of peaches and other fruit crops since its appearance in the north central states in the mid-1920s. When first introduced, the pest caused heavy losses that threatened the fruit industry. In recent years, losses have been less severe because more effective insecticides are available.

■ Life Stages

Egg: The egg looks like a small, flat scale adhering to the leaf or fruit. It is the size of a pinhead, 0.5 to 0.7 mm across, usually white, often semi-transparent and faintly reticulated.

Larva: The newly hatched larva is white with a black head and measures about 1.4 mm in length. When full grown, the larva has a brownish head and a pink body and measures 10 to 11 mm long. The head capsule is 1.1 mm wide.

Pupa: The pupa is brownish, turning nearly black just before the adult emerges. It is about 6 to 7 mm long.

Adult: The adults are small, grayish brown moths, with wings silvery on the undersurface and figured with light, wavy lines above. They are inconspicuous when the wings are folded. The male and female are similar, but the male's abdomen is more slender than the female's. The wingspread is 12.5 mm; body length is 4 to 5 mm.

■ Host Range

The Oriental fruit moth attacks peach, apricot, nectarine, almond, apple, quince, pear, plum and cultivated cherry. It also attacks many woody ornamental plants. The Oriental fruit moth is found in all areas where peaches and nectarines are grown.

■ Injury or Damage

The larva attacks the twigs and fruits of most host plants and is now a common pest of apples, regardless of whether peaches or nectarines are grown in the area.

Twig Injury

During May, June and July, when the terminal parts of rapidly growing twigs are succulent, they are frequently attacked by the Oriental fruit moth. Succulent peach twigs are exceedingly attractive to the larvae. Plum, apple and cherry may occasionally be moderately infested. Young trees are usually more heavily attacked than old bearing trees, and rapidly growing trees have more injured twigs than stunted trees.

In peach, a newly hatched larva usually enters the tender growing twig at its tip near the base of a young leaf, whereas a half-grown larva that has abandoned an old injured twig may enter a new one at the axil of a fully developed leaf. After entering the twig, the larva consumes the central part and gradually works its way down the shoot for

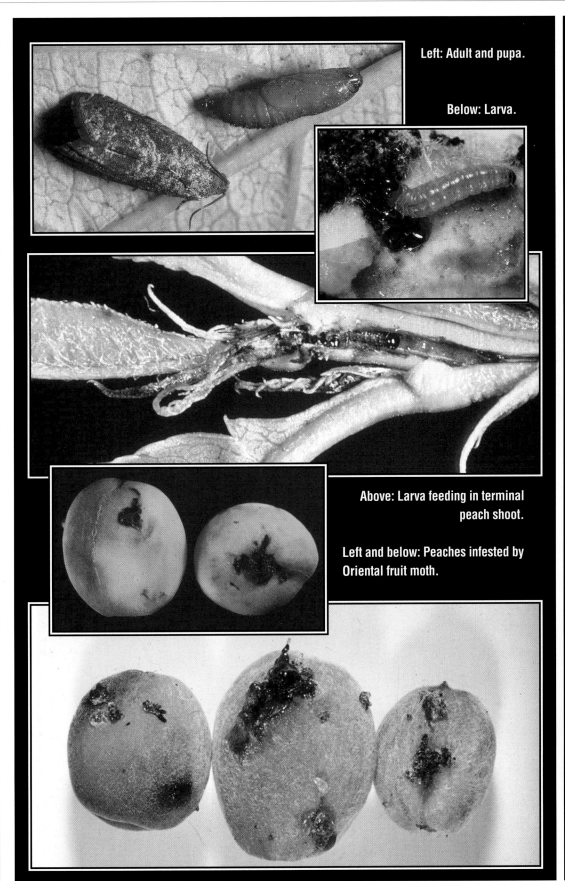

Left: Adult and pupa.

Below: Larva.

Above: Larva feeding in terminal peach shoot.

Left and below: Peaches infested by Oriental fruit moth.

2 to 6 inches. When a twig is no longer desirable as food, the larva makes an exit hole somewhere along the gouged-out channel and emerges. If it needs more food to complete its development, it may enter another twig or a fruit. One larva may enter two to five twigs or even more. On emerging from a twig, a full-grown larva will seek a place to spin a cocoon.

Twigs infested by larvae usually have one or more wilted leaves. When an upright twig has one small wilted leaf, it means that a larva has recently entered it, probably 24 to 28 hours before the time of observation. As a larva progresses down into a twig, successive leaves become wilted, with the number depending on the distance the larva penetrates. Injured twigs with dark-colored or dry leaves and exudations of gum no longer harbor larvae.

The only fruit trees in which Oriental fruit moths are likely to cause conspicuous injury to the twigs are peach and apple. In young trees when terminal twigs are attacked, several lateral shoots will appear below them and grow rapidly. Some of these shoots may also be injured by later generations, and then secondary lateral shoots will be produced. Under severe and continued attack, the tree may become somewhat bushy. In nurseries, the rapidly growing shoots of recently budded peach trees are sometimes severely attacked. The result is crooked stems.

Fruit Injury

In harvested peaches, two distinct types of injury are visible. One is caused by feeding on or entrance into the side of the fruit early in the season when the fruit is small. Frequently called "old injury," this is usually caused by larvae that have abandoned the twigs and gone to the fruit. It may take place where two peaches are touching, where a leaf rests against a peach or on the open surface of the fruit. As the peach grows, gum exudes from the point of entrance. The exudations turn dark as the season progresses, and a black blotch will be present on the peach at picking time. The infested fruit of early varieties usually shows a high percentage of side entrances; other types of entrance are not so common.

Injury caused by entrance at the stem, sometimes called "new injury," occurs when the fruit is almost full grown, especially in late varieties. This injury is caused by newly hatched larvae that go directly to the fruit. As a larva wanders over twigs and leaves in search of food, the first part of the peach it reaches is likely to be tissue near the stem end. The outside skin surrounding the stem is tender, and the larva promptly enters at this point and leaves a small pile of frass, which is easily overlooked unless the fruit is examined carefully. When fruit is sorted in packing sheds, this type of injury goes unnoticed unless it is prominent. Stem entrance in late varieties may be found in more than half of the infested fruits. Generally, the later the variety of peach, the greater the percentage of stem entrances and the smaller the percentage of side entrances.

A type of injury characterized by no visible entrance is called "concealed injury." About half the injury in late peaches may be of this type. In orchards where fruit injury is severe, it is possible to examine a peach with great care and find no external sign of injury, yet when the peach is cut open it contains a larva feeding on the inside tissue. The larva under these conditions entered the fruit through the green stem. In the orchard, it has been repeatedly noted that a newly hatched larva may enter the side of the stem and work its way down into the fruit without in any way injuring the skin. When the peach is picked, the short stem remains on the tree, and all evidence of how the larva entered the fruit is destroyed. Concealed injury is apparently produced by newly hatched larvae, not by larvae that have abandoned the twigs.

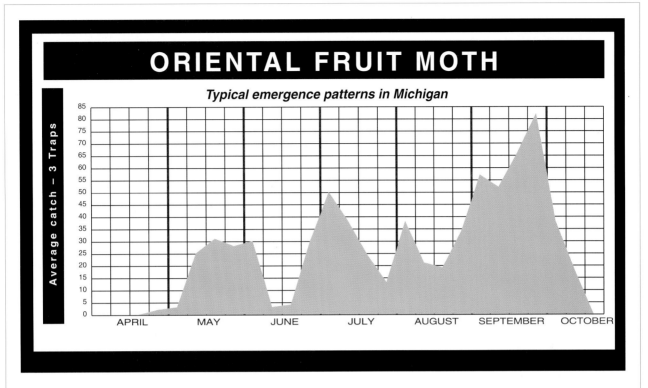

ORIENTAL FRUIT MOTH

Typical emergence patterns in Michigan

Average catch – 3 Traps

APRIL MAY JUNE JULY AUGUST SEPTEMBER OCTOBER

Once a larva has entered a fruit, it may make a long, irregular channel through the soft tissue or confine its activities to a small area. It frequently does much of its feeding around the pit and characteristically leaves much sawdustlike frass in this area. Its feeding in ripe or nearly ripe peaches is thus distinguishable from that of the plum curculio, which is more likely to cut cavities in which the frass is relatively inconspicuous. Unless the infestation is severe, there is usually only one larva to a fruit, though third-generation larvae frequently enter fruits through the conspicuous black, gummy side injury caused by an earlier attack. When a larva has completed its development in a peach, it tunnels to the surface and leaves the fruit through a clean hole.

So far as is known, a larva will not leave one partly consumed fruit to attack another and will not abandon a fruit to attack a twig. Early in the growing season, some of the larvae enter very small peaches. When infested at this stage, the fruit always drops, usually before the larva has issued from it. Brown rot infection in peaches frequently starts at the entrance or exit holes of larvae.

■ *Factors Affecting Abundance*

Oriental fruit moths are most active on quiet, fair days toward sundown. Maximum egg production occurs at 70 degrees F and above. A succession of days when the temperature is below 60 degrees F will inhibit egg production; temperatures of about 80 degrees F will retard egg deposition.

Wet weather following a dry spell kills many of the larvae in the twigs. They apparently drown in the flow of sap that occurs. Severe winters may kill up to 90 percent of overwintering cocoons, but usually enough survive to produce a normal spring generation.

Natural parasites, such as *Trichogramma minutum* (an egg parasite) and *Macrocentrus ancylivorus* (a larval parasite), may parasitize 50 to 90 percent of the Oriental fruit moth eggs or larvae. Growers cannot rely on parasites for commercial control of this insect, however.

■ Life History

The Oriental fruit moth has three full generations and occasionally a partial fourth generation each year in the Midwest and the northeastern peach-growing regions. The moths overwinter as full-grown larvae in cocoons in tree bark crevices, weed stems, trash on the ground, fruit containers and packing sheds. Most of the larvae that over-winter on mature peach trees are found on the lower 2 feet of the trunk; the remainder, on the upper parts of the tree.

In the spring, the larvae change into pupae. Pupation begins about mid-March. The adults begin to emerge about the time Alberta peach blossom buds show pink. Though they will continue to emerge for about two months, peak emergence of the first generation occurs about the last week in May or in early June. On peach trees, the great majority of the eggs are laid on the leaf surfaces; the rest are laid on fruit stems and bark.

The Oriental fruit moth, like the codling moth, has a marked daily flight period in the evening. That's when the eggs are laid. Females lay from 30 to 60 eggs. The incubation period averages about seven days in July and August, with a minimum of four days.

On hatching, most of the first-generation larvae bore into the twigs; only a few attack the fruit. First-generation larvae usually damage two or three twigs before reaching maturity. The length of the larval feeding period can vary from 10 days to 10 weeks, with an average of about three weeks. During the summer, the average length of the developmental period from newly deposited egg to adult emergence is about six weeks, with a minimum of 24 days during very hot weather.

The second generation of adults generally begins to emerge about July 1, with increases or decreases in numbers dependent on weather conditions. Larvae of this generation attack both peach twigs and fruits. As the twigs harden, the partially grown larvae leave them and enter the fruits. Fruit injury in July or early August is indicated by the exudation of large masses of gum mixed with frass. Second-generation larvae usually attack three or four twigs before reaching maturity.

Adults of the third generation emerge in early to mid-August, depending on weather conditions. The third-generation larvae appear about mid-August and may continue to hatch in large numbers until mid-September. This generation is the major cause of wormy fruit at harvest, often with little or no external sign of injury. The majority of the third-generation larvae grow to maturity, spin cocoons and remain in them over winter. In very warm seasons, a few may pupate and emerge as adults that may produce a few eggs and larvae late in the season.

■ Monitoring

Using 45 degrees F as a base, degree-days (DD) for Oriental fruit moth activity* are:

175 DD	first adult emergence.
250 DD	first eggs laid.
325 to	
425 DD	peak adult emergence.
525 DD	peak egg laying.
950 DD	first emergence of second-generation adults.
1,100 DD	first eggs laid by second generation.
1,300 to	
1,425 DD	peak emergence of second-generation adults.
1,500	peak egg laying by second-generation adults.
1,900 DD	first emergence of third-generation adults.
2,200 to	
2,450 DD	peak emergence of third-generation adults.
2,500 DD	peak egg laying by third-generation adults.

*Data from MSU PETE model.

■ *Control*

Use pheromone traps to monitor adult activity and to time spray applications. Pheromone disruption of Oriental fruit moth is now legal in some states. Hang traps in early April and count and remove moths twice weekly. Use 10 traps for a 10-acre orchard, with two traps inside and the rest as border traps. Place traps at least 100 feet apart to prevent interference between traps. Sprays to control the first generation should be applied about six days after the first peak adult emergence. This application usually coincides with sprays for plum curculio control. Apply sprays for the second generation three days after peak adult emergence to coincide with peak egg laying of the second generation.

The braconid wasp *Macrocentrus ancylivorus* is an important parasite that destroys many of the first- and second-generation larvae.

Growers spraying for the third-generation fruit moth need to take into consideration expected harvest dates of their cultivars. Because ripening peaches are most susceptible to fruit moth attack, third-generation larvae are largely responsible for wormy fruit at harvest. To protect ripening peaches, sprays should be applied 10 to 12 days before harvest. If peak emergence of third-generation adults occurs some weeks before harvest, sprays should be applied about three days after peak emergence of adults to coincide with peak egg laying. Additional sprays may be necessary, depending on harvest dates.

Common Name—

Green Peach Aphid

Scientific Name—
Myzus persicae (Sulzer)

Family—
Aphidae

THE GREEN PEACH APHID IS A NATIVE European pest. It was first described as a peach pest in Europe in 1761.

■ Life Stages

Egg: Eggs are shiny black, about 0.50 mm long and 0.25 mm wide.

Nymph: Young nymphs look yellowish green and have three darker green lines on the back of the abdomen.

Adult: Stem mothers, which appear in the spring and fall, are deep pink. The adults developing from the stem mothers are pear-shaped, about 1 to 5 mm long, and yellowish green with a median and two lateral dark green stripes that pass over the abdomen. A pair of cylindrical cornicles are present at the end of the abdomen.

■ Host Range

The green peach aphid feeds on a variety of host plants, including peach, plum, apricot, cherry, ornamentals, vegetables and flowering plants.

■ Injury or Damage

Green peach aphids feed on leaves and extract sap, causing the leaves to turn yellow and drop. Honeydew is excreted as a waste product and acts as a foundation for a black, sooty fungus that causes smutting of leaves and fruit. The green peach aphid transmits a variety of diseases on other crops, particularly vegetables. It is not uncommon to find hundreds or even thousands of aphids per tree.

■ Factors Affecting Abundance

Aphids have a high reproductive potential. Weather, including wind, rain and cool temperatures, regulates populations. A number of predators and parasites, including ladybird beetles, lacewings, syrphid fly larvae and chalcid wasps, prey on them.

■ Life History

The green peach aphid has a complex life history, with five distinct morphological forms and two behavioral forms. This pest also needs to complete several generations during midsummer on host plants other than peach. As cold weather approaches in the fall, females fly to peaches and give birth to female nymphs. These females mate with males as they return from summer host plants and either lay eggs under peach buds or overwinter as adults without laying eggs. In the spring when the first peach leaves appear, the overwintering females establish themselves as stem mothers. This spring generation triggers two or three more generations of females on peach; the females give birth parthenogenetically to wingless young. By June, winged adults appear and the aphids leave the peach trees by July to migrate to

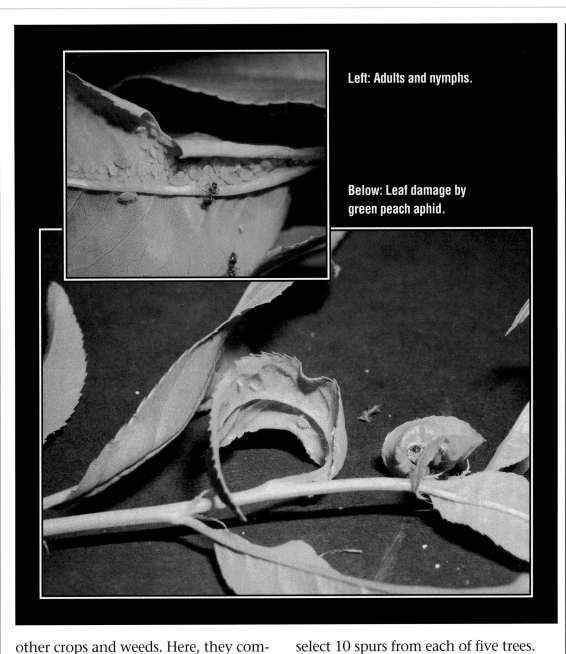

Left: Adults and nymphs.

Below: Leaf damage by green peach aphid.

other crops and weeds. Here, they complete several summer generations of their life cycle before returning to peach trees in the fall to lay eggs or overwinter as adults.

■ *Monitoring*

Aphids are a problem early in the season and remain on peaches for two or three generations — until about the middle of June — before leaving for other crops. The aphids feed on the undersides of the leaves. In a block of peaches, select 10 spurs from each of five trees. Treatment is recommended if an average of one colony or more per tree is found.

■ *Control*

This pest is difficult to control because it has developed resistance to many pesticides. Encourage the buildup of predators and parasites. When using an effective pesticide, thorough coverage, particularly of the lower leaf surfaces, is necessary.

THE PLUM CURCULIO IS A MAJOR PEST OF STONE FRUITS, AFFECTING (IN RANKING ORDER) NECTARINE, PLUM, CHERRY, PEACH AND APRICOT. OVERWINTERING ADULT BEETLES ATTACK THE FRUIT SOON AFTER IT FORMS AND EAT HOLES THROUGH THE SKIN AND FEED ON THE PULP, USUALLY NEXT TO THE PIT.

For complete information on this pest, see page 35.

The female makes distinctive, crescent-shaped wounds on the skin when laying eggs. In many cases, the beetles introduce spores of brown rot fungus to fruit during feeding. Infested fruits usually fall prematurely, though cherries remain on the tree until ripe. In early peach varieties, the fruit matures about the same time as the curculio larvae, and larvae may be found in these peaches at harvest.

To distinguish between larvae of plum curculio and Oriental fruit moth, examine the leg area. Plum curculio larvae have no legs; Oriental fruit moth larvae have three pairs of true legs and five pairs of prolegs on the abdominal segments.

To distinguish between cherry fruit fly larvae and plum curculio larvae, examine the head capsule. Plum curculio larvae have distinct, hard, brown head capsules with well developed opposable mandibles. Cherry fruit fly larvae (maggots) do not have head capsules and have curved mouth hooks rather than mandibles (jawbones). Furthermore, cherries infested with maggots will sink in water cooling tanks at harvest; cherries infested with curculio larvae will float because of large air spaces left around the pit during feeding. Cherries infested by plum curculio may be floated off the rest of the cherries and disposed of.

Plum curculio is capable of causing great damage and is considered a difficult pest to control. Unfortunately, there are no pheromones for this insect and no reliable monitoring methods other than jarring branches over a beating tray or light-colored ground cover for collection and identification. If using this monitoring method, do so during the petal-fall or shuck-split stage or during the first-cover period, especially after a few days of warm weather. Select trees near wintering hibernation areas such as woodlots, fences or ditches.

Apply sprays at the petal-fall and shuck-split stages. Be aware that if the weather is unfavorable during bloom and shuck-split, adults may not leave hibernation quarters until after shuck-split is over. Under such conditions, you may need a first-cover application and possibly a second-cover spray.

THOUGH THE TARNISHED PLANT BUG IS THE MAJOR PEST OF PEACHES, A NUMBER OF OTHER PLANT BUGS ALSO ATTACK THIS STONE FRUIT. THESE INCLUDE THE OAK PLANT BUG, *LYGOCORIS OMNIVAGUS* (KNIGHT); THE HICKORY PLANT BUG, *LYGOCORIS CARYAE* (KNIGHT); AND THE GREEN STINK BUG, *ACROSTERNUM HILARE* (SAY). PLANT BUGS ARE MEMBERS OF FAMILY MIRIDAE; THE GREEN STINK BUG BELONGS TO THE FAMILY PENTATOMIDAE.

For complete information on tarnished plant bugs, see page 90.

Injuries caused by these pests can be classified into general categories, including blossom injury and fruit drop, cat-facing injury, scarred injury, water-soaked injury and gummosis. Blossom injury, fruit drop and cat-facing are the most serious kinds of damage caused by the tarnished plant bug.

Blossom injury and fruit drop include blossoms that drop as a result of plant bug attack and the fruit that drops as a result of feeding injury between the petal-fall and shuck-off stages. The tarnished plant bug causes blossom and fruit dropping by piercing and injuring these parts in feeding activities. This can take place from the bloom stage until about a month after bloom. About one-third of blossom dropping is caused by tarnished plant bug injury.

Cat-facing injury includes all types of injury involving fruit deformation. Cat-facing results from plant bug feeding between the shuck-split stage and the time when fruits reach a diameter of about 20 mm. The damage usually consists of shallow to deep depressions that are covered with a brown, corky tissue. Except for small, scattered patches of grayish or brownish fuzz, these depressions usually are free of fuzz. There is usually a mass of gum located in the center of the injury. Scars vary from 2 to 26 mm in diameter. Fruits attacked early usually drop, though those larger than 20 mm in diameter tend to remain and exhibit no other fruit deformation at harvest except scarring.

The peak of cat-facing injury from tarnished plant bug occurs within a few days after shuck-off.

In typical scarred injury, damage consists of a group of brownish scars concentrated in a relatively small area. Except for small patches of discolored fuzz and a small mass of gum that is usually found in the center of the injury, the brown, corky scarred areas are normally free of fuzz. The width of the scars varies from 1 to 2 mm, although in some areas, numerous scars blend to form larger scars that can measure up to 9 by 25 mm. Some scars may have a concentration of reddish pigment in the skin around the edges.

Fruits with water-soaked injury have small, dark green areas that appear water-soaked. Water-soaked areas are round and range from 2 to 3 mm in diameter. When the skin of the fruit is removed, the injury shows as dark green, water-soaked areas in the flesh. Flesh injuries are about 2 mm deep and have the same size and shape as skin injuries.

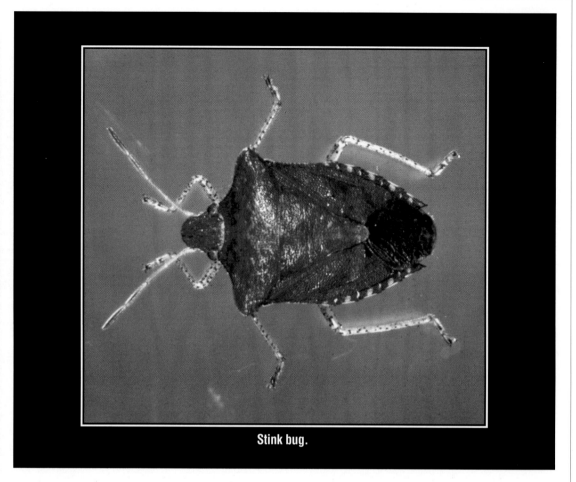

Stink bug.

Gummosis injury is characterized by an oozing of clear gum after the epidermal tissues are punctured by feeding insects. Though gummosis is often associated with cat-facing and scarring, it can occur alone. Early in the season, injured fruits exude gum in long strings. This is usually followed by cat-facing or scarring unless the fruit drops. Late in the season, when gummosis occurs without other injury, the gum pours out in small droplets and is sometimes darkened by the growth of a sooty fungus. Scarring and gummosis injury inflicted by tarnished plant bug occur from five to 10 weeks after bloom. Some peaches, especially those attacked by the tarnished plant bug between seven and 10 weeks after bloom, may show both water-soaked and gummosis injury.

Tarnished plant bugs are most abundant at peach bloom. Their numbers gradually decrease as the season progresses.

The oak plant bug overwinters in the egg stage and the eggs hatch at about the time that oak leaves appear. The nymphs feed on the oak and mature in early June. The adults gradually migrate from the oak to the peach trees from four to 10 weeks after bloom, with the greatest numbers found from five to six weeks after bloom. Numbers then decrease rapidly. Because the oak plant bug does not appear in the orchard until a month after bloom, cat-facing damage caused by this pest is minimal, and even when it occurs, the deformity is much less severe than that caused by the tarnished plant bug. The most visible injury caused by the oak plant bug is scarring and gumming that occur from five to six weeks after bloom. Water-soaked injury inflicted by this pest occurs from six to eight weeks after bloom, while gummosis alone occurs from seven to 10 weeks after bloom. The various types of injury caused by the oak plant bug are similar to and cannot be distinguished from those caused by the tarnished plant bug.

The hickory plant bug has a life history similar to that of the oak plant bug except that the eggs are laid on species of hickory. The hickory plant bug migrates to peach orchards at about the same time as the oak plant bug, and the seasonal incidence of the various types of injury produced is similar to that of the oak plant bug.

The green stink bug is generally not a serious pest. Injury from them is usually sporadic and confined to trees bordering woodlots. Peaches attacked by this pest have sunken areas or pits. The skin is not broken, although the fruit is often badly deformed. When the fruit is attacked near maturity, the injury may appear as shallow, water-soaked depressions, although the skin does not have the dark brown scars or masses of gum characteristic of injury caused by other plant bugs.

Adult stink bugs are bright green, flat and shield-shaped, and measure about 16 mm long. They emit an odor when handled. They overwinter as adults among fallen leaves and other debris, mostly in woods, then emerge in the spring to lay their eggs on various wild trees and shrubs, including elder, basswood, wild cherry and dogwood. Eggs are seldom laid on peach trees. Most of the injury caused by this pest is from green stink bugs that breed on wild plants and disperse to peach orchards after they have matured in late summer.

The adults feed on the fruit early in the season; later, the nymphs cause some injury. Because of the adults' bright coloration and large size, visual inspection of trees can help you detect their presence. Monitor green stink bugs by jarring the branches over a ground sheet or beating tray. For plant bugs in peaches, hang reflecting, white, rectangular sticky traps about 3 feet from the ground. If possible, hang the traps along the periphery of a block near wooded areas. Use three traps per block, or one trap for every 3 to 5 acres. Monitor weekly from pink stage until midsummer. The threshold level for peaches is one plant bug per trap.

Insects that bore into the trunk, branches, twigs or roots

THE BORERS ARE MAJOR PROBLEMS OF STONE FRUITS. THE PEACHTREE BORER IS A major pest of young trees, and a single larva can kill a tree. The lesser peachtree borer can weaken mature trees and provide openings for diseases such as valsa canker.

Chapter 11

Common Name—
Peachtree Borer

Scientific Name—
Synanthedon exitiosa (Say)

Family—
Sesiidae

THE PEACHTREE BORER KILLS MORE PEACH TREES in the United States than any other insect. In the north central states, where there is a high incidence of valsa canker and winter injury, the lesser peachtree borer probably ranks higher as a general pest than the peachtree borer. However, control programs for the peachtree borer must begin the year young trees are planted and must continue for the life of the planting.

■ Life Stages

Egg: The egg is about 0.65 mm long, chestnut brown or reddish brown, ellipsoidal and slightly flattened at the sides, with light-colored, waxlike, elevated lines that form hexagonally sculptured areas on the egg surface.

Larva: The larva is white or cream-colored with a yellowish brown to dark brown head. It has three pairs of segmented thoracic legs. Abdominal prolegs are present on the third, fourth, fifth, sixth and last abdominal segments. All of the prolegs have two rows of crochets (hooks) except the last pair, which have one row of crochets. The larvae vary in size from 1.6 mm for newly hatched larvae to 38 mm for full-grown larvae.

Pupa: When full grown, the larva leaves the burrow under the bark and constructs a cocoon made of silken threads and bits of wood or frass. Approximately 90 percent of the cocoons are found in the top layer of soil within 2 inches of the tree, but some may be found attached to the tree near the ground line. In infested trees, cocoons may be found in the burrows. Female pupae average 19 mm long (slightly larger than male pupae), are darker and show an orange band on the fourth abdominal segment just prior to adult emergence. Female pupae have one row of spines on the seventh abdominal segment; male pupae have two rows of spines. The length of the pupal stage varies from 18 to 30 days, depending on temperature.

Adult: The adults are clear-wing moths (only the veins and edges are colored). The females are slightly larger than the males — the wing span of the female is 30 to 33 mm and that of the male, 25 to 28 mm. The general color of the moth is dark steel-blue. The fourth or fourth and fifth abdominal segments of the female's body are covered by bright orange scales. The female's body is usually more robust than the male's, especially when filled with eggs. In the male, various areas of the third, fourth, fifth and sixth abdominal segments may be fringed with white or yellow scales. The slender abdomen of the male terminates in a wedge-shaped tuft of scales tipped with white.

■ Host Range

The peachtree borer is a major pest of peaches but sometimes causes serious damage to cultivated cherry, plum, apricot, nectarine and related ornamental shrubs. The peachtree borer has been reported in all fruit-growing areas of the United States and Canada.

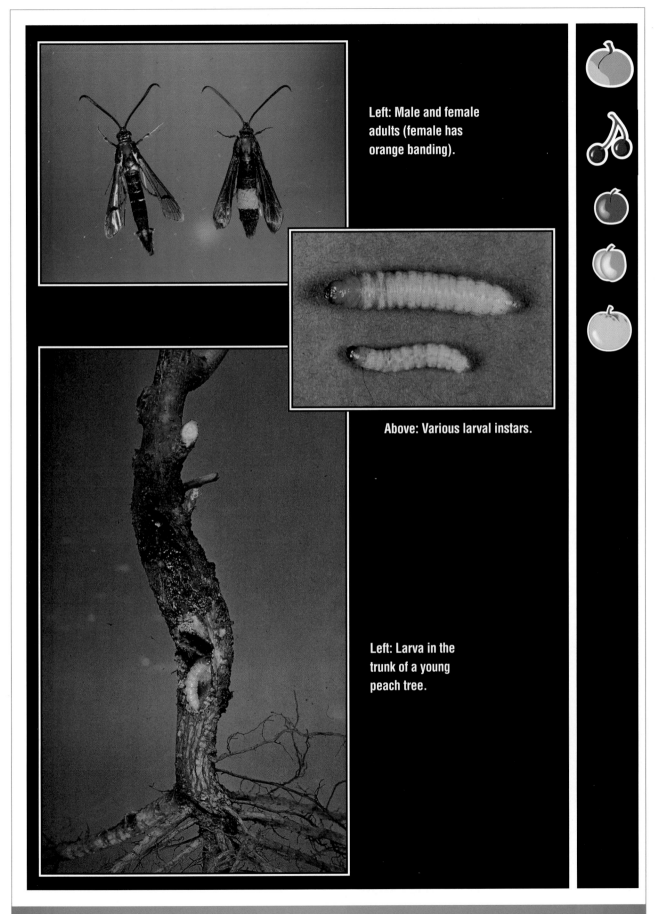

Left: Male and female adults (female has orange banding).

Above: Various larval instars.

Left: Larva in the trunk of a young peach tree.

■ *Injury or Damage*

The principal damage is done by the larvae, which feed on the cambium, or growing tissue, and inner bark of the tree. Most of the larval activity is confined to the trunk area from a few inches above to 6 inches below the ground line. Larval feeding may completely girdle and kill young trees. Older trees are less likely to be girdled but are often so severely injured that their vitality is lowered so that other insects, diseases and environmental conditions can complete their destruction.

Borer-infested trees bleed or exude gum during the growing season. The frass or sawdustlike excrement in the exuded gum indicates the presence of borers. Trunk injury by diseases or environmental conditions will usually produce clear gum.

■ *Factors Affecting Abundance*

Warm, sunny days favor the emergence of adults from their pupal cases; darkness retards emergence. Moist soil also favors adult emergence. The greatest emergence usually occurs the day after a rain.

■ *Life History*

The peachtree borer overwinters as larvae on or under the bark of trees, usually below the ground level. The larvae become active and begin to feed on the inner bark when the soil temperature reaches 50 degrees F. When full grown, the larva constructs a cocoon and pupates, usually during late May and June. Moth emergence begins in early July and continues into September. The moths mate immediately after emerging and the female begins to lay eggs within 30 minutes.

The majority of eggs are deposited the day of emergence and mating. Eggs may be deposited singly or in bunches on all portions of the tree, but the majority — up to 85 percent — are deposited around the bases of the trees or on the trunks. Each female deposits between 200 and 600 eggs during the six or seven days she is alive. Egg deposition occurs between 9 a.m. and 4:30 p.m., with the majority of eggs deposited the afternoon of the day of mating. Females lay few eggs after the third day.

The egg incubation period averages nine to 10 days during warm summer days and up to 15 days during colder periods. The young larvae bore into the bark at the base of the tree. Once beneath the bark, they feed in the cambium and inner bark of the tree. Generally, only one generation occurs each year in the north central states. Some larvae, however, may require two years to complete development.

■ *Monitoring*

Examine the bases of trees for frass or sawdustlike excrement in the exuded gum. Place pheromone traps in trees early in the season. Depending on location, this may vary from early May to late June.

Identification of the peachtree borer adult male is important; pheromones are not specific for this pest, and other clear-wing moths such as the dogwood borer and lilac borer may be caught in pheromone traps meant for the peachtree borer. Note that the lesser peachtree adult borer is not attracted to the same pheromone traps as the peachtree borer; pheromones for the former are specifically designed to trap only that species.

■ *Control*

A hydraulic gun is used to direct an effective chemical at the base of the tree at low pressure before the eggs hatch. One or two years' protection can be provided to newly planted trees by dipping the trunk and roots into an effective chemical solution before planting. The young trees should be inspected for crown gall before using the dip method. Pheromone traps are used to time sprays.

Common Name—
Lesser Peachtree Borer

Scientific Name—
Synanthedon pictipes (Grote & Robinson)

Family—
Sesiidae

THE LESSER PEACHTREE BORER WAS FIRST reported in Pennsylvania in 1868. Since then, it has been found in all sections of the United States and Canada. In many respects, the lesser peachtree borer is similar to the peachtree borer. It differs from the peachtree borer in that the moths emerge over a long time during the summer. Also, the larvae do not confine their activity to the trunks of the trees but can be found in the trunk, scaffold limbs and branches.

■ Life Stages

Egg: Eggs of the lesser peachtree borer are cinnamon- or rust-brown and oval in outline, and they average 0.62 mm long by 0.39 mm wide. The surface of the egg is finely netted. Egg incubation takes from 7½ to 8½ days.

Larva: The larva of the lesser peachtree borer is similar to that of the peachtree borer and other clear-wing moths. The length of the full-grown larva is 20 to 26 mm. The head is yellowish brown, the cervical shield is light yellow, and the body is creamy white, sometimes tinged with pink and slightly translucent. The larva has three pairs of short thoracic legs. Abdominal prolegs are almost absent but bear one transverse band of crochets (hooks).

Newly hatched larvae are about 0.65 mm long. The head is yellowish brown and the body is translucent white. Larval growth is completed after six larval stages, or instars.

Cocoon: Cocoons are from 12 to 20 mm long and elongated. They are constructed from chips of bark and frass held together by silken strands. New cocoons are light yellowish brown; older ones are rust-colored. The pupation period during May averages about 23 days.

Pupa: Pupae vary from 10 to 17 mm long. They are elongated and cylindrical and light tan. The head has a hard chitinized cutting plate for cutting through the cocoon. Wings, legs and mouthparts are identifiable on the ventral (underside) side of the pupa. Abdominal segments have rows of sharp spines that enable the pupa to push from the cocoon to the surface of the bark. Male pupae have two rows of spines on the seventh abdominal segment; female pupae have only one row.

Adult: Both sexes have clear wings; the only colored areas are the wing edges and veins. The head, thorax, body, legs and antennae of both sexes are metallic blue-black with pale yellow markings. The female wing span measures 15 to 26 mm; the male wing span measures 15 to 23 mm. In both sexes, the second and

Above: Female adult (left) and male adult.

Left: Larva.

Below: Adult on peach limb. Note frass on limb, which results from larval feeding within the limb.

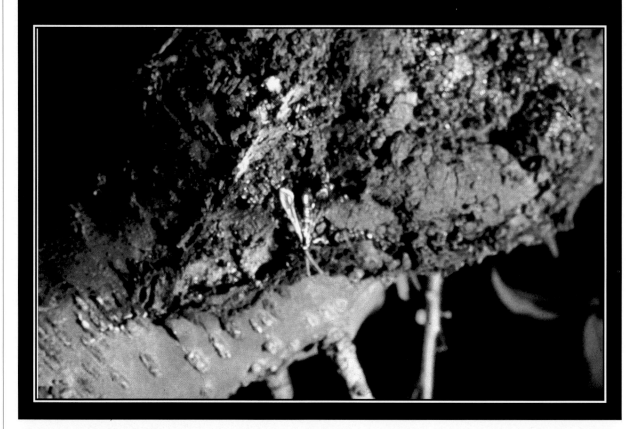

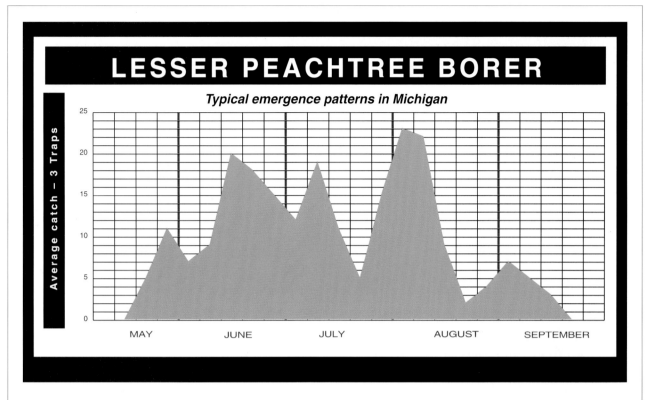

LESSER PEACHTREE BORER

Typical emergence patterns in Michigan

Average catch – 3 Traps

MAY JUNE JULY AUGUST SEPTEMBER

fourth abdominal segments are bordered in pale yellow bands. In general, the male is slightly smaller and more slender. The finely tufted antennae of the male make it easy to distinguish between the two sexes.

Both the male and the female lesser peachtree borer resemble the male peachtree borer. However, the second and fourth abdominal segments of the lesser peachtree borers bear yellow bands, while the male peachtree borer has a yellow band on the posterior margin of each abdominal segment.

Male and female lesser peachtree borers appear quite similar. The finely tufted antennae of the male distinguish it from the female and her simple antennae. The abdomen of the female is also more robust than that of the male. The female has two long, slender spines, which rise from the base of the hind wings and are concealed by the front wings. The male has a single, shorter spine.

■ *Host Range*

Cultivated food plant hosts include peach, plum, sweet cherry, tart cherry, apricot and nectarine. Wild crop hosts include wild black cherry, wild red cherry, beach plum, wild plum and Juneberry. The lesser peachtree borer occurs in all fruit-growing sections of the United States and Canada.

■ *Injury or Damage*

The larvae of the lesser peachtree borer commonly occur under the bark in wounded or injured portions of the tree. They may be found in injured or diseased trunks, scaffold limbs or branches. Pruning wounds, valsa cankered areas, insect-injured areas, sun-scalded bark or winter-injured areas are locations of infestation. The lesser borer can become established only in tissue previously injured by some other cause — it cannot establish itself in healthy tissue.

Once established in an injured area, the larvae feed freely on the tender growing bark at the margins of the injured area. If not controlled, they may enlarge the wounded area by feeding until the entire branch or limb is girdled, resulting in death of the limb. Borer-infested trees are especially susceptible to attack by the valsa canker fungus organism.

The presence of borers is revealed by the sap flowing from wounded areas, which contains brown frass from the larvae.

■ *Factors Affecting Abundance*

Temperature, principally during the spring, probably influences the development of the pupae and the emergence of the adults more than any other factor. Also, favorable high temperatures during the summer induce a partial second generation late in the season. Tree injury from mechanical harvesting that results in bruised or open wounds in the bark of the limbs and trunk of the tree has been chiefly responsible for changing the status of this insect from a minor to a major pest of cherries.

■ *Life History*

The lesser borer passes the winter in various stages of larval growth from the second to the sixth instar. In the spring, the larvae feed for a while, then burrow to the surface of the outer bark, leaving only a thin disk of bark over the mouth of the burrow. The larva constructs a cocoon in the burrow from bits of frass and bark. The pupa, with its head directed toward the mouth of the burrow, pushes through the cocoon and disk of bark. The pupal case splits and the adult moth emerges, usually before 10 a.m. The time spent in the pupal stage varies from 20 to 30 days.

During favorable weather, mating occurs within an hour after the moths emerge, and oviposition takes place shortly after mating. The female deposits eggs in cracks and crevices near injured areas. Usually two to four eggs are deposited at a single location. Almost 98 percent of the eggs are deposited in injured areas between ground level and 8 feet up, with the highest percentage being deposited within 3 to 4 feet of ground level.

Depending on the temperature, egg hatching occurs in seven to 10 days. Then the young larvae invade the wounded tissue and start feeding.

Moths of the lesser peachtree borer are in flight from late May through September in the northern states. In the southern states, emergence occurs earlier in the season and there are two complete generations in a year. In the north central states, peak emergence may occur from early June to mid-July, depending on the location. There is a single continuous generation each year, but in some years in some locations, a partial second generation may occur.

■ *Monitoring*

Examine the trunk, scaffold limbs and exuded gum for frass. Place pheromone traps in trees early in the season. Depending on location, this may vary from early April to mid-May. In southern locations where there are two generations, replace the caps and traps for the second generation. Because the lesser peachtree borer emerges over a period of five months in locations where there is a single generation a year, the pheromone traps will have to be replaced during this emergence. Because the pheromone for the lesser peachtree borer is species-specific, other clearwing moths such as the peachtree borer and dogwood borer will not be caught in these pheromone traps.

■ *Control*

A hydraulic gun with low pressure is used to apply an effective pesticide to the trunk and scaffold limbs. The first application should be made about 10 to 14 days after first emergence. Spray to runoff. Pheromone traps should be employed for timing of male emergence.

Common Name—
Peach Bark Beetle

Scientific Name—
Phloeotribus liminaris (Harris)

Family—
Scolytidae

THE PEACH TREE BARK BEETLE IS A native of America and has been recognized as an enemy of peach trees since about 1850. It first came into prominence as a supposed cause of the peach tree disease known as "yellows," a supposition that was not borne out by subsequent investigations. The insect is very similar in form and habits to the shothole borer.

Life Stages

Egg: The egg is milky white, hard, elliptical and opaque, and measures about 0.5 mm long and 0.25 mm wide.

Larva: The larvae are about the same length as the egg but more slender. Initially, they are white but later become pink. The larval stage lasts about one month.

Pupa: The pupa is white and measures 2.5 mm long and 1 mm wide.

Adult: The adult is about 2.5 mm long and about 0.75 mm wide. The brown body is punctured, with yellowish hairs arising from the punctures.

Host Range

Peach, cherry and wild cherry are the main hosts, though the beetle can infest plums. It is found in Canada and the United States in most areas where stone fruits are grown.

Injury or Damage

The beetle tunnels into the bark and cambium wood. It weakens the tree and can kill it. It generally attacks trees already weakened by disease, insects or injury.

Factors Affecting Abundance

Peach bark beetles will seek out and breed in unhealthy trees — those in poor vigor as a result of insect damage, diseases, root damage from mice, trunk damage from rabbits, and broken limbs from wind or other causes.

Life History

Unlike the shothole borer, this insect winters in the tree as an adult. The adult beetle is a little less than 2.5 mm long and light brown to nearly black. Some of the beetles — those that transform to the adult stage late in the fall — winter within their pupal cells in dead or dying trees. Others, which transform earlier in the fall, leave the host tree and bore into healthy or unhealthy trees just beneath the outer layer of bark. They make hibernation cells (averaging 12 mm long) at the inner terminus of the burrows. Great numbers of such burrows are often made in growing trees, and during the following season, a large

Cherry branch damaged by feeding of peach bark beetles.

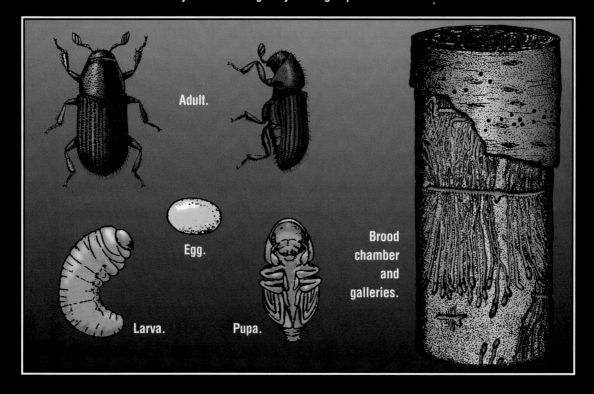

Adult.

Egg.

Larva.

Pupa.

Brood chamber and galleries.

amount of gum will flow from the numerous wounds.

After leaving their hibernation quarters in the spring, the beetles make short burrows in healthy trees, either to obtain food or to form brood chambers. The constant flow of sap from such wounds eventually weakens the trees to such an extent that brood chambers can be constructed without interference from gum formation, after which the larvae make short work of the trees.

The beetles leave their hibernation cells early in the spring and migrate to other trees, brush heaps of prunings or any suitable wood wherein eggs can be deposited. The female bores into the bark, forming a hole very similar to that made by the shothole borer but distinguished from it by the particles of excrement held together by fine threads of silk that partly fill the mouth of the burrow. The brood chamber may be anywhere from 1 to 2½ inches long. It may be distinguished from holes made by shothole borers because invariably it is made to cross the grain of the wood instead of running parallel to it, and because a short side tunnel branches from the main chamber near the inner end. This side branch enables the female to turn around within the burrow and is occupied by the male at mating.

The small, white eggs are deposited in little pockets excavated from the walls of the brood chamber. A female places from 80 to 160 eggs in a single chamber. Eggs from the first generation of beetles require 17 to 20 days to hatch. The larvae bore at right angles away from the brood chamber, forming burrows from 37 to nearly 75 mm long. Larvae are white, often with a pinkish cast due to the contents of the digestive tract, and have yellowish heads and darker mouthparts.

In 25 to 30 days, they attain full growth and then pupate within the bark. They pass from four to six days in the pupal stage, after which they transform into beetles. The adults of this generation issue about midsummer and provide eggs for a second generation, the beetles of which appear in the fall and hibernate. During the summer and fall the two generations overlap, so all stages of the insect may be found in trees at one time.

■ *Monitoring*

Examine weakened trees for small holes filled with frass. Removing bark will reveal brood chambers running at right angles to the length of the tree; galleries from the brood chambers will run parallel to the length of the tree.

■ *Control*

Eliminate breeding places, not only in the orchard but in land adjacent to orchards. Apply fertilizer to restore vigor of weakened trees. Remove trees that will not recover. Apply effective pesticides when the beetles are active.

Common Name—
Shothole Borer

Scientific Name—
Scolytus rugulosus (Muller)

Family—
Scolytidae

THE SHOTHOLE BORER, INTRODUCED FROM Europe, was first recognized as a pest in North America in New York in 1878.

■ Life Stages

Egg: The eggs are milky white when first deposited, later becoming translucent or clear. They are oval and about 0.52 mm long and 0.36 mm wide.

Larva: The larva is a cylindrical, footless grub. It is whitish, often tinged with pink and transversely wrinkled, with a small, yellowish head. When newly hatched, the larvae are only about 0.56 mm long, but when full grown, they are from 3.5 to 4 mm long.

Pupa: The pupa is a trifle less than 3 to 3.5 mm long and dull white to pinkish.

Adult: The adult is about 2.5 mm long and one-third as wide. It is black except for the tips of the wing covers and lower parts of the legs, which are russet-red. The wing covers are grooved, and the depressions are fitted with lines of minute punctures. The posterior margins of the wings have a saw-toothed edge. The body is covered sparsely with short, yellowish hairs. The thorax is smooth and shiny but shows numerous punctures under a hand lens. It is lined along the posterior and lateral borders with a slightly elevated line.

■ Host Range

The shothole borer is a pest of peach, cherry and plum. It is found in all areas in Canada and the United States where stone fruits are grown.

■ Injury or Damage

Except in cases where the bark beetles are excessively abundant, they do not normally attack and breed in healthy trees; neither do they feed and deposit their eggs in wood that is entirely dead. Trees that have been greatly weakened by unfavorable conditions or that are dying afford the most acceptable food for the beetles and their larvae. Where a great quantity of dying wood exists — such as prunings and trees that have been injured by the San Jose scale, the yellows, freezing or root troubles — the beetles will breed in great numbers.

After their supply of preferred food has been exhausted, the beetles will sometimes attack vigorous trees. At first the attacks may not make much impression on sound trees, but a continuation of the injuries may eventually weaken the trees to such an extent that they become acceptable food for the larvae, which can then develop within the bark and eventually kill them.

When the beetles attack healthy peach, plum, cherry and other stone fruit trees, the flow of gum will often check the entrance of the beetles and will prevent the development

Exit holes in fruit tree made by adult shothole borers.

of larvae when eggs are deposited. The formation of gum at the wounds will diminish, however, as the tree is weakened. After a period during which the beetles have inflicted slight but numerous injuries, the condition of the tree may become exactly right for the deposition of eggs and the growth of larvae.

The pest attacks the trunk, branches and twigs of suitable trees, and all the inner bark and the surface of the sapwood is converted to dust in a very short time by the primary wounds of the beetles and the more extensive burrowing of the numerous larvae.

Factors Affecting Abundance

The presence and abundance of breeding places provided by trees dying from neglect, diseases, insects or animals favor the beetle.

Life History

In early June, the beetles appear on suitable trees and begin to excavate brood chambers between the bark and the sapwood. In preparing the chamber, the female beetle gnaws a round hole about 1 mm in diameter through the bark and then extends a slightly enlarged (35 to 50 mm long) burrow nearly or quite parallel to the grain of the wood. This burrow or brood chamber is made partly in the bark and partly in the wood, and during its construction, the female mines small niches out on both sides. Into each of these she deposits a minute, white egg. A single female will produce from 75 to 90 eggs.

The eggs hatch in three or four days. The small, footless, grublike larvae are white with reddish heads. When full grown, they are about 2.5 mm long. The larvae burrow between the bark and the

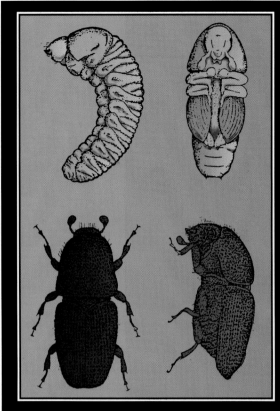

Clockwise from top left: Full-grown larva, pupa, and dorsal and side views of beetle *Scolytus rugulosus*.

Right: Brood chamber and galleries of *S. rugulosus*.

sapwood, first at right angles away from the brood chamber, and form centipede-like figures in the wood that are disclosed by removing the bark. The completed larval burrows average 3 or 4 inches in length and are filled with dustlike, reddish brown frass. After feeding from 30 to 36 days, the larvae attain their full growth and pupate within specially constructed cells just beneath the surface of the sapwood.

The pupal period lasts seven to 10 days. Then the beetles gnaw out through the bark, making their escape through small, round holes similar to the entrance holes made previously by the females.

Within a few days after emerging, these young beetles begin to deposit eggs, giving rise to a second brood of larvae that feed in the trees during the latter part of the season.

The second-brood larvae winter in the trees, pupating early in the following spring. Two generations of the insect occur annually.

■ *Monitoring*

Examine weakened trees for small holes without frass. Removing bark will reveal brood chambers running parallel to the length of the tree; galleries from the brood chambers will run at right angles to the length of the tree.

■ *Control*

Eliminate breeding places in the orchard and in land adjacent to orchards. Apply fertilizer to restore vigor of weakened trees. Apply effective pesticides when the beetles are active.

PEST CONTROL

Integrated pest management

INTEGRATED PEST MANAGEMENT (IPM) IS AN APPROACH THAT USES ALL AVAILABLE techniques to manage pests at acceptable levels. The concept of pest management applies to any form of pest population manipulation where the objectives are to optimize control of the pest while achieving overall economic, social and environmental goals. The three major components that are integrated into pest management in tree fruit production are biological control, chemical control and, to a lesser extent, cultural control.

Chapter 12

■ IPM Techniques in Managing Fruit Pests

In fruit orchards, IPM helps manage fruit pests below an economic injury level by combining or integrating biological, chemical and cultural controls. "Economic injury level" is the level at which the cost of control equals the cost of sustained damage. This implies that eradication is unrealistic and unattainable. The economic action threshold level is a population level somewhat below the economic injury level that allows for the delay between the recognition of a damaging population and the time it takes to get it under control. Economic injury level or economic action threshold for the grower usually involves a known population of a pest. If the population density rises above the economic action threshold, biological control is unreliable in suppressing potential orchard damage, and chemical control must be used. Unfortunately, economic injury thresholds are known for very few orchard pests.

In developing IPM programs, it is important and necessary to identify which species are present in orchards. Although an orchard is a relatively stable structure, arthropod populations fluctuate in orchards as in all environments. This leads to species variations both within and between years in any given orchard. Similarly, adjacent orchards can vary considerably in species present and population levels.

Growers know their orchards better than any other person does. They are familiar with every tree and can very quickly detect even subtle changes. With some training, growers could very quickly become the world's best consultants for their own orchards. They can use modern techniques such as bait traps and pheromone traps and, by keeping records, could diagnose problems and trends in only a few hours a week. Even if growers are uncertain about the interpretation of the data, if they have the information at hand, they can simplify their county Extension agent's or their consultant's job in recommending a sound management program.

■ Population Dynamics in Orchards

A number of factors affect population densities; all are important in orchard pest management. Theoretically, population densities are adjusted by four major biological factors: mortality, natality, short-range movement and generation time.

Mortality (death) is the most important of these factors. Pesticides, as well as parasites and predators, act to increase the mortality of a pest species. Unfortunately, because they seldom act cumulatively, most pesticides regulate parasites and predators along with the pests.

Natality (birth rate) is rarely used to control pest populations in orchards. The sterile male technique is the best known method to manipulate this factor. It involves releasing large quantities of sterile males that mate with receptive females. The result, of course, is that no progeny are born. Severe limitations make the sterile male technique impractical for most orchards, though this technique has been used with limited success to manage codling moth.

Range movement — movement from alternate hosts or new orchards — may add significantly to orchard pest populations and parasites. Such migrations can speed up changes in orchard pest populations, but they rarely have rapid positive influences on biological control agents. In orchard situations, available time seldom lends itself to manipulation. This factor is usually under the influence of weather.

A major cause of pest outbreaks is the condensing of generations when favorable weather conditions speed up the development rate and increase the number of generations that occur in a given time period.

Biological Control

Biological control involves the management of pest insects and mites by natural enemies. Biological control agents are usually density-dependent — their numbers are maintained and influenced by the pest population. Under natural conditions, many tree fruit pests can be maintained at low population levels with predators and parasites. At present, however, biological control of fruit pests alone cannot supply the quantity or quality of organically grown fruit to satisfy consumer and industry demand. Though each area is unique and pests and diseases can vary widely, most fruits must compete in a common market. Regardless of the conditions in which the fruit is grown, the end product must appear pleasing and pest-free to the buyer.

In commercial orchards, beneficial species are often eliminated because of their susceptibility to pesticides. Careful management is needed to conserve and enhance beneficial species so they can be used to the grower's benefit.

Once established, biological control offers more permanent control than chemical control. Biological control reduces environmental pollution by minimizing pesticide use, which, in turn, reduces farm workers' exposure to toxic pesticides. Biological pest control can also slow the development of pest resistance to insecticides because it reduces the selective advantage for resistance to pesticides.

To get the best results from biological control, growers must maintain sufficient pest populations to support the biological control population while, at the same time, avoid injury to the fruit or trees. Because some pests must be necessarily present, biological control is most effective against indirect pests such as aphids, leafhoppers and mites. It is less effective against direct fruit-feeding pests such as codling moth, apple maggot and plum curculio.

Biological control agents differ in effectiveness. Some are effective at pest densities that are too high to prevent damage, while others are effective at low pest densities and maintain pest populations below levels that require chemical control. By changing orchard management practices, growers can often encourage biological control. It is often helpful to conserve protective habitats within the orchard for predators. For example, ground cover at the bases of apple trees is necessary if the predator mite *Amblyseius fallacis* is to overwinter successfully and find prey before migrating into the apple trees in late spring or early summer.

Proper choice, timing and placement of pesticides can have a major impact on predators. To have the most effective impact, growers should monitor trees and fruit regularly to determine the presence of beneficial insects as well as pests.

Cultural Control

Cultural control is the use of techniques that modify the environment to reduce the impact of pest species or encourage the production of beneficial arthropods. For example, the removal of neglected or wild apple trees near the orchard will eliminate the movement of orchard pests from this source into the orchard.

Host plant resistance is another method of cultural control that can have a major effect on pest populations. Host plant resistance was the forerunner of biotechnology. An insect-resistant plant is one that sustains less damage at a given level of infestation than the average for the same species grown in the same environment. Natural resistance is one of the safest, most practical and most economical approaches to cultural control and pest management.

Factors involved in plant resistance are complex and vary with the pest and the crop. In general, however, resistance is the result of three interrelated factors that are genetically transferable: antixenosis, anti-biosis and tolerance.

Antixenosis refers to a situation where the plant is not acceptable to the insect for food, oviposition or shelter. Antibiosis is any process by which plants adversely affect development of the insects. Tolerance describes a state where plants show less damage than their susceptible counterparts.

In the past, resistant varieties have been obtained using two general methods: selecting superior individuals from large wild or domestic populations, and hybridizing superior plants to transfer resistant characteristics or germ plasm to desirable varieties. There has been considerable research on host plant resistance. Some apple varieties have been developed that are resistant to apple scab, while other varieties are less attractive to such pests as mites and apple maggot.

Formerly, progress in host plant resistance was measured in decades. Today, because of biotechnological advances, dramatic results can be achieved in a very short time. When chemicals or host plant resistance alone will not provide adequate protection, a combination of both sometimes will.

■ Chemical Control

Unlike biological control agents, pesticides act primarily as density-independent factors. Hence, they are effective under most conditions against pests and beneficial parasitoids. At present, only chemical controls can guarantee an acceptable fruit product, and nothing in the foreseeable future will replace them. However, a number of disadvantages are associated with chemical control, including cost, pest resistance and ecological problems.

Chemical control programs are costly and make up a significant portion of production costs. Because they are one of the few production costs that are not fixed, however, good pest management offers potentially great savings to the grower.

Insect and mite populations develop resistance or tolerance to chemicals after various periods of use, so chemical control may not work for all pests. Some growers have approached this problem by seasonally or annually rotating compounds that have different modes of action. This option is no longer as effective as it once was, though, because pests have become cross-resistant to diverse classes of compounds, including chlorinated hydrocarbons, organic phosphates, carbamates and pyrethroids.

■ Improved Ways To Integrate Chemical Controls Into IPM Programs

To maximize the use of parasites and predators as an integral part of a successful IPM program, it is important to minimize use of spray programs. Because IPM emphasizes the importance of the biological components, it is advantageous to be highly selective and use pesticides that can effectively manipulate pest populations without eliminating biological control agents. Few available chemicals have these properties, and it is currently not economically feasible to develop very selective chemicals.

Currently, many growers prefer to use broad-spectrum pesticides because they can control a wide range of pests with a single spray. Unfortunately, they also have an adverse effect on many beneficial predators and parasites. The most practical way to balance these concerns and still produce a clean, marketable crop is to reduce spray programs. The amount that can be reduced will depend on the individual orchard situation, its pest history and its proximity to sources of infestation.

Spray calendars must necessarily be written for the worst possible situation and the least skilled and most neglectful grower. Spray calendars assume that all pests in that region are present. If properly applied, spray calendar recommendations are expected to produce clean fruit under the most severe insect infestations. Pest situations in the most well cared for orchards do not warrant this intensive preventive control. Unfortunately, many growers find it easier to follow a spray guide because they feel insecure about their knowledge of the biology that goes on in their orchard. Therefore, they feel more confident routinely applying the sprays as scheduled in the spray calendar.

■ Spray Programs

Growers currently have a number of options to reduce the amount of chemicals used during a season. These are:
- ■ Extended-interval spraying.
- ■ Alternate-middle spraying.
- ■ Reduced-dosage spraying.
- ■ Spray-as-needed methods.
- ■ Tree-row volumes.

Extended-interval spraying

This program consists of a petal-fall spray followed by three or four cover sprays at approximately 21-day intervals, instead of the standard six to eight cover sprays at 10- to 14-day intervals. Timing of sprays depends on the season, with the most important application occurring at petal fall. This spray is necessary to control a number of pests, including the white apple leafhopper, tarnished plant bug, green fruitworm, plum curculio, redbanded leafroller, obliquebanded leafroller, fruittree leafroller, lesser appleworm, spotted tentiform leafminer and first-brood codling moth adults. In a relatively pest-free orchard, this application has a reasonable chance of success unless aphids or San Jose scale are major problems.

The next critical spray would be timed for apple maggot. Normally, apple maggot is not a resident pest, and it may move into the orchard anytime between the beginning of July and early August. Application should take place when the apple maggot, second-brood codling moth, or obliquebanded or redbanded leafrollers appear. Growers who have problems with tufted apple bud moths or variegated leafrollers may have to apply sprays in June.

Alternate-middle spraying

This involves a split application in which the spray is applied down the middle of every other row. For best results, make a complete application at petal fall and split the cover sprays on a 10- to 14-day interval. In a clean orchard, the alternate-middle cover sprays should protect against mobile insects. The more difficult species to control are non-motile pests, such as mites and aphids. It is important to spray the outside rows and end trees during each spray application to maintain a protective chemical barrier against pests migrating into the orchard.

Reduced-dosage spraying

This type of spraying is based on the premise that spray calendars and chemical dosages are written for maximum pest pressures. You can reasonably assume that fewer chemicals will be needed to protect clean commercial orchards.

This program should be initiated on a few orchard blocks rather than the entire orchard. A starting point might be a 50 percent reduction in chemical rate on a full-cover 10- to 14-day interval or a half-rate on an alternate-middle seven-day spray interval program. Experienced growers will learn when they have cut the rates too far if they experience additional fruit and foliage damage.

Spray-as-needed methods

This concept is based on need rather than prevention. It assumes that the grower or consultant has made observations in the orchard, appraised the situation and determined the need for a spray application. Effective monitoring devices available for most major orchard pests now make this approach more feasible and generally less costly than standard calendar applications.

Tree-row volumes

This spraying concept is based on the need for a method that will determine chemical dosage rates per acre for different sized trees. With the introduction of dwarf and semi-dwarf trees, it is no longer practical to spray all trees at the same gallonage and dosage. The application rule of thumb for midwestern and eastern orchards is 1 gallon of spray solution per 1,450 cubic feet of orchard foliage. A mature standard apple orchard in the midwestern and eastern United States generally has trees that measure an average of 19.5 feet high and 23.5 feet wide. When spraying, dilute and apply a total of 400 gallons per acre. Base rates of gallonage and chemical dosages on the following formula:

$$\frac{43,560}{\text{Row width}} \times \frac{\text{Tree width}}{580,000} \times 400 \text{ gal/acre} \times \frac{\text{Leaf density}}{(1.2-0.7)} \times \frac{\text{Pesticide rate/100 gal}}{\text{dilute (lb, pints, oz)}} = \text{lb, pints or oz/acre.}$$

Leaf density depends on foliage: 0.7 represents early season before foliage is fully expanded; 1.0 represents a typical well pruned Red Delicious apple tree in midseason; 1.2 represents a Red Delicious with heavy foliage in midseason.

■ Orchard Pest Management in the Future

At the time this manual was prepared, a new class of chemical compounds was being introduced that could have a profound effect on pest management. These pesticides are known as insect growth regulators (IGRs). Some are chitin inhibitors, while others are juvenile hormones or juvenile hormone mimics. Chitin inhibitors work by interfering with the formation of chitin, which makes up part of the external skeleton or exoskeleton of insects. Juvenile hormones work by interfering with the insects' molting process. All

insects must molt to grow, and interference with this process is often lethal.

New IGRs are being evaluated, and it is anticipated that many more will be synthesized in the coming years. Most are unique in that they have a very low mammalian toxicity and prolonged residual action. They are also effective at very low dosages. Some are much less detrimental to parasites and predators than other classes of chemical compounds currently in use. In the future, IGRs may provide growers with better opportunity than ever to successfully implement pest management in the orchard.

Biotechnology will be an important factor in the production of fruit in the future. A number of apple varieties have been developed that show disease resistance and more tolerance to mites and other orchard pests. Unfortunately, these varieties are not commercially acceptable. When the genes for resistance and new ones for additional resistance and tolerance have been identified, it is possible, through gene splicing, to transfer these qualities to acceptable commercial varieties.

Pheromones will play a more important role in future IPM programs. Pheromones are released by insects for intraspecific communication, and sex pheromones are used as a means of communication between male and female insects of one species. The major use of pheromones in current IPM programs is in monitoring and detection. With the development of controlled-release systems, mating disruption using sex pheromones has been used to control Oriental fruit moth, grape berry moth, lesser peachtree borer and peachtree borer.

A greater understanding of the biology and ecology of pests is necessary to develop strategies that exercise control by interfering with pest behavior. Studies in the future will involve the behavior of synthetic pheromone formulations in the field and try to relate this to pest behavior. Increased knowledge in both of these areas will lead to the design of controlled-release devices that will improve the manipulation of pest behavior within certain physical and climatic parameters of the pests' environment.

Beneficial insects and mites

With the help of color photos of insects, growers may more easily recognize beneficial parasites and predators in the orchard. Following are descriptions and photos of some of the most common of these beneficial insects and mites.

Chapter 13

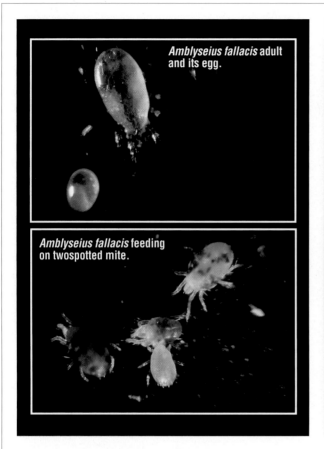

Amblyseius fallacis adult and its egg.

Amblyseius fallacis feeding on twospotted mite.

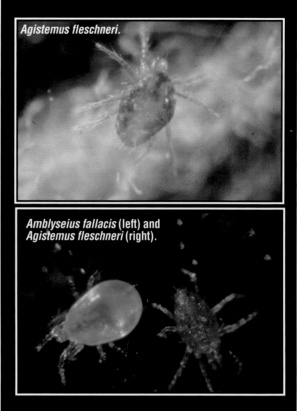

Agistemus fleschneri.

Amblyseius fallacis (left) and Agistemus fleschneri (right).

■ *Amblyseius fallacis*

This insect is about the same size as a spider mite but is longer and has a broad abdomen. Its color will vary from white to pinkish. When exposed to direct sunlight, this predator, which is usually found on the underside of the leaf, will move rapidly across the leaf surface. Its eggs are larger than twospotted mite eggs, oval and almost transparent. The insect lays between one and five eggs per day, usually along the leaf midrib or near leaf hairs.

Like the adults, the immature stages are transparent or colored. Development from egg to adult takes about a week at 70 degrees F. Populations can multiply within two to three weeks from 10 per 100 leaves to 200 to 500 per 100 leaves. Adult females overwinter at the bases of apple trees or in ground-cover litter. In the spring, they feed on twospotted or other plant-feeding mites on the ground cover until around mid-June or July before migrating into the apple trees.

In summer, this predator is most commonly found on the undersides of leaves on spurs in the lower and innermost portions of the tree. As populations increase, *A. fallacis* will disperse throughout the tree. The insect has the potential to nearly eliminate phytophagous mites from apple trees.

■ *Agistemus fleschneri, Zetzellia mali*

These two mites are very similar. The eggs of both species are round, smaller than twospotted mite eggs and bright yellow. These mites later turn reddish yellow after feeding on pest mites. Adults are almost oval but have a more pointed posterior than spider mites, and they are slightly smaller than either adult spider mites or *A. fallacis*.

Both of these predaceous mites feed on all stages of spider mites and rust mites.

A. fleschneri and *Z. mali* require nearly double the time that phytoseiid mites, including *A. fallacis*, require for egg-to-adult development. Both also have a much lower intrinsic rate of increase, a longer generation time and a much lower reproductive rate. They consume about one to two mite eggs a day.

Though these predaceous mites have neither the reproductive potential nor the high prey consumption potential of phytoseiid mites, both can maintain themselves at low densities. Under detrimental environmental conditions, they can develop high population densities in orchards. To some extent, the relatively large populations of these predator mites compensate for their relative inactivity, and they can considerably reduce overwintering phytophagous mites. Both species can survive pyrethroid applications.

Stigmaeids do not interfere with phytoseiid mites' control of phytophagous mites. There is little direct predation between these predator species and relatively little overlap between preferences for European red mite stages. In controlling the European red mite at low densities, a combination of one stigmaeid and one phytoseiid per leaf is nearly as effective as two phytoseiids, even though the maximum phytoseiid rate is about four times that of stigmaeids.

■ *Stethorus punctum*

This insect is considerably larger than phytophagous and predator mites. Both the larval and adult stages feed on spider mites in apple trees. The larva is about ³⁄₁₆ inch long when full grown. Color varies from light black to brown. Stethorus pupae are black, flattened and generally fastened to the upper sides of apple leaves.

The adult beetle is jet black, has wings, and is very round and shiny. In the winter, adult Stethorus hibernate in debris at the bases of apple trees and in fields and woodlands adjacent to the orchard. In summer,

Stethorus punctum adult (top).
Stethorus punctum larva (bottom).

adults fly to the apple leaves where high densities of mites are present. Here, on the lower surface of the leaves, they lay about 95 percent of their whitish, elongated eggs.

They need a minimum of five mites per leaf to stay active and eight to 10 mites per leaf to encourage reproduction. They will feed on all stages of mites. They typically feed on European red mites early in the season, and then on both European red and twospotted mites later in the summer. *S. punctum* larvae feed on motiles. The adults prefer eggs and can consume up to 60 eggs.

The development from egg to adult requires about a month at 70 degrees F. Depending on the location, two or three generations are produced in a season.

S. punctum requires large spider mite populations and will leave a tree in search of new spider mite populations when the phytophagous mite population declines. *S. punctum* will generally not lay eggs until there are eight mites per leaf. When *S. punctum* is the major predator, miticides should not be applied until there are at least 15 mites per leaf, and perhaps not then if it appears that *S. punctum* is present in sufficient numbers to control the phytophagous mites.

Climatic conditions appear to limit the spread of this insect — it is not abundant in many northern apple-growing regions.

Nabid adult.

Ladybird larva feeding on aphids.

Reduvid adult.

Ladybird adult.

■ *Nabids and Reduvid bugs*

These are predaceous bugs whose adults and nymphs feed on aphids, leafhoppers, scales and caterpillars. Many true bugs are pests, such as the tarnished plant bug, but some have adopted predaceous habits. The predaceous bugs have modified front legs that can grasp and hold prey, and short, stout beaks that help them feed on prey. Their salivary glands produce poisonous or paralyzing secretions that subdue the prey.

■ *Ladybird beetles*

These beneficial insects can be found worldwide. They are very efficient predators of aphids, scales and mites. Adult ladybird beetles are generally hemispherically shaped and brightly colored, although some, such as *Stethorus punctum*, are completely black.

Adults overwinter in sheltered locations such as tree holes and other natural hiding places. They become active in the spring and lay their eggs on the undersides of leaves that are usually near aphid colonies.

Eggs are yellow and spindle-shaped, and they stand on end. A single female can lay hundreds of eggs. The larvae, which resemble tiny alligators, have well developed legs and are quite active. They are usually brightly colored, with various protuberances on the body segments. The larvae develop through four instars, then pupate on a leaf or branch by attaching the body to the leaf surface. The larval skin splits along the upper surface and is pushed to the bottom of the pupa. The pupa then stands erect on the leaf or branch until the adult emerges. The life cycle takes about one month. Depending on location, there are two or three generations a year.

■ *Lacewings*

These can be easily recognized because of their distinctive characteristics. Adults have lacy, net-veined wings, metallic golden-colored eyes and a strong defensive odor. The

Green lacewing adult.

Tachinid larva emerging from tufted apple budmoth larva.

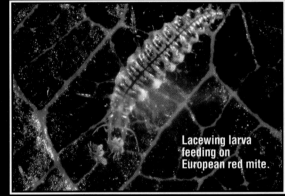
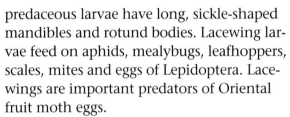

Lacewing larva feeding on European red mite.

Braconid adult.

predaceous larvae have long, sickle-shaped mandibles and rotund bodies. Lacewing larvae feed on aphids, mealybugs, leafhoppers, scales, mites and eggs of Lepidoptera. Lacewings are important predators of Oriental fruit moth eggs.

Mature larvae overwinter inside cocoons situated in bark cracks or on leaves on the ground. Adults become active in the spring, laying eggs on tree trunks and branches. Each oval egg is situated at the tip of a long, erect stalk. When larvae hatch, they climb down the stalks and seek out prey. The stalks offer protection from egg parasites and predators and help reduce cannibalism by newly emerged larvae.

Larvae often adorn themselves with the remains of their prey and other debris. The trash placed on top of their bodies is lost at each molt and a new accumulation is then started. The life cycle is completed in about one month. Depending on location, two or three generations are produced a year.

■ *Tachinids*

This is a large group of flies that are nearly all parasitoids. They are valuable because they have a high biotic potential. This rapid increase in numbers can be effective in biological control. Tachinids commonly parasitize lepidopterous larvae and beetle larvae and adults.

Tachinid adults are medium to large flies with dull coloring and prominent bristles. Tachinids generally overwinter in the pupal stage in the soil or leaf litter. Adults emerge in the spring and feed on insect honeydew and flower nectar. After mating, the female seeks out hosts to parasitize.

The larvae feed internally in the host, often consuming all but the skin of the host. Only one larva usually develops in each host, but if the host species is large, more than one larva may successfully develop. When the larva completes feeding, it bores out of the host and pupates.

Brachonid (genus *Opus*), parasite of fruit flies, including apple maggot.

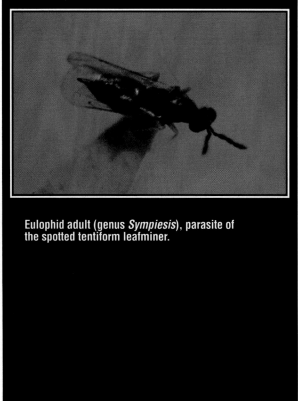

Eulophid adult (genus *Sympiesis*), parasite of the spotted tentiform leafminer.

Some species of tachinids have only one generation a year, while others have multiple generations a year and require about a month for development of each generation.

■ *Ichneumonid and Braconid wasps*

These are large groups of wasps that closely resemble one another and parasitize beetle larvae and adults, fly larvae, lepidopterous larvae, sawflies and aphids. Most of the braconid and ichneumonid larvae develop inside the hosts' bodies. When the host is concealed, however — which may be the case for such pests as leafrollers or wood-boring beetles — the parasitic larvae may remain outside the hosts' bodies, feeding externally.

Eggs of many pest species are parasitized by very small wasps, most of which are from the trichogrammatid family. In some cases, up to 90 percent of lepidopterous pest eggs are parasitized.

■ *Eulophid parasites*

Under natural conditions, these egg parasites can have an almost 100 percent control effect on spotted tentiform leafminer.

anterior — front.

arrhenotokously parthenogenetic — unfertilized females produce only males.

arthropod — an animal that belongs to the phylum *Arthropoda*.

beating tray — a tray, usually about 20 inches in diameter, into which insects/mites fall after a tree branch is struck so the pests can be collected for identification.

beneficial — a term used to designate species that are useful in managing pest species.

brood — a group of individuals of a given species that have hatched into young or have become adults at approximately the same time and live together in a defined and limited area.

burr knots — the sum of partially developed root initials that usually occur in clusters at or below a branch's graft union.

calyx — the external green or leafy part of a flower.

cambial — referring to the cambium, the thin layer of tissue between the xylem and phloem of most vascular plants.

cephalothorax — the body region that consists of the head and thoracic segments.

chitinous — referring to the hard material covering parts of an insect's body.

cocoon — a covering composed partly or completely of silk spun by many larvae to protect them during the pupal stage.

colony — a cluster of aphids.

crawler — an immature developmental stage in which an organism has legs and is able to move. In later stages, the organism will become permanently affixed to one site.

crochets — curved spines or hooks on the prolegs of caterpillars.

degree-day (DD) — a unit of accumulated heat equal to 1 degree F above an average daily temperature for one day (24 hours), often used to help predict and monitor pest activity.

density dependent — the relationship between a pest population and a predator population.

deutonymph — the third instar in the molting or growth of a mite.

deuterogony — the occurrence of two types of females.

deutogyne — a female mite that has no male counterpart.

Glossary

dimorphic — occurring in two distinct forms.

dorsal — top surface.

economic injury level — a pest population level sufficient to cause economic losses greater than the cost of a spray treatment.

economic threshold — the level at which a pest population begins to cause economic losses to a crop that are greater than the cost of a spray treatment.

flight — a period of adult moth flying activity.

frass — solid larval insect excrement.

hardshell stage — the fifth nymphal stage of pear psylla.

hibernaculum (pl.: hibernacula) — a sheltered place in which a larva hides or hibernates. The larva may construct a hibernaculum of a leaf or other material, or use an existing place.

honeydew — a sugary, syruplike substance secreted by aphids and pear psylla.

instar — the period or stage between a larva's molts.

integrated pest management — a control approach that uses all suitable techniques and methods in as compatible a manner as possible to maintain pest populations at levels below those causing economic injury.

integument — an insect's covering layer.

larva — a young insect that leaves the egg in an early developmental stage. Differs in form from an adult.

lenticular — lens-shaped.

lepidopterous — referring to moths and butterflies, which belong to the order *Lepidoptera*.

meristematic — referring to plant tissue made up of small cells that are capable of dividing indefinitely to produce similar cells.

mesophyll — the leaf substance that lies between a leaf's upper and lower surfaces.

metamorphosis — the series of changes through which an insect passes in its growth from egg to larva to pupa to adult.

mine — a hollowed-out area between the upper and lower surfaces of a leaf that is caused by insect feeding.

molt — the process of shedding skin.

morphology — the science of biology that concerns the form of living organisms.

motile form — the form or stage in the insect life cycle in which the insect is capable of movement.

negative temperature coefficient — when a pesticide is more effective in colder rather than warmer temperatures.

nymph — in certain insects, the stage of development immediately after hatching in which the insect resembles the adult but lacks fully developed wings and sex organs.

oviparous — the process of reproduction in which living young hatch from eggs outside the mother insect.

ovoviviparous — the process of giving birth to living young that hatch from eggs retained within the mother insect.

palpus (pl.: palpi) — a mouth feeler.

parasitoid — a parasite of the order *Hymenoptera*. Parasitoids eventually kill their victims.

parenchyma — a layer of cells located just below a leaf's surface that store food or carry out photosynthesis and have the capacity to divide even when mature.

parthenogenesis — a process by which female insects and mites give birth to living young without mating.

pest management — an approach to pest control in which populations are monitored and integrated control methods are applied at times that most effectively hold pests at manageable levels.

petiole — a slender stem that supports the blade of a plant leaf.

pheromone — a substance secreted externally by an insect that is produced to affect the behavior of other members of the species (ex., sex pheromones attract members of the opposite sex).

phytophagous — feeding upon plants.

phytoseiids — predaceous mites that belong to the family *Phytoseiidae*.

popcorn stage — a stage of early bloom in cherry when the unopened blossom begins to show color.

posterior — rear.

preoviposition — the period between the time an adult female emerges and the time she begins to lay eggs.

prolegs — appendages that serve as legs on the abdomens of larvae.

protogyne — a female mite that has a male counterpart.

protonymph — the second instar of a mite.

pupa — the resting, inactive instar in insects; usually the intermediate stage between larva and adult.

quiescent — inactive.

reticulated — meshed, netted or covered with a network of lines.

senescence — the process of becoming old.

setae — slender, hairlike outgrowths of the integument.

spur — a spinelike process of the integument, connected by a joint to the body wall.

thorax — the middle region of an insect's body (between the head and the abdomen), which bears the legs and wings.

tortricids — moths that belong to the family *Tortricidae*.

ventral — lower surface.

viviparous — giving birth to living young.

water sprouts — rapidly growing, upright shoots found on a tree's trunk as well as large branches on the inside and top of the tree.

white-bud stage — the stage of early bloom in cherry when the opening blossom begins to show some part of the white blossom.

■ Common Name Index

American plum borer, 11, 142, 145, 174, 193–198

Apple aphid, 8, 16, 66–68, 70–73, 77

Apple curculio, 11, 39–42

Apple grain aphid, 11, 66–70, 73, 77

Apple maggot, 8, 10–11, 16, 21, 25, 31–34, 44, 154, 170, 233–235, 244

Apple rust mite, 11, 61–63

Black cherry aphid, 11, 77, 187–188

Black cherry fruit fly, 11, 31, 170–173

Braconid wasps, 44, 205, 207, 244

Brown mite, 58–60, 63

Cherry fruit fly, 10, 11, 31, 154, 169–173, 210

Cherry fruitworm, 178–180

Cherry leafminer, 189–191

Cigar casebearer, 130–131

Codling moth, 10–11, 14, 16, 21–27, 29–30, 43–44, 164, 206, 232–233, 235

Destructive prune worm, 174–177

Dogwood borer, 141–145, 196, 218, 222

Eulophid parasites, 244

European fruit lecanium scale, 11, 82–83

European red mite, 10–11, 46–53, 56–60, 63, 241, 243

Eyespotted bud moth, 101, 119–121

Forbes scale, 88–89

Fruittree leafroller, 16, 108, 110–113, 118, 235

Fruitworms, 11, 16, 108, 123–126, 181, 235

Grape mealybug, 159–161

Green fruitworm, 11, 16, 108, 123–125, 181, 235

Green peach aphid, 11, 77, 208–209

Green stink bug, 92, 211–213

Hickory plant bug, 211, 213

Ichneumonid wasps, 244

Japanese beetle, 11, 132–134

Lacewings, 208, 242–243

Ladybird beetles, 11, 81, 208, 242

Lesser appleworm, 11, 16, 22, 27–30, 43–44, 178, 235

Lesser peachtree borer, 11, 142, 194, 198, 215–216, 219–222, 236

Mineola moth, 174–177

Nabids, 242

Oak plant bug, 211–213

Obliquebanded leafroller, 11, 16, 97, 100–101, 106–110, 112, 118, 123, 235

Oriental fruit moth, 11, 22, 27, 29–30, 43–44, 201–207, 210, 236, 243

Oystershell scale, 11, 85–87

Peach bark beetle, 223–225

Peachtree borer, 11, 142, 198, 215–219, 221–222, 236

Pear leaf blister mite, 162–164

Pear psylla, 12, 151–154, 246

Pear rust mite, 11, 155–156, 184–186, 240

Pear sawfly, 157–158

Pear slug, 157–158

Periodical cicada, 146–148

Pistol casebearer, 127–129

Plum curculio, 10–11, 16, 21, 35–42, 169, 201, 205, 207, 210, 233, 235

Plum nursery mite, 184–186

Plum rust mite, 184–186

Pyramidal fruitworm, 123, 125–126

Redbanded leafroller, 7, 11, 16, 98–102, 104, 108, 116, 118, 235

Reduvid bugs, 242

Rosy apple aphid, 7, 10–12, 16, 64–68, 71, 73, 77

San Jose scale, 11, 45, 53, 78–81, 88, 226, 235

Shothole borer, 223, 225–228

Speckled green fruitworm, 123–125, 181

Spirea aphid, 73

Spotted tentiform leafminer, 11, 136–139, 235, 244

Tachinid flies, 243–244

Tarnished plant bug, 10–11, 90–92, 211–213, 235, 242

Tufted apple bud moth, 11, 104, 114–118, 121, 235

Twospotted spider mite, 11, 55–57, 63, 240–241

Variegated leafroller, 103–105, 118, 235

White apple leafhopper, 10–11, 93–95, 235

White-striped fruitworm, 123

Woolly apple aphid, 11, 74–77

Yellow-striped fruitworm, 123

Indexes

■ *Scientific Name Index*

■ *Subject Matter Index*

(For discussions of specific pests, see common name and scientific name indexes)

North Central Regional Extension Publication #63

North Central Regional Extension publications are subject to peer review and prepared as a part of the Cooperative Extension activities of the 13 land-grant universities of the 12 North Central states, in cooperation with the Extension Service - U.S. Department of Agriculture, Washington, D.C. The following states cooperated in making this publication available: University of Illinois, Purdue University, Iowa State University, Lincoln University, Kansas State University, *Michigan State University, University of Minnesota, University of Missouri, University of Nebraska, North Dakota State University, Ohio State University, South Dakota State University, University of Wisconsin,

*Publishing state

For copies of this and other North Central Regional Extension publications, write to: Publications Office, Cooperative Extension Service, in care of the university listed above for your state. If it does not have copies or your state is not listed above, contact the publishing state (marked with an asterisk).

Printed and distributed in cooperation with Extension Service, U.S. Department of Agriculture, Washington, D.C., and Arizona, Arkansas, Colorado, Connecticut, Delaware, Florida, Georgia, Kentucky, Louisiana, Maine, Maryland, Ponape ECI, Mississippi, Nevada, New Mexico, New York, Oklahoma, Oregon, Puerto Rico, Rhode Island, South Carolina, Tennessee, Texas, Vermont, Virginia, Washington, West Virginia, Wyoming.

Programs and activities of the Cooperative Extension Service are available to all potential clientele without regard to race, color, national origin, age, sex, religion or disability.

In cooperation with NCR Educational Materials Project.

Issued in furtherance of Cooperative Extension work, Acts of Congress of May 8 and June 30, 1914, in cooperation with the U.S. Department of Agriculture and Cooperative Extension Services of Indiana, Iowa, Kansas, Michigan, Minnesota, Missouri, Nebraska, North Dakota, South Dakota and Wisconsin. Gail L. Imig, Director, Michigan State University Extension, Michigan State University, East Lansing, Michigan 48824-1039.

October 1993

Michigan State University is an affirmative action/equal opportunity institution. Produced by Outreach Communications, MSU.